For Brother Jan, a
brother I have chosen..
with love.
yamow

THE BONE BRIDGE

THE BONE BRIDGE

A Brother's Story

Yarrott Benz

DAGMAR
MIURA

Published by Dagmar Miura
Los Angeles
www.dagmarmiura.com

The Bone Bridge: A Brother's Story

First published 2015

Library of Congress Copyright Registration: TXu 1-325-302

ISBN: 978-1-942267-04-1

Portions of this work appeared, in both slightly and significantly different forms, in the following:

Montréal Review: "The Heart of Florence"

Gulf Stream: "Wars"

Existere: "Clear Water"

Vanderbilt Poetry Review: "Noon with a Dying Brother"

For CMB
enemy, friend, *brother*

"In the very act of connecting, bridges
emphasize difference."

—Jan Clausen

Contents

PART THREE

Acknowledgments

The genesis of this memoir occurred in a dark theater in New York City in 2005, while watching a reading of a beautiful play by my good friend Jennifer Fell Hayes. Titled *Endurance*, it was based in part on conversations Jennifer and I had had about my brother's illness and my role in it. I was touched by her remarkable artistry of breathing life into the characters, particularly those based on my family and me. In the following days, I realized that there were many more parts that I had forgotten, and a much larger story to tell—one that only I could recount. I thank Jennifer for helping me to realize the importance of our story and for demonstrating, quite literally, its dramatic resonance.

I would like to thank the many people who were willing to return to the 1970s with me. John Sergent gave me a moving account about Charley's first days in the hospital and the dilemma my parents faced. Terri Griffith Shine remembered numerous important details about our friendship in the early 1970s. Mike Blim, with whom I lived half of the story, offered invaluable insights. Vickie Erickson Dash revisited her heartrending eighteen months with Charley and provided warm encouragement to me during my year of writing. My brother, Eddy, recalled medical details and my sister, Angela, carefully retraced her steps to provide glimpses into our family's life.

Many people encouraged my writing about this story when I wasn't so sure I could do it or that it even merited it. Longtime friends Draper Shreeve and Christopher Bram, together and separately, told me decades ago that I needed to get this story on paper. Chris's reminder *to not explain, but to describe* the story was probably the single best piece of advice I received, particularly as it relieved me from the burden of fully understanding what I, myself, lived through.

My first editor Meg Blackstone and I immediately established a bond during our first conversation on the telephone in 2006. Her editorial recommendations kept the book on its early course despite my occasional blinding fog. She became an essential muse for the first draft. Others who read the early drafts were Beth Taylor, Tina Petrig, Dagmar Pfander, Dom Cappello, Daniele Ford, Linda Pelcher, Cecilia Gutierrez, Susan Rhoades, Rachel Siegel, Jerry Jaffe, Rob Anker, Jan Tussing, John Byrne,David Krantz, Elizabeth Rosen Mayer, and Scott Williams. All provided insights and warm encouragement.

I received tremendous words of wisdom from poet and memoirist Jan Clausen.

My dear friend Pepi Strahl read my first draft and got it in the hands of agents Erica Silverman and Martha Kaplan who worked with it for two years. Sid Wagner and Christopher Church helped relight the fire to get the book published after I had put it away for several years. Teja Watson edited the final manuscript masterfully and Chris laid out a gorgeous text.

I thank all of these wonderful people from the bottom of my heart.

Part One

ONE

In the Spotlight

In the summer in 1972, I had just graduated from high school when a reporter from a Nashville paper called. He had heard of the Benz brothers through a doctor at Vanderbilt Hospital and wanted to talk to us about our situation. He saw a story in it.

On the phone Mother was formal and protective. "Yes? That's correct. They are. They do. May I ask why are you writing this? Uh-huh. Yes, it is. Quite the testimony to modern medicine."

The reporter came out to the house with a staff photographer who had a cigar hanging between his lips. I remember the brown-stained fingers clutching the big camera. With our incongruously paired mother and father, respectively stylish and egghead, Charley and I sat in a circle with the reporter in the living room. As he loped his way around us, looking for good angles, the photographer banged against Shaker tables and brass floor lamps, stopped himself and stepped carefully over one of our dogs, and then continued his circling. Charley and I smiled at each other. Getting this sort of attention, with an actual newspaper reporter taking notes as we talked, swelled our heads. I felt like we were Jack and Bobby Kennedy sitting on the turquoise sofa.

By the time that reporter visited the house, Charley had been sick for two years already. But it was the summer and we were both tanned and relaxed. Despite what was going on, we looked fit and healthy. Both of us had hair swooping across our foreheads, his chestnut-colored and mine blond. I remember the reporter's first question. "Now, which of you good-looking boys is the sick one and which one is his lifeline?"

Dad did the explaining, in a monotonous, scientific voice. He was full of terminology that the reporter had never heard before.

"Blood platelets? What are they, Dr. Benz?"

Dad answered, "White cells, red cells, and platelets—they are the three components manufactured by the bone marrow, which has, in Charley's case, suffered a catastrophic failure called aplastic anemia, the cause of which is still unknown." Dad was a geek, but a sweet one, with his thick glasses and his white hair in a crew cut. Hardly anybody had crew cuts anymore. He continued to drone in a matter-of-fact voice, "While Charley gets all of his red cells from the Red Cross, Yarrott supplies all of his platelets twice a week, every week, all year round, through a centrifuged procedure called a pheresis. That's *fuh-REE-sus*. It's a four- to six-hour procedure." The reporter looked a little bewildered. Then Dad said, "Without Yarrott's platelets, Charley would die in about a week." Suddenly the reporter sat up straight and scribbled in his notepad.

Charley was grateful to me in front of everyone. I was modest about my role in his survival. We sounded upbeat, hopeful, and brave. It was a good time for a photograph.

On the following Friday the article came out on the front page of the Living section of *The Nashville Banner*. A big photograph of Charley and me covered the top quarter of the page. The article described a situation like Mother described: upbeat, hopeful, and brave. It made a lot of people feel good to read about such fine boys demonstrating a dramatic fraternal bond, and it was read all over middle Tennessee. My parents received dozens of extra copies from their friends and relatives.

Then the tabloids got hold of it and gave the story their particular spin for a national audience. Under a headline, Charley and I sat there in the same picture again, tanned and smiling out to all the readers. My aunt in Kentucky came across it while getting her hair done. She tapped at our picture with her bright painted nails and screamed, "My nephews!" The other ladies gathered around her with their reading glasses. In her hand *The*

National Tattler headlined in bold letters, HE AIN'T HEAVY, HE'S MY BROTHER.

Back at home, I wanted to hide. I knew this hero stuff was blown way out of proportion. I remember thinking something was wrong the instant the flash bulb sent shadows around the living room. *You know how heavy a damn locomotive is? That's how heavy my brother is.*

TWO

A Siren in Lexington

Every life has a shape to it, which you, the bearer of that life, cannot see until somehow given some distance—age, psychotherapy, very discerning friends, or maybe even a visit to a mystic. Like being tricked by those gargantuan ancient earthworks in Central America—whose rolling, continuous hills reveal themselves from the air to be man-made forms in the sacred shapes of snakes and bears—we are blinded by our closeness.

My life has certainly had its share of remarkable patterns, symmetries and asymmetries, coincidences that have left me wondering on the ground just what my life looks like from a distance—seen from the air, does it reveal a scheme? I have heard myself mulling over this question many times while growing up. But now that I'm well into middle age and have reached the age my mother was when one son's illness ensnared a second one, I look down from the air and am astonished at the landscape.

She must have awakened in the mornings and asked herself, "Good Lord, why is all this happening?" In 1972 my mother was fifty-four years old. A Scots-Irish child of Kentucky, she was once tall and radiant, with black hair and olive skin, a very pretty girl by all accounts. Then she was crippled in a car wreck as a teenager and, later, despite her injuries, became a nurse. As young nurses sometimes did, she gave up her hospital job to become a doctor's wife, and by 1972 she was a silver-haired mother of four almost-grown children. Elizabeth Ann McElroy Benz was my mother, The Lovely Lady on Crutches. She already had a full plate in front of her—even without what had been going on with my brother Charley and me for two years already.

Her tight-knit world in Nashville was dominated by her own precarious health and her concern for all four of her children, each one off to a rocky start. There was my oldest brother, Eddy, a brilliant and eccentric student, fresh from dropping out of one medical school and trying to start another one. Then my sister, Angela, an explosive tomboy, trapped and angry in a lady's role that other girls embraced so keenly in the South in those days. Then came Charley, the stubborn macho jock, brought to his knees by a blood disease, who despised his life more with the passing of every day. And then finally, there I was, the youngest, the artistic one, confused about myself from every angle, and the key player in Charley's survival.

I used to blame my mother for what I saw as her shortcomings: her quiet distance, her anger that flared when I needed help, her blind self-righteousness, and her refusal to challenge the status quo of Southern society. I used to think she chose to be the way she was. Now I see that she must have survived her life the only way she knew how. For her, life was always complicated and hard. Her body failed her in big ways and in important times. And I hate to say it, but a lot of the time Dad was not much help to her. Edmund Woodward Benz, MD, was off being a popular surgeon at Vanderbilt Hospital, off helping other people's families with *their* problems. Yet Mother needed him, too, in more ways than one. In the scripted manner of their era, he was the provider, the professional husband, and she was the dependent, jobless wife. And by fifty-four she had to accept a body already in decline from arthritis, watching her remarkable good looks disintegrate, waking up in pain and not being able to turn off her worries at night.

Hers was a life complex enough I cannot imagine it.

My own life, so many years later, feels very simple at times. Perhaps that's because I am in good physical shape and don't have children, healthy or sick. I am fortunate that my life ultimately has become, at least in a few important ways, dynamic. Literally. As in full-of-motion. I have moved a lot. Since leaving home in Nashville, I've lived in six major cities. I've made and shown my art, owned a gallery, taught high school, and have been an AIDS activist. I've gotten up and left when I didn't like the person I was with or where I was living. I speak Italian, a little German, and a little Spanish. I've seen a good piece of the world.

But my mother's life was very different. Hers was stationary, weighed down by a hip joint ruined in the car accident at fourteen. The summer afternoon of her wreck is rooted in my own memory as clearly as if I had been there myself. The accident is part of family lore, a bloody and violent episode that we found fascinating as kids, but irrevocably changed Mother's life, and influenced the life of her family to come.

They had gone swimming for the day in Lexington and were headed home. Her aunt, Calloway McChord, was driving the fancy coupe on Paris Pike when it veered out of control, ran down a ditch, and struck a telephone pole. Mother and her first cousin, Hood, had been sitting in what was called a trundle seat, a folding exterior seat that rose out of the back end of the car. At the moment of impact, they were ejected like gangly rockets of skin and bone. Aunt Calloway clung to the steering wheel and moaned through her blood pouring from a gash in her forehead while passersby pulled to the shoulder to help. Hood lay in the grass with a deep gash on his forehead. Mother came to ten feet in front of the car with her right leg broken in three places. Her younger sister, Beck, having sat in the front next to Aunt Calloway, received the most serious injuries and needed immediate attention. As Beck's head went through the windshield, her neck was cut open to her jugular vein, and the doctor in the ambulance had to concentrate on closing the wound. He abandoned my mother in the grass with her skirt scissored open to her waist and her legs splayed apart. More excruciating to her than her physical injuries was looking up from the ground, helpless and told to remain still, as a trolley car packed with passengers idled overhead, an audience poking through the windows and pointing at her. Much worse to her than her broken leg was that she was having her period and she feared the whole trolley car would know it. She was a young lady, after all.

The damage to her leg would begin to haunt her in her thirties. Periodic operations on her thighbone and hip joint temporarily relieved the immediate problems, but arthritis developed so badly at the site of the trauma that it spread to other joints. My father, the doctor, would give her pain medication whenever she asked for it, and she became addicted to a host of drugs, including Darvon and Dilaudid. Walking became increasingly difficult without a cane or a crutch, and she began using a wheelchair at home when I was a small child. This was normal life for our mother, compromised and painful, and it became the backdrop for her future. She had a temper and could be impatient and angry—she was no saint, but she often pushed through her physical obstacles, like a ship breaks through frozen ice. She carried on with social commitments to her family and friends, with going to church, and with volunteering for the hospital auxiliary. "After all," she would say, "there's no point in giving up. Life does not assign us a limit on worries. They keep coming."

THREE

Geronimo and White Cloud

We called our mother's father Popo. He called us scally-wags. In 1964 his Mercury Monterey was as sleek and modern as his birthplace at Pleasant Run, Kentucky, was old and obsolete. His long, white car was heavy with fins and chrome trim, and its iconoclastic rear window slanted inward instead of outward. Popo lowered the window by pressing a button on his console, and I felt cool air on my neck. Smoke from his Lucky Strikes swirled over our heads and disappeared behind us. Tapping his handsome gold pinkie ring on the huge steering wheel, he said to himself, "Dang it, you scallywags. I know the road's here...somewheres."

There was a two-volume set of books in my father's study entitled *World War II: A Pictorial History*. The books stuck out from a shelf, oversize and teetering, so heavy you needed both hands to lift each one. I always felt a strange attraction to them, one book with its blue spine and the other green, because they held a mix of titillation and horror. On one page there was a picture of naked American soldiers on a beach in Italy, hairy and wet, arm in arm, and bathing the war off themselves. On the next page, more men, injured in combat and denuded like burned trees, wheeled in a circle for the camera in the heat of the South Pacific. I wondered if all wars meant that men had to get naked, lock themselves in a sweaty embrace, and then have their bodies ruined. That kind of sacrifice seemed crazy to me.

At home I watched with a child's eye as my older brothers, one by one, grew pubic hair and developed muscles. I wondered when they, too, would be leaving to fight in a war. I looked at myself, towheaded and androgynous, and hoped I could escape war by looking like an angel.

I felt like I came from a different world than my brother Charley. He sensed it too. Perhaps it was simply my being different that made him despise me so much when we were young. Being different—like being Communist is different from being American, Negro from White, Indian from cowboy, or girl from boy. Just being different. It was wrong to be different and that was that. "You stay on that side of the line, where your world is weird like you, and I'll stay on my side, where the world is normal like me." That might have been it. He saw it as a *crime* not to be like him. And what had encouraged that notion? In the segregated American South in the middle of the twentieth century, what on earth had encouraged that notion?

In Popo's car on Columbus Day in 1964, I sat miserably between my brothers in the back seat and twitched. Ever since a series of ear infections in the second grade, I had been beleaguered with tics. I flared my nostrils and jerked my head from side to side. I could not stop doing this to save my life, despite the humiliation it brought, particularly from my siblings. Eddy was older than me by eight years, and Charley by three. Angela, my sister, was five years older and sat obediently in the front seat next to Popo. I was ten, so my siblings were thirteen, fifteen, and eighteen at the time. And Popo? This was just before his stroke, so he was eighty-two.

From my grandfather's perspective in the front seat, we looked like we were behaving ourselves in the back, but Charley scowled and threatened me with a closed fist in his lap, "I'm not finished with you...you dipshit, you dumb-ass." He was always doing that, disapproving of me, and I was always throwing my hands up to defend myself. We were total opposites in *every* possible way. Again, I think that's what boiled his blood. We had radically different personalities, and radically different looks, too. Despite our having the same prickly crew cuts, you would never have thought we were brothers and came from the same set of parents. Both he and Eddy

11

were dark, like they were Italian or Spanish or even American Indian. But I was fair, like Angela, like a little Nazi. Charley proudly called himself Geronimo, and derisively pointed to me and yelled, "White Cloud!" To him dark was manly, like Tarzan, like Johnny Weissmuller. Blond was inferior, feminine, like Leslie Howard, or worse: Liberace.

You would never have guessed that just that week, back home in Nashville, in a back room in the basement, Charley had shown me how to masturbate. While gawking at Jayne Mansfield's bosoms slipping out of her dress in a magazine, he nudged me and said, "Look how big mine is. Something, huh? Look at yours. Don't worry, it'll get bigger one day." He stroked up and down on his, and I jerked away on my little finger of flesh. I agreed that his was something. Then he finally rolled his eyes back and some stuff poured all over the cot. I just looked straight ahead and thought we ought to clean up the mess he had just made. Suddenly nervous, suddenly a different person, he jumped up, tossed the *Playboy* into a cedar trunk, and said, "If you tell anybody about this, I'll beat the crap out of you."

"Shoot, Charley, you're the one who wanted to do it."

"Dumb-ass," and he let the slatted door slam in my face.

Popo's white and chrome sedan sailed across the rolling hills and one-lane roads, aiming for Pleasant Run. In his lifetime Popo had seen the shift from kerosene to bulbs and from horses to cars. He pointed to a big house with six white columns that his father had built in 1858. Its current owners now had a TV antenna on the roof and an air conditioner in a window. The car purred to a stop at the intersection of another dirt road, and I could see a tiny brick church standing primly across the field in front of us. It had once been fancy and proud, showing off the prosperity of its Scots-Irish parishioners. We drove straight across the grass to a yew tree in the middle of the churchyard. A marble obelisk stood over the grave of Popo's father, the first Yarrott. Popo was the second. His son, my mother's brother, was the third. And I was fourth. Not everyone agreed on giving the name to me. When I was an infant and baptized in Nashville, my father's big-knuckled, Germanic aunt complained, "Such a big name for a little baby."

"Well, it's all that's left of Pleasant Run," answered my mother.

In Eddy's snapshot of us in the graveyard on that October afternoon in 1964, Charley glared at me across the grave, while I smiled faintly into the camera, trying to figure out what I had done to make him so mad. Angela smiled too, but obligingly, like a hostage. I knew she would rather have been throwing the football with my brothers in the fields. Instead her rugged little hands were neatly clasped in front of her the way Mother had always instructed. Even her tomboy hair was rolled into a formal and wavy permanent, suggesting a scrappy little version of Queen Elizabeth.

Popo stood with his hat in his hands, a sure sign of respect at his father's grave, but his mouth was a blur. He was caught saying something while the shutter clicked, as if he was claiming the last word. This was the last time he would be in the company of his father, and it would be the last time we would be in the company of a lucid Popo. The camera caught the moment in a click. Orbiting all around us in the photograph were gravestones and other obelisks and, beyond the stone wall, cattle dotting the fields, the very same fields the first Yarrott had ranched a century before, at the time of the Civil War. Standing there with my father's World War II books on my mind, I wondered how many men had fallen down and died in those fields during the Civil War, bloody and naked. I twitched my head, desperate for psychic relief. Eddy moved around the graves with the Nikon in his hand while Popo remained at his father's grave, his hat off and his head lowered. I looked at Angela, standing ladylike and obedient, waiting patiently for us to return to the car. Then I heard Charley behind me, pulling on the branch of the yew tree and stripping the needles with his thumb. I turned around and there he was, again, glaring at me.

FOUR

Building Blocks

Weird to feel my front tooth broken. Breathing through it hurts. Why'd Angela have to go and do that? She didn't have to push me—not in the car. And my face had to go and hit the car door. I want to stay down here. I like hearing the furnace. It's saying something to me. Don't want to go up for dinner. Much safer here. Got to stay away from them. Shoot, I can't help what I'm doing. Stop twitching, head! Stop it, right now! Stop it? Can't stop it. It's wearing me out.

There, put the long block on the square one. Looks good. Center it. Looks even better. Careful...don't knock it down. Slide this fat one under the long one. Don't like it. Try this other one. There. Looks like the front porch at church. Put a triangle on the long one. Really looks like church now. I'm feeling better. My head's not twitching now. I'm feeling good. Really good. How can I keep feeling good? You're not so dumb, Yarrott. Bet Charley couldn't figure out how to make this. Bet Angela couldn't either. I don't know about Eddy. He might. Yeah, put the steeple on now. Wow, that's beautiful. Okay. What about some steps up to it? Have to lift the whole thing up for that. It's okay. Do it.

Mother called down to me in the basement. "Yarrott, dinner. Come on, now. Don't hold up the rest of us. You can play with those blocks anytime."

Shoot. I don't want to eat. Not hungry. Don't want to sit across from Charley and Angela. Yesterday they called me a baby. They'd cry, too, if I could slug as hard as they can. The bruise on my arm hurts. No fair. Now look at this stupid mess I made. Doesn't look like a church at all. Looks like a damn mess. Take *this. Yeah, fly across the room, you stupid blocks.*

The door at the top of the stairs swung open angrily. "Yar-rott! I said come to dinner at once, little man. If I have to come down there and get you myself, you're going to be sorry. Do you hear me?"

I looked up the stairs and called back, "Yes, ma'am. Be right there."

Why can't you just leave me down here by myself?

FIVE

Tissue and Starch

Mother noticed that I calmed down when I made things with my hands. When I was in the sixth grade, she located some art classes for me at a lady's house. On Saturday mornings in 1966, there was a quiet rumble of activity in Mrs. Tibbott's basement. I was the oldest boy in a class of a dozen kids eleven and twelve years old.

Mrs. Tibbott designed sets for the Children's Theatre and had constructed a panoramic scene of a Jamaican fishing village in a large alcove of her studio. I stood in front of it, imagining being there in the Caribbean. It was backlit with a setting sun. The open windows in the hillside cottages glowed with electric light inside. Floating on the sea in the distance were the lights of fishing boats, tiny electric bulbs screwed into a Masonite backdrop painted deep blue. At the side of the vignette, a large fish net hung from the ceiling and gathered at the floor with a starfish caught in it. I stood in front of the alcove, quiet and happy. Mrs. Tibbott's creativity seemed to have no limits. She amazed me.

To say she was an enthusiastic teacher would be an understatement. "Y'all are so special," she would remind us every week. "You've got to remember that. Each and every one of you. Listen now, kids, be as creative and different as you can be. Don't be afraid to be yourselves." She willowed over us with dangling scarves, a prominent nose, and expressive dark eyes. She looked like a Gypsy.

"Yarrott, honey, think abstract," she directed me one morning. "Don't be afraid to think different."

What the hell does she mean? Think abstract? Different?

She laid ten big pieces of colored tissue paper in the middle of the table and passed out a plastic gallon jug of liquid starch, and we each filled a paper cup. Brushing starch on both sides of the tissue paper made it transparent, allowing us to make combinations of colors when layering the paper. It reminded me of the combined colors you see inside plaids.

"Kids, I want you to interpret the fruit on the table in front of you. You've got lemons, limes, pears, apples, and bananas. But I want you to just use the tissue and starch, brushing both sides. Just that. Okay, kids? Remember, think different."

I felt like I was in a race on the playground. I tore the paper crudely, not even bothering to make round shapes for the spherical contours of the fruit. Instead, I composed the forms by stacking the layers in a graduated curve, accumulating darker shades, which suggested round masses in three dimensions. It happened quickly and unconsciously. Mrs. Tibbott passed behind me and looked over my shoulder. "Good golly, Yarrott, that's just gorgeous!" I turned around to her and caught her excited grin. I felt wonderful. "That's just absolutely fabulous, darlin'. Fabulous!" She squeezed both my shoulders and passed on to the next student.

Eddy drove over to pick me up at noon that day. I was late cleaning up and he waited impatiently between mothers in station wagons. He saw me gathering my things inside and honked angrily for me to come out. The mothers in front and back of him glared at him. When I hopped in the car, he blurted, "That stupid cow kept you fifteen minutes late. Mother told me you'd be waiting. What the hell happened?"

"Hey, don't call Mrs. Tibbott a cow. She's really nice."

"I don't care. I'm busy this afternoon and don't have time to sit in a car waiting for you. You understand that? Jesus."

"Yeah. Sorry, Eddy."

Mrs. Tibbott was an exotic bird in Nashville, a free spirit and somewhat antiestablishment. I caught her frowning when she saw Mother or Dad or Eddy or any other representative of 1120 Tyne Boulevard coming to pick me up, and I got the distinct impression that she wanted to protect me from something.

SIX

Bullitt

Four inches of snow fell in Nashville on Christmas Eve, 1968. The slope of the hill at 1120 Tyne Boulevard was pristine except for a few manic zigzags left by Hansel and Gretel, our two black dachshunds. A giant wreath hung from the second floor and our big home looked solid, gracious, and warm. It was quite the magazine cover.

The holidays meant an escape from academics and athletics at the boys' school, Montgomery Bell Academy. In the ninth grade, Algebra was one of many big obstacles that I could not overcome. Since I could not see the mathematical problems in front of me or even imagine them in my head, I could get nowhere in figuring out their solutions. Everyone seemed to be standing around me tapping their feet impatiently and insinuating *Why can't you get it?*

Early in the semester, the teacher, Mr. Albright, who seemed to love math for an unfathomable reason, and who normally spoke in his class with a breathy, excited-about-math tone, had been abruptly lowering his voice when he called on me. It was clear that I was disappointing him. I was making an F for the quarter and probably for the semester, too. The narrative reports Albright and others had sent home from the school were humiliating, all saying the same thing: "Yarrott does not live up to his promise. Is he happy?" Most recently, though, he hadn't been calling on me at all. He had given up and I was relieved. I could now hide behind the huge head of the red-haired guy sitting in front of me.

It didn't help that the math teacher was a live version of

Dudley Do-Right. With his perfect teeth, cleft chin, and sexy tuft of chest hair escaping from his collar, he was an impossibly masculine model of a man. I was about to fail the model of man's Algebra class. Along with my crooked teeth, skinny face, and hairlessness, I was a pathetic misfire at a school whose brass yearbook seals promised *Gentlemen, Athletes, and Scholars.* Well, maybe I could still learn how to become a gentleman, even despite my stupidity and ineptness.

Angela had come home for the holidays from Centre College in Kentucky all fired up about her psychology class. She and Mother and I stood around the kitchen one evening chopping carrots and pouring Jell-O, when Angela stopped and watched me for several moments and then exclaimed, "I read in *Psychology Today* that facial tics often accompany latent homosexuality." Turning bright red, I concentrated with all of my being on keeping my head still.

Mother looked at Angela with a surprised expression, "Why on earth do you have to bring up such a subject?"

Angela continued to stare at me. I held my breath. Finally I blurted, "I think the toilet's running, I better go shake the handle," and ran upstairs to the bathroom. Locking the door, I sat on the edge of the tub with my head twitching angrily in my hands.

My *habits,* as Mother scornfully called the tics, seemed to haunt me most insidiously when I was under pressure, which in my ninth grade year was all the time, asleep and awake. The question asked that winter by the teachers—"Is Yarrott happy?"—was one I could not have answered, because the concept of happiness was beyond me. What does that mean to a ninth grader who is failing mathematics, who cannot concentrate, who feels awful about liking the hairy nakedness in the locker room, whose own body in sports feels paralyzed, who sees the handsomeness of the other boys but he, himself, feels invisible with plainness? The question of pressure, however, was one I probably could have answered. "Yes, I feel pressure. Pressure in my head, pressure in my school, pressure in my home. *Everywhere* pressure."

Mother had already called me to her room before Christmas vacation. She was propped up on the bed with a book in her hands. She had the same scowl familiar to me in the photographs of her own family. A fold of skin in the shape of a keystone was wedged between her eyes, an unmistakable sign that she was not pleased. "Yarrott, I want to talk to you... about something I've noticed since you've been at Montgomery Bell."

My heart stopped. She now knew what I was afraid of all along: that I was stupid. That my grades were terrible. That I was not sports-worthy. That I failed at making friends. I did not have a thing I could hide behind. "Yes, ma'm?"

She slapped hard at the bed. "Look at the way you're standing there, Yarrott. One foot askew. Favoring one hip. See that? This is exactly what I wanted to talk to you about. You have suddenly become so...so *effeminate*. Since you've been going to Montgomery Bell. It's appalling. Tell me what that's all about."

In 1968, Charley and I loathed each other with ferocity. To me, he was the embodiment of the boys who know how to fit in, and I was their opposite. He was attending a different school, Battle Ground Academy, a less polished private school (however, equally conservative). I had seen how happy he was with his many friends there. I had sat in the BGA bleachers during many of his games and watched the tight camaraderie among the team players and their families. During his senior year, he lettered in three varsity sports: football, basketball, and baseball. Meanwhile, the year before I had left all of my lifelong friends at Burton, a public school, to attend the exclusive Montgomery Bell Academy, and had not made any significant new friends. I had enrolled at MBA because my parents believed it would be better for Charley and me, given our profound differences, not to be in the same school. That would have created, they said, a combination ripe for explosion.

To compound our dislike for each other, during Charley's senior year his football team had suffered a particularly bad season, and my school had won the state championship. Not that it mattered a blade of grass to me. To Charley, however, it was a crushing humiliation. It didn't help that the group of three boys I shared a ride with every day to and from MBA got particular pleasure in reporting on each and every mistake Charley's team made in the playoffs, repeating them slowly in my ear and then gleefully trumpeting our own school's graceful wins. The boys—the single-syllabic Matt, Hal, and Fred—while strutting around in a men's club unity, in fact came from vastly different economic strata. From my dog-paddling viewpoint down in the water, however, they were all princes. They were all safely on board a boat going somewhere, whereas I had fallen overboard.

Their ridicule of my brother's team was stifled on the days when my mother drove the carpool. These boys, after all, were not stupid. One day, however, Hal forgot who was in the driver's seat and let slip a sarcastic reenactment of a bad play by BGA during a game the night before. I saw my mother's jaw tighten and she swerved to the shoulder of the road. She twisted slowly around, put one arm over the back of the seat, and jabbed her finger at Hal's chest. "I want you to shut your mouth this instant. You're talking about my son and Yarrott's brother."

We called her *Mother*, after all. She was nobody's fool. She was beautiful but she was tough. Being crippled when she was fourteen never stopped her from becoming a nurse, driving a car, having a family, or climbing up ladders into places most people would consider scary. She was fearless despite her crutches and I was enormously proud of her, this handsomely dressed, silver-haired lady with a backbone, a doctor's wife who matched her husband in brains and guts. But when she defended Charley with a jab of her finger right toward Hal's ninth-grade sternum, I was just as stunned as the rest of the carpool. The truth is I never felt the loyalty to defend Charley or his BGA football team. I was detached from his accomplishments and his failures. I had no brotherly proprietary interest in him. We had nothing in common, did not enjoy each other's company, felt no support from the other. Simply put, Charley and I did not give a shit about each other. Therefore, the slurs from the carpool did not register with me very deeply. I just remember looking out the window at Nashville's billboards thinking, "Why bother trying to piss me off by insulting my brother and his football team? Who the hell cares?"

The snow during the Christmas vacation had been exciting on December 24, but after forty-eight hours sparks began to fly in the house. Sure, it was great to be away from my demeaning school life for two weeks, but it was no pleasure being trapped under the same roof with my family.

If I had only known my father then, I might have felt at home on Tyne Boulevard. He was in many ways kinder to me than my mother, but he was most often absent. As a surgeon, each day he rose at five o'clock, disappearing to the hospital by half past six and not returning home until seven at night. I grew close to my father in adulthood, about the time I turned thirty, but in my childhood he was something of a shadow constantly slipping out of the room. As I later discovered, he and I were very much alike, and we developed a deep regard for each other, but I would not know that until it was almost too late.

My parents had invited a roomful of relatives to dinner the day after Christmas. To me, that meant an evening of patriotic talk by the men supporting the Vietnam War, of more handwringing about the church's loss of influence in our drifting society, and of more negative innuendoes about black people. Charley and I looked for other things to do. We promised Mother that we would get along and see a movie together. *Bullitt* was playing at the movie theater nearby. I could not, for the life of me, in the ninth grade at least, understand his fascination with Steve McQueen. Except for the ruggedly sexy face, I thought of McQueen as having the same anti-charisma as John

23

Wayne, another star whose public appeal I did not get. Listening to them act was like watching golf on TV: slow, deliberate, and monotonous. But Charley wanted to see the car chase scene through the hills of San Francisco and there was not much else playing. The only other choice that night was *The Lion in Winter*. For my brother, that was out of the question.

On the night of December 26, the roads leading to Hundred Oaks Shopping Center were covered in a half-frozen gray mush. Driving was reduced to a crawl. Charley was an excellent driver, even as a teenager. He was confident and smart in his decisions on the road.

You would think he and I would have had lots to talk about. He, too, had been having an awful year at school. This was his senior year and his grades were not much better than mine. Even his varsity prowess, which he had been proud of for three years, was stumbling and in a publicly humiliating way.

I don't remember much about *Bullitt*. What I remember was in the car heading home, Charley was hyped up by the chase scene in the movie and gunned the engine a few times to make us slide and skid down Franklin Road. I yelled at him to slow down and he dismissed me, disgusted. "Look at you. A scared pussy."

"Look who's the loser, asshole. If your driving's as good as the way you play football, we're as good as dead."

He pulled the car over and stopped. He sat looking straight ahead and I was afraid for a second that I had really hurt him. Instead he slowly turned and looked at me with contempt. In a burst, he grabbed the collar of my coat and yanked me closer to him. He raised his fist slowly and then let loose on my face. I felt his knuckles pummel my cheekbone and pound at the side of my head. I pushed back from him and curled up against the car door, trying to block his attack with my hands and legs, but his rage kept flying. I swung the door open and fell backward into the wet snow. He jumped on top of me and continued slugging. I could feel the dirty slush on the side of the road coming through my cap, my heavy coat, and into my shirt. This was not a jealous brother beating me up. This was not roughhousing. This was years of pent-up anger, disgust, embarrassment, and disappointment let out in a single flash of honesty to prove that I, the entity of me, was something that he utterly hated. My lips and teeth hurt and I tasted blood in my mouth. But the rest of me was numb.

I hadn't hit him. Not a single time.

I curled up in a ball on the seat, sniffing back a bloody nose as he drove us home. The cars of the relatives lined the driveway. The house was filled with company.

"Oh, shit." Charley realized how embarrassing this would be for Mother and Dad.

"Open the garage door," I demanded. "I want to go to Ida's bathroom. I'm staying in the basement."

I locked the slatted door of the maid's room behind me and collapsed on the toilet in the dark. I released the anger and hurt from the ordeal, weeping uncontrollably and rocking back and forth on the toilet.

When I stopped, I could hear the muffled talking of adults. From the heating vent I could hear what they were saying. From the heating vent they had heard me crying. I had let loose and they all had heard it in the dining room. My parents and my aunts and uncles had all heard it. "We should go check on what's happened, Ed." As they excused themselves from the table, my parents sounded more concerned than embarrassed. I felt relieved that they read the incident as serious. After they left the room, I could hear the relatives' cautious laughter trying to play down the embarrassing moment with "boys will be boys."

I don't recall now what my parents said to me or what they might have said to Charley. I only remember what my mother said to both of us together. "You two have to find a way to get along or something much worse than this is going to happen and then you'll have to live with it for the rest of your lives." I dismissed it as church talk. *God will punish you if you don't behave. God will punish you if you don't get along. You are brothers and you must love each other.*

Church talk. That kind of rationalizing made no sense to me. Particularly as those who lived by the words of the Bible seemed to be condoning a war that nobody could explain and seemed to be standing by idly while the blacks of their communities were exploited and angry. The adults in this world seemed to be hating and distrusting somebody new every chance they could get. Instead of church talk, I wanted my parents to prevent these outbursts of Charley's so I wouldn't have to fear for my life again. I wanted them to have him arrested and taken away so I could sleep that night. I wanted them to take my side, to see that I had done nothing wrong, and that I had not caused this. They did no such thing.

The snow melted the next day, December 27, and the air turned warm enough for Charley and me to wash the gray dirt off the car in which we had driven to see *Bullitt*. Without speaking, we morosely hosed down the white Impala in the driveway. I soaped up the sponge with detergent and wiped my own brown blood off the door from the night before, a handprint smeared in a wide, desperate arc.

SEVEN

Hair

Flunking out of MBA in 1969 was not the end of the world. It was the best thing that could have happened to me. I studied Algebra again in the summer at another school in Nashville, Peabody Demonstration School, a liberal-minded institution in the 1960s' alternative mold. I found it easier and made an A. I could not understand what had made it so hard before. Of course it would be easier the second time around, and no doubt it would be easier at Peabody than at MBA, but to go from an F to an A?

At Peabody, I finally enjoyed some of the other students in the class. It was the first time I had ever had black classmates and I found it a stimulating challenge to cut through my shyness in order to get to know them. It was entirely new to me to know middle- and upper-middle-class blacks, given that up to that point the only blacks I knew were servants. At Peabody, with student backgrounds being so widely varied, politeness was automatic.

No more fathers who were all members of the same clubs. At Peabody there was some sort of democratic spectrum. It had been two years since I had been in a classroom with girls. It felt wonderful to have cohorts nearby with whom I did not feel competitive and defeated. Many of the boys had grown their hair to their shoulders and smelled like cigarettes. I liked the break from the buttoned-down, conservative standard. Many students wore blue jeans. There was a range of bodies, of beauty, of ethnicities, of economies. After two years of feeling apart from the other students in my classes at MBA, I finally felt at home inside all the variations of people in the room. I liked learning more about the other students and especially so when I discovered how different our lives were.

I bought some new clothes that summer, colored T-shirts and my first pair of Levi's blue jeans. I noticed that the shirts were suddenly tighter on my arms—I was finally starting to fill out and take on a masculine shape. I observed myself for the first time with two mirrors and saw myself as others did, from the side and the back. There were some features I hated and some I liked, but it was all weirdly exciting, like visiting a new country. I was able to be objective about who I was for the first time in my life. Like listening to one's own voice on a tape recorder for the first time: there is a moment of revulsion followed by a certain amount of acceptance, until finally one simply gets used to it. In my eyes, I was looking a little more like a guy, not a sexless angel. Being fair-haired, skinny, and smooth all of my life, androgyny had been one of my biggest sources of humiliation.

By the end of the summer, I had applied and been accepted to Peabody. I could now try school again and this time with no previous baggage attached. Whenever I drove by Montgomery Bell Academy after that, I looked at it on the hill and wondered what would have happened to me had I remained. Had I passed Algebra I.

The first day of the tenth grade at Peabody was chaotic with lines for books, lines for schedules, lines for meal tickets, and lines for lockers. I was still nervous and shy, but I voluntarily threw myself into the matters at hand. Halfway through the day, I ran up the main staircase for an appointment with a teacher and bumped into Draper running downstairs toward the lobby. We had gone to kindergarten and then Burton School together, until he entered Peabody in the fourth grade. We had played as children and always enjoyed each other's mischief and humor. I hadn't seen him for five years, two of which had been the unhappiest of my life. His eyes burst with recognition and we stood laughing at how we had ended up together there, in that stairwell.

That night, Draper called and we talked for over an hour,

most of it spent laughing. To this day, Draper and I have not let our connection break since that moment in the stairwell. Almost forty years later, he and I still spend an inordinate amount of time laughing.

The first month at Peabody Demonstration School was an antidote to the two years spent at Montgomery Bell Academy. First of all, I discovered that I was not stupid. The woman who taught the English class, Eleanor Hitchcock, was an imposing, sophisticated woman in her midfifties. She was a northerner, a Yankee, who had gotten a master's degree at Columbia and was not one to smile without reason. Like my mother, she suffered no fools. Period. During the first weeks of school, the entire class was intimidated by this crusty and world-weary woman, a cross between Agnes Moorehead and Pearl S. Buck. As we got to know her, though, she opened up in meaningful ways and respect for her replaced the fear. For the first time, I understood how to think analytically about what I read. Shortly into the first semester, Mrs. Hitchcock took me aside and said, "I like the way you think, Yarrott. You are independent and you are a fine writer." I was surprised.

Now I realize that my previous interpretation of learning had been confused with obeying teachers. The two processes are often mutually exclusive. You cannot think fully while you simply obey. You cannot think when you are being told *what* to think. The key was that at Peabody we were encouraged to have our own opinions, not to adopt a club's motto or pledge of like-mindedness. We were encouraged not to confine our thinking or our loyalties to our race, our sex, or our social status. At Peabody, particularly in Mrs. Hitchcock's class, I developed opinions, threw them into the class discussion, and learned how to defend them.

Maybe the mouse could learn to roar.

In the first semester, because my cumulative grades were near the top of the class, a group of psychologists from Peabody College for Teachers, the parent institution of the Demonstration School, included me in a study of gifted students. I buried the previous two years at Montgomery Bell and rarely spoke of them again.

One of the biggest surprises to me that year was a romance with Natalie. She was in my class with Mrs. Hitchcock and sat across the room from me. Physically beautiful, with radiant olive skin, pale green eyes, and straight brown hair to her waist, she had a perfect small woman's body. I was amazed that she was attracted to me. I saw myself as a boy, yet here she was, this *woman*. Natalie was a perpetual honor student. For her, straight A's were as expected as tomorrow's lunch. I didn't let on how my grades of that year were brand-new developments. I felt the past was something best overlooked, along with my surprise that she liked me, and along with my pounding pulse in the boys' locker room.

I was hesitant when I first started making out with Natalie, unsure of what I wanted or what I could do, but I became bolder each time we found ourselves in a secluded place. We tasted each other's tongues and explored each other's mouths as deeply as we could. I forgot about my crooked teeth and the braces weaving in between them. Natalie liked me as I was. *Maybe I'm not so bad.*

I got excited making out with her and started slipping my hands under her bra, trying to get to her nipples. *I know she can feel how turned on I am. Is that okay?* She encouraged me to take as much as I wanted. She made it clear that her body was my territory to explore. The problem was that I was not sure what sort of territory I wanted. At the point when I had her nipple in my mouth, at the point when I felt dizzy from equal measures of excitement and fear, I would stop. I would pull away and cross my legs and say, "It wouldn't be right to go any further. I just can't do that to you." She would open her eyes and look at me, astonished and flushed, but she accepted what I claimed.

Natalie was Jewish, and though my parents had Jewish friends I didn't understand what being a Jew meant until Natalie explained it to me. In Nashville, the concept of religious or cultural differences among polite white people was, in my parents' circle at least, kept somewhat hidden, as if noting differences among people and their histories was somehow rude. I was not aware, for example, that there had been classism and bigotry in the United States toward Irish Catholics. Since President Kennedy, the Crawfords in the big house down the street, and my own patrician grandfather McElroy in Kentucky all were Catholics, I had assumed that the American Catholic church was chiefly composed of wealthy aristocrats who had always enjoyed privilege and power. As for Jews, I abstractly knew of but didn't understand the Holocaust of World War II and understood nothing of historical anti-Semitism occurring before that. Bigoted comments about Jews from the Episcopalian family down the street were completely lost on me. They spoke in euphemisms that I simply did not understand. Since Uncle Louis, my father's office partner for forty years, his wife's family, and many other Jewish families in Nashville were civic leaders and quite prosperous, I assumed that all Jews were wealthy civic leaders and were happily woven into the fabric of every American community. The ethnic divisions I did see were only between whites and blacks. In many ways, until the tenth grade I was as blind as a bat about everything political, social, and cultural. Until then, I had responded to what was in front of me purely spontaneously and intuitively, with no greater contextual understanding.

One can't fault my old prep school Montgomery Bell for having tried but failed to drill into a stone. It simply was not the way to the middle. Mrs. Hitchcock knew how to do it, though, by looking me in the eye and with utmost confidence convincing me that I had something to say. She led me out of my myopic self.

At home, life was quieter in the tenth grade than ever before in my life. With Angela back at Center College, in Danville, Kentucky; Eddy at Washington University Medical School, in St. Louis; and Charley now at University of Tennessee, in Knoxville, not only did I suddenly find myself enjoying school, but I had the house and my parents to myself. I celebrated this new independence by painting my room and moving the furniture around. I cleared out the empty aquarium from the corner and finally threw away a huge ten-year-old old Coke bottle from the dresser top. I replaced them with a stereo record player and a bottle of Brut cologne. I believed the sun would shine brightly on a shade of white called Timothy I found at the Sherwin Williams

31

paint store. I floated furniture in the middle of the room instead of jamming everything against the walls and arranged separate areas for sitting, studying, and sleeping. I bought huge red paper flowers from The Shop of John Simmons and gathered them in an old wine bottle on a table beneath the psychedelic White Rabbit poster. I memorized the entire album of *Hair*. I cleaned out my closet and straightened the clothes on the hangers. I prepared myself to take hold of this new life.

When Charley drove off to Knoxville, I felt a palpable sense of relief. While he and I had been tolerating each other more that summer, particularly once I had settled into Peabody, there was still a territorial tension in the air.

Charley had a superb sense of style in high school, one that was based on the young conservative male's concept of good clothes, a polish acquired through reading *Esquire*, *Playboy*, and *Sports Illustrated*. With his dark tan and straight dark brown hair, he had the muscular good looks of one of The Beach Boys in prep school clothes. A yellow Oxford cloth shirt gave Charley the élan of a sexy hotshot. He had been grooming himself well since his first year in high school, and his room with all of his clothes and things were left untouched in his absence. Otherwise, he would be infuriated and I would catch the heat for it.

I talked with Draper and Natalie every night on the phone. We tied up the line so often that my father's patients began complaining. Even the notorious Hazel Atkins, the woman who interrupted our family dinners, had the nerve to complain. Through our laughing fits, Draper and I would resurrect the day's cast of characters we had just seen at school. We regurgitated every hilarious moment we could remember and when we finished talking, my stomach muscles sore, I would then call Natalie. By the time I got off the line, at least two hours had passed. Natalie and I once stayed on the phone from one o'clock A.M. until after sunrise. I bragged that I had spent the night with her.

My parents were relieved that I was laughing now instead of hiding away in a sullen state, so they allowed my outrageously long phone conversations to continue. However, I soon had to pay for my own separate telephone line for the bedroom, so the real emergencies of Dad's patients would not have to stand in line behind my laughing fits. All the hours of talking apparently did not take a toll on my grades, as they continued to rise as the school year went on.

Draper and I shared a view of the world in which, behind all the humor we cultivated together, the issue of sexuality remained a mutual Achilles' heel—something we carefully avoided with each other until college but both knew was there. We had identified a safety within each other's company as quickly as a hummingbird finds a patch of red. I think we knew something was up when we each admitted to having memorized the words to *Hair*. This said something about our sensibilities—artistic, poetic, and emotional—that we understood immediately in each other. We needed to break some important social rules, even if we were not sure which ones they were. We wanted to act how we felt, not how we were told. The album of *Hair* screamed that message into our ears. It was the Age of Aquarius, damn it.

We had steady girlfriends, we even seemed to enjoy all that, but there was something else, something more. In the tenth grade, I was very proud of myself for having become involved with a beautiful girl and it felt, at the time, very real. Having Draper as a best friend stimulated me intellectually and socially, but Natalie's attraction to me repaired my self-confidence more than any other single change in my life. I learned fast in those relationships, observing behavior and absorbing social skills to make up for the critical time lost in the previous two years.

During the spring semester of my tenth grade, however, the calm seas at home—which had been so essential for a fundamental change in me—began to roil. A squall of unimaginable proportions was gathering on the horizon.

EIGHT

The Instincts of a Dog

Charley had called from Knoxville several times since Christmas to tell my parents school was not going well. He was unable to pinpoint what was happening, but it was something physical. He had lost his appetite, was unable to concentrate, and had very little energy. In March, Mother and Dad finally suggested that he come home to be tested for mononucleosis. Immediately, as soon as he brought his bags up to his room, he and I began to argue about territory. I had transgressed in a big way by moving a few things out of my room and into the hallway. I was instantly resentful that he was back home, even for a short visit.

The medical examinations were conducted in the office of his internist, Dr. Kingsley. They pinpointed no specific problem and mononucleosis was ruled out. It was recommended that Charley return to school to prevent falling further behind in his classes. He returned to Knoxville the next morning.

Ten days later, he was back home.

I overheard him confiding to Dad on the porch, "I don't know what's wrong. Sometimes I just feel incredibly flat, you know, really low. I can't make myself concentrate in class or read the material. I've made lots of friends, but they want to go out partying and I don't have the energy. I don't know what the hell is wrong with me." Despite my lifelong distaste for Charley, I couldn't help but feel something for him now. He was not so much the arrogant, volatile teenager who made me terrified for my life. He seemed somehow humbled by the past several months.

Dr. Kingsley suggested a wider battery of tests that would require a few days in the hospital, so Charley gathered together some pajamas in a gym bag and Dad admitted him to Vanderbilt. After his first twenty-four hours, I visited him during evening visiting hours. I arrived at his door at nine P.M. to hear a conversation between him and our first cousin, Bert, a young Baptist minister considered dynamic and popular in his church in Maryland. Bert's voice was raised, high-pitched and impatient. "You've got to get a hold of yourself, guy. You're letting yourself and your parents think you're sick. You know as well as I do that's not true. Truth is, you're just letting them down. I know how much you've hated school all your life. So what, guy. You've still got to do your job and get through it. You know the phrase *mind over matter*, fella?"

I pushed the door open and stopped the tirade. Bert lifted his voice another octave. "Well, well, well, look what the cat dragged in. Long time no see, guy." Bert was sitting across the room in the big chair and had an open Bible on his knee. Charley's face was flushed. He looked embarrassed.

"Hey, Bert. Yeah, long time. I just came by to see if Charley wanted anything from outside. Before they kick us out. Because it's past visiting hours." I saw relief sweep over Charley's face.

After Bert finally left, Charley stuck out his hand to shake. "Want to thank you, little brother, for helping me out tonight. Man, you appeared just in time. I couldn't have taken another minute with him."

"Wow. He upset you that much, huh?" I asked.

"Shit, Yarrott. Maybe Bert's right. Maybe there's nothing wrong with me except that I don't want to go back to school." Charley crossed his arms and stared ahead. "Maybe he's right. Maybe I'm just scared or depressed or something."

Further demoralizing him, no causes for his symptoms were discovered during the hospitalization. The day after his release, he returned to Knoxville, adamant about facing his invisible demons at school. While his friends had been skiing in the mountains, he had lost the bulk of his spring vacation trying to figure out why he felt so bad. Bert's hospital visit, which he found deeply humiliating, continued to haunt him.

My week of spring vacation started a few days after Charley returned to school. I had decided to use this time in early April to breed Gretel, so that she could deliver puppies before school ended and I could care for them in the summer. Hansel had been neutered, but Dad's secretary, Mrs. Buford, had a black male dachshund named Troy and she agreed to oblige us with a weekend visit. Gretel's heat was in full swing on Friday afternoon and she was more than happy to meet her muscular little visitor. By Monday, she was ready for Troy to return to the place from which he came. It would be a few weeks before we knew if the mating was successful or not.

Meanwhile, Charley was losing his struggle in Knoxville. Catching up with his studies had proven impossible with an energy level that fluctuated erratically. In addition, his dormitory was located directly across the river from a paper mill, and its fumes were making him nauseated in the morning and making it difficult to get out of bed. He had what he figured was the first migraine headache of his life. He continued to lose weight. His friends, who were frequent partiers, drinking most nights and often smoking grass, had grown tired of reaching out to him and being rebuffed. Charley had become a drag to them.

By the end of April, he had withdrawn from UT and moved all of his things back to 1120 Tyne Boulevard. Mother and Dad were sympathetic and believed that he had tried his best to deal with an invisible problem. They agreed with Charley that there must be a physical cause for his symptoms. For the time being, he would move home and try to recuperate from whatever he was suffering from. Our cousin Bert was kept at bay.

Gretel's belly had begun swelling by the middle of April and her due date was the first week of June. Charley occupied himself with caring for her. He and Mother fed her morning shakes of eggs and vitamins and took turns brushing her coat in the afternoons. Between the two of them, they provided an idyllic environment for Gretel during her nine weeks of pregnancy. Meanwhile, I was finishing my second semester at Peabody and preparing for exams. The year had gone so well at school I found it hard to believe.

Earlier in the spring, Mr. Stubblefield, the gym teacher, had announced that he was recruiting a new gymnastics team for Peabody. I tried out and made the team, alongside Draper, and we began practicing several afternoons each week after school. Learning how to accomplish moves that seemed to defy gravity became my theme for the year. I was now doing what everyone, including me, had assumed I could not. My life at that moment—academically, physically, and socially—seemed to be mirrored on the parallel bars: I had begun with my feet stuck to the ground, but with encouragement from new friends and teachers, and with a burst of self-confidence, I had learned to swing myself up into a handstand.

Early Wednesday morning, June 3, an enormous Gretel began digging in her bed, rooting around restlessly. She circled her spot on the mattress and nestled, then got up and repeated herself. My mother knew the signs. She called me at school and asked me to come straight home after my last class. By the time I returned at four P.M., no puppies had yet appeared. Instead, Gretel had begun whining with discomfort. Clearly she was in labor, but nothing was moving. Our veterinarian urged us to bring her to his office at once and determined that one of the puppies was blocking the rest from passing through the birth canal. He performed a Caesarian immediately. The next morning I carried Gretel home in my arms in an old blanket, while Charley carried a shoebox with her five black, squirming pups. Watching Gretel come back to life from her groggy, post-Caesarian fog and know immediately, naturally how to mother her pups was the most straightforward display of instinct I had ever witnessed. Ignoring her pain from the incision the night before, she put her offspring before herself, gathered them in a pile, feverishly licked each one, and then rolled to her side to let them get to her teats. She knew what to do. Somehow.

NINE

July 31, 1970

The summer noise on Old Hickory Lake vibrated like a distant machine, an unidentifiable sound like the incessant hum of a big city. Shouts, music, echoes, and motorboats scattered across its surface like lace on a tabletop.

On our brown shoulders that Friday, decades ago, the erotic mix of sweat and Coppertone got us ready for a broiling sun. Our long hair was stuck to our faces. Eddy, Charley, Angela, and I had finished the lunches we had brought from home. We laughed in small clouds of cigarettes, arms behind our heads, our feet propped up in the boat, the anchor dropped. Angela and I slipped in and out of falsetto harmonizing in "Ladies of the Canyon." Charley objected, "You two. Aren't you sick of Joni Mitchell yet? Why don't you ever sing Dylan?"

"I've got an even better idea," Eddy interrupted. "Let me find Dylan on the radio."

The construction of Old Hickory Dam in 1952 revolutionized how Middle Tennesseans spent their summers. Houseboats were lowered onto the new lake by the thousands. Cabins were built along the adjacent hillsides. A number of boating clubs emerged with docks and restaurants along the water, all designed from top to bottom with lacquered knotty pine and outfitted with screen doors that slapped loud and hard.

In 1963, my father bought the small outboard runabout that had belonged to his secretary. He began driving us back and forth to the lake, pulling the white boat on its trailer.

Although he never learned to swim, Dad often drove the boat and convinced us to be at home in the water. All four of his children became strong swimmers and water-skiers, and when we became teenagers we made our trips to the lake by ourselves and spent the days screaming in the wind, fighting with one another, listening to folk and rock on a transistor radio, getting stoned and sunburned, and polishing our slalom.

Over time, at the lake, there developed a warm esprit de corps among us four siblings. We continued to argue, but not like we did at home with the doors closed and the air conditioners on. Perhaps it was the independence we felt at the lake, without our parents, stretching our physical selves with more and more skillful waterskiing. Perhaps on that day, July 31, 1970, it was the rope swing to which we had come, hanging from a tree on a high cliff. I had never seen it before. Neither had Angela or Eddy. Charley had discovered it with his high school football buddies the weekend before and had come home with excitement in his face, beer on his breath, and a few big bruises on his legs.

"Incredible. You won't believe it. It takes you way out over the water, must be fifty feet high, then you drop."

"Do you think it's dangerous? That high, I mean?" I was cautious.

"Nah. You'll love it, Yarrott. Except you've got to remember to let go before swinging back toward the cliff."

It was as he said it would be. High, so high, up a hill and then over to the edge of the cliff. The tree hanging over the edge was gnarled and old, but still green. The rope was a heavy-gauged type used for docking houseboats and was tied to an upper branch of the tree. Charley stepped up to the rope first, showing us what to avoid below when we dropped. He pushed off the cliff, gripping the rope, and swung away from us by fifty, sixty, seventy-five feet. At the farthest point of the swing, he let go and remained in a seated position, calm and still, as he dropped. Then he hit the water, making a clean splash, and disappeared for a few seconds. When he surfaced he was laughing hysterically. "Oh, man! I love it!"

The three of us added to his screaming and Angela scrambled up to grab the rope. "Okay...now it's my turn."

"Be careful, Angela," I warned.

"Stop your worrying, Yarrott," she said, looking disgusted with my concern. Then she jumped into the air, holding tightly to the rope. "Sayonaraaaa!" She followed Charley's arc and did exactly as told, dropping from the highest point, but making an enormous splash. "Oh, hell, that hurts!" she screamed to us when she surfaced. "Whatever you do, don't flop! It'll kill you!"

Eddy went next, without hesitation, and at the top of the arc, dropped straight and clean into the water with little noise. He surfaced a moment later. "That's unbelievable! It's fantastic!"

I held onto the rope and stood there on the cliff. From the height I could see water-skiers and boats across the water. My siblings were quiet, watching to see what I would do. I knew that if I stood there and thought about it too long I wouldn't jump. The height was terrifying and I was suddenly very aware of my knees. They were as tense as my knuckles were white. Then Charley yelled to me, "Okay, little brother, your turn! You can do it. Don't worry. We're all down here waiting for you." At that, I lifted up on my toes and lost contact with the cliff, soaring out over the water. "Okay, drop now! Goddamn it, drop, Yarrott!" I waited until I was starting back to the cliff and then let go. The view from up there was gorgeous. The moment of looking down and seeing my siblings, eyes glued on me and cheering, gave me a novel courage. I hit the water on my side and, like Angela said, it stung like hell. But it was a small price to pay, I figured, for an enormous thrill.

By the end of the afternoon, we were dropping cleanly into the water, one after another. We had honed the skill and were worn out. Charley quit first and struggled back on the boat, collapsing on the seat. "I don't know about you guys, but I'm beat. I mean it. I'm finished." Hanging his head, he rested his elbows on his knees, his shoulders drawn narrow. He suddenly looked smaller.

Angela noticed several red patches on his arms and back. "I think you've gotten burned, Charley. Better put on your shirt."

"Man, I'm feeling shitty. For some reason, I'm really shaky. Maybe I need to eat. Let's head home."

We didn't talk much on the way home in our Volkswagen bus. Angela gently massaged Charley's back with sunburn lotion, as she did for all of us when we turned red. She remarked that it didn't look like a sunburn to her. "It's something else. A rash, maybe?" Eddy drove the bus and I sat in the back seat breathing in the hot wind off I-40. It took us an hour to reach home. The sun at five P.M. on July 31 was blistering in middle Tennessee, the humidity thick and stifling. We had no air-conditioning in the bus. The long ride home after skiing all day always made me feel queasy. Charley sat in the front passenger seat, dazed and staring ahead quietly.

Mother and Dad were not home when we got back; their white Impala was gone. Eddy and I unhitched the trailer and pulled it to the side of the driveway while Angela gathered up the towels and all our other gear. She removed the water from the rear of the boat by pressing the big sponge onto the floor and letting it swell with bilge water, then squeezed it out on the grass.

I checked on the puppies in the pen and put Gretel in to nurse. On my way upstairs, I threw the towels in the washer and changed into dry shorts and a T-shirt.

Angela called up to me, "Yarrott, see if Charley's upstairs, will you? And ask him to give me a hand putting the cover on the boat. I think it might storm tonight." The canvas tarp had metal snaps, which were rusting and becoming more difficult to line up with their mates on the topside of the boat. It took brute force and experience to accomplish what normally should have been a simple job.

I stuck my head in his room, next door to mine, and found him in bed, lying on his side and facing the wall. His window shade was drawn and the room was dark. "Angela wants some help with the boat cover, Charley. Can you do it?"

"Give me a minute," he moaned slowly. "I've got a splitting headache."

"Hey, no sweat. Take a nap. I'll take care of it." I noticed a dark shadow across his pillow and lower face. It turned bright red as I moved closer.

"Charley, you've got a nosebleed. Holy shit, there's a lot of blood. What happened?"

He tried to sit up and, sighing, dropped his head back on the pillow. He slowly moved his hand to his nose and felt the blood. "Nothing. Nothing happened at all. I don't know what's going on."

I ran to the banister and yelled down to Angela and Eddy to come up. Eddy had just finished a year of medical school in St. Louis. He took one look at the quantity of blood and was alarmed. Turning on the overhead light and raising the shades, he told Angela and me to get ice and a stack of towels. We returned and began mopping up the blood.

"Hey, Charley, can I see inside your mouth?" Eddy pulled back Charley's lips and exposed his teeth. Blood was oozing from the gums around the base of each tooth. Eddy cursed under his breath. It had turned the inside of his lips red and was beginning to dry at the corners of his mouth. "Can I look at your hands, Charley?" Eddy took one, looked closely at a fingertip and began squeezing it. He squeezed several times, but the pink did not return to the nails.

"What the hell you doing?" Charley softly asked, annoyed.

"Just checking your color. That's all."

Then Eddy instructed me to make an ice pack with the towel and apply it to both sides of Charley's nose. He told Charley to keep an ice cube in his mouth as long as he could stand it. He asked Angela to track Mother and Dad down. She thought they were having dinner at our Aunt Mary and Uncle Brad's house. "Call them and tell them to come home."

"Gosh, Eddy, is that really necessary?"

"Goddamn it, Angela. Do what I say. It's something serious."

TEN

Downpour

I remember the short space of time before our parents returned home. I leaned against the counter in the kitchen to watch a storm gathering outside the window. Part of the sky was covered in a dark gray blanket, a powerful storm front, the kind that whips tornadoes off its edges. It was the kind of sky we were taught to fear. Inside the house, there was another tension growing, a peculiar kind of waiting—as if the house were holding its breath. Hansel sat on his haunches in the front hall, looking up the stairs as if waiting for someone to descend. The icemaker in the new refrigerator whirred and dropped ice into the bin, and refilled itself with water. I withdrew the bin from the freezer and dumped it in a Tupperware bowl. Running back upstairs, I felt something like a brewing storm inside the house as well, though not altogether bad. Something was causing us siblings to relate to one another today, first at the lake, and now with this crisis. It was one of the few times that I could tell we actually cared about one another. I could see how competently we all worked together in an emergency. I was proud that we were not afraid of the blood and we could figure out what to do. Outdoors, the sky was filling with blue-gray clouds. The leaves on the trees were turning upside down. A major summer downpour was beginning. I hurried outside to gather up Gretel and her puppies and brought them into the kitchen.

At the back door, we heard the metallic clicks of Mother's crutches in the rain, then the swinging open of the screen door against the wind. I ran down to meet them. "Hey, where is everyone? Yarrott, do you know what's going on with Charley? Where is he?" Mom said, wiping her glasses. Dad appeared behind her, coming up the steps, concerned.

"He started to feel bad at the lake so we came home early. Then he got a headache and a really bad nosebleed."

"Well, let's have a look, Elizabeth." Dad navigated through the puppies, then ran up the stairs in front of Mother, who climbed the steps cautiously with her crutches. I could hear Dad's stock greeting as he entered a patient's room: "What do we have here, old man? A nosebleed?"

A few minutes later, I heard Mom's crutches on the stairs again, this time moving much

more quickly and emphatically. "Yarrott, honey, we're taking Charley to the emergency room. Daddy's pretty concerned. Will you call Aunt Mary and tell her we won't be returning to the dinner party?"

After Charley, Mother, and Dad left, the house seemed to stand still and wait. The storm outside continued in a greenish haze of humidity and lightning. Eddy and Angela showered and changed into dry clothes. With little appetite, we picked at odds and ends from the refrigerator and darkness descended. Without paying attention to it, the three of us watched a nighttime sitcom on the miniature Sony propped on the breakfast table. The storm ended outside. I fed the dogs. At ten o'clock, Angela turned on the porch lights and I put the puppies back in their pen outdoors. We watched the news and then a rerun of *The Tonight Show*. At midnight, the phone rang. Eddy and I shared the extension in his room and Angela got on the phone in the kitchen.

"Charley's just now been admitted." Mother's voice was subdued. "They got his nosebleed stopped. Now a house officer and a couple of interns are examining him. They've taken all sorts of blood tests but won't know anything until tomorrow."

"How's he feeling?" Angela asked.

"Terrible. The headache's gotten much worse. Frankly, your father and I are worried. You know those red spots on his skin? They're clusters of broken capillaries, something called petechiae." She repeated the pronunciation slowly, "You pronounce it like pa-*TEEK*-ia. Daddy knows what they are. He's also afraid that his blood counts might come back with some very low numbers tomorrow."

"What about his headache?" Eddy asked.

Her voice lowered, she sounded tired. "Well, it might be related to the bleeding."

"Intracranial stuff?" Eddy was one of them now, a medical professional. "They suspect a subcranial hematoma?" To me, he whispered, "Bruising and bleeding inside the brain."

"They think so." Mother's voice was that of not just a nurse, but a very worried mother. "I'll keep you informed as we learn anything. We're staying with him until we feel things are under control. If there is bleeding inside Charley's skull, it's developing pressure on his brain. It can be extremely painful, that is if he remains conscious."

After hanging up, Eddy turned to us and explained what he knew about intracranial bleeding. "It's a critical situation and can result in brain damage, disruption of vital functions, and could even kill him. Jesus Christ, you all. Charley's in bad shape."

Angela looked at me with her eyes welling up. "We were just swinging like maniacs from the rope swing a few hours ago. How could this just happen out of the blue?"

Eddy broke in, "Hate to say it, but the jumping probably caused it. Remember when the rash started on his arms and legs? Right after he landed hard on the water. But I want to know what's making him so fragile."

I stayed awake most of the night, my mind racing. At four o'clock I went to the kitchen for orange juice and saw that Eddy's bedroom light was on. He had taken down Dad's medical textbooks from the shelves in the living room and was reading the chapter on hematology in bed. "So what do you think it could be, Eddy?"

"Not sure until we get the results of his blood back. Could be a couple of things, from a simple kind of anemia to the worst form of leukemia. Lots of conditions make your gums bleed."

At six o'clock, I heard the back door swing open, followed

by the familiar clicks of Mother's crutches. Dad was carrying a puppy in one arm and Charley's bloody clothes in the other. "You need to bring in the pups," he ordered me. "They shouldn't have stayed in the pen all night. It's too wet." He dropped the clothes into the washing machine on top of the damp towels from the lake, filled it with cold water, and turned it on.

Eddy and I joined them in the kitchen. With a tired face, Dad explained. "They gave him platelets at three-thirty and brought his bleeding under control, so we came on home to get some rest. His headache has stopped. Your mother and I need to go back in a few hours." Turning to me, Dad explained further, "Platelets are one of three blood components made by the bone marrow. You've got red cells, white cells, and then platelets. They are essential for clotting to happen."

"You mean like factor VIII for hemophiliacs?" I asked, proud that I had remembered something from my biology class.

"Not exactly, but something like it. Factor VIII is a protein substance you must have so your blood will clot. Platelets are actual cell-like structures that collect together and attach to one another. That's when your blood aggregates or clots."

"Any idea what's causing this, Dad?" Eddy asked.

"Not yet. They'll know better after the hematology department takes a look at his results. Give them a few hours."

"Do you know any of those guys?"

"Sure. John Flexner, the department head. We've had patients together in the past. He's very good. Known him for years. There's also a new house officer who's on the case. Young guy named John Sergent."

Mother added, "He's great. A really dynamic guy. Stayed up all night with us. Charley likes him and they've been talking a lot this morning. Especially after the bleeding stopped. He's also from Kentucky—Frankfort."

A procession of doctors and medical students quietly gathered in his room. Groggy from medication and blood loss, Charley lightly scratched at his IV. The small needle inserted into the top of his hand was taped tightly, but a blue hematoma was beginning at the site of the insertion. A common accident, the needle had been pushed through the vein, then pulled back into its proper place during the initial stick. He had received three units of red cells and two of platelets. Some of the infused fluids had leaked out of the vein through the puncture and had settled in the surrounding tissue. He had been given 50 milligrams of Benadryl to lessen his body's reaction to the foreign blood and 500 milligrams of acetaminophen to reduce his headache. His nose was packed with gauze and his lips were gray, despite the suntan from the day before.

While he was not very alert at that moment, he was nevertheless embarrassed to hear his situation being explained to six students only a few years older than himself. Without asking, the doctor raised the sheet to expose Charley's inner thighs and the constellations of broken capillaries, the petechiae, gathered near his groin. "Please. Don't," he insisted to the doctor. "C'mon. There's girls with you."

The silver-haired doctor stopped his hand in the air for a moment and looked over his glasses. "Charles, you're going to have to get used to women looking at you. You know from your father that this is a teaching hospital. These are all medical students and nothing they'll see is new to them. May I now raise the sheet?"

Charley reluctantly agreed.

"And now will you please roll over so we can see the petechiae that have occurred on your buttocks?"

Charley groaned but did as asked. One of the female students thanked him and he turned around and looked at her. She was slim, like a runner, with shoulder-length brown hair parted down the middle. He cringed when he saw how attractive she was.

ELEVEN

A Circle Around the Bed

Mother and Dad returned to Vanderbilt after breakfast. An hour later, Eddy, Angela, and I drove the VW bus to join them in Charley's room. We stopped at a light on the corner of 21st Avenue and Blair Boulevard and I heard the radio from the car in the next lane. The song of the summer was playing, the insipid "Close to You" by The Carpenters.

Reflexively, I felt my gut tighten. The song, regardless of whether I liked it or not, affected me like a significant smell. It instantly brought me back to a moment that had occurred a few days earlier. I remembered the dark-blond guy across the pool at the Sequoia Club and felt my stomach sink. I remembered the curve of his lower back disappearing under his blue trunks, the thick golden hair on his forearms, his Adam's apple, pronounced and jumping as he threw his head back to drink a Coke. The thoughts stirred me. I wanted to hear his voice again, listen to his deep, hollow voice, and feel the coarseness of the hair on his neck. *Why am I thinking of that guy now, when all this is happening to Charley? What is wrong with me?*

We parked behind the hospital at Dad's office and walked across to the back entrance of the hospital, down a corridor from the 1940s, through the round wing of the 1960s, then up to the hematology floor and back again to the 1940s. I could hear Mother's lilting, animated voice as we approached the room.

Charley was in the bed with a faint smile on his face. He was listening to the conversation across his bed bouncing from one side to the other. Mother was discussing the baseball game earlier in the week at Wrigley Field in Chicago, between the Atlanta Braves and the Chicago Cubs.

"I've always been a fan of the Cubs, Dr. Sergent. But the Braves sure trampled them yesterday."

"How about Jackson's home run, Mrs. Benz? Fa-a-antastic!"

Mother continued smiling as we gathered in the room. "Oh, hey, you all, this is Dr. Sergent, the house officer I was telling you about. Daddy is making his own rounds right now, but he'll be back in about a half hour. You just missed him."

John Sergent was twenty-nine years old, a tall, handsome, and engaging man with an enormous personality and, despite a Southern accent, a rapid-fire talker. The room immediately fell into a lively discussion around the bed and, for a time, we seemed to forget why we had assembled there. Charley was the physical center of the room, but was drifting in and out of the conversation. His faint smile remained. I looked at him and saw that he was vastly improved from the night before, when his face was streaked with blood and his lips had turned gray. But he still did not look good today. Better, but not good. With his dark tan, his skin color seemed to have become a dark yellow, as if all the pink had been drained from his face and hands.

His being confined to a hospital bed seemed wrong to me, given how healthy he had seemed just the day before. I hated to see this transformation; it was a change that seemed weirdly threatening, otherworldly. If this could happen to Charley, of all people, it could happen to any one of us. I did not know what to talk to him about, so I joked with him. He joked back. Wanly, we smiled at each other, and he rolled his eyes as if to say, "Can you believe all this?"

When Dad returned from his surgical rounds, Dr. Sergent suddenly became serious and addressed us, now that the whole family had assembled in Charley's room. "We think we have a name for what's going on with Charley. We'll be able to confirm it tomorrow after a bone marrow biopsy this afternoon, but we're pretty sure. It's called aplastic anemia, which is a malfunction of the bone marrow. Don't let the word anemia fool you into thinking that this is not serious. Aplastic anemia can be every bit as deadly as leukemia. The marrow normally produces much of your red cells, white cells, and platelets, but it can shut down. We don't know what causes it. Charley's counts suggest that he has a good number of white cells, but is very low in red cells and platelets. We can infuse him with those from the stockpile at the Red Cross, but poor matches for platelets make them almost worthless to him. It's the luck of the draw how well they work. One good thing: Aplastic anemia can be a temporary condition. It comes and then it can go. It sometimes occurs in old people as a passing problem. Sometimes in pregnant women. I have to say, though, the extremely low level of Charley's counts is pretty serious. His spontaneous bleeding is a real problem and we have to find a way to stop it. We will be doing a bone marrow biopsy on him in about an hour and we expect that to confirm our suspicions."

There was a silence among all of us, including Mother and Dad. It was not simple news. It was not altogether bad news, because Dr. Sergent had said that the condition could be temporary. On the other hand, Charley was in a dangerous place with regard to his bleeding. Worse still, the doctor had compared this to leukemia. I knew about leukemia. It was a word that scared me to death. Nobody survived leukemia. Not in 1970.

"Will the bone marrow biopsy be painful or difficult with Charley's bleeding?" Angela asked.

"No, there won't be much pain. The procedure is not pleasant, but he'll have a local anesthetic at the site of the withdrawal. We use a very large needle and push it right into the pelvic bone and extract a sample there. It's not complicated. There won't be much bleeding."

Eddy, Angela, and I remained in the room until it was time for Charley's bone marrow biopsy and then returned home before noon. Hansel and Gretel needed to be let out, the puppies had to be fed, and I had promised to cut the grass in the side yard. In the late afternoon, to kill time as we waited for word from the hospital, Eddy and I drove the seven miles to the Sequoia Club for a swim. It was hotter than the day before at the lake. Saturdays were always crowded at the pool and this one was particularly so. There were no chaises free, so we lay on the grass on our towels. Someone's radio wafted top forty songs.

I propped up on my elbows and looked at the crowd through the legs of the chaises. Same crowd as always, but today they looked entirely different to me. They seemed simple, monotonous, happy and one-dimensional. I thought of Charley. *Was anyone else sick like that here? Did anyone else have a brother in the hospital? I doubt it. I bet the worst thing these people have to think about is what they're going to put in their salads tonight.*

Then I saw the dark-blond guy across the pool. My heart raced and I could feel the pounding in my neck. *What the hell is going on with me?* I tried to obliterate my thoughts of the guy's shoulders, the wavy dark hair on his neck becoming gold over his ears. This guy had eyes I could read across the pool. Enormous, expressive, with thick, dark eyebrows. *Damn it, think of Natalie, Yarrott. Change the channel. Remember how Natalie's white bikini clings to her when she climbs out of the water. I can see the darkness of her nipples through her top. I can see their pointed shapes pushing at the cloth. Think about Natalie, Yarrott.*

Over the water, from the length of the entire pool, the Carpenters' hackneyed song "Close to You" floated across to bite me like a horsefly. I felt an instinctive, unconscious grip in my stomach. The dark-blond guy threw his head back and laughed at his girlfriend. *Yes, his girlfriend, Yarrott, his damn girlfriend. He's probably screwing his girlfriend. What you should be doing to Natalie, Yarrott, if she weren't away at camp.*

I jumped in the pool and held myself on the bottom with my eyes opened. *This water is so much better than the lake's. I can still see the sky. I can see people swimming over me. Think of Charley, Yarrott. What he must be feeling right now. He's stuck in the hospital. He is really sick, Yarrott. You're sitting here under the water and the sun. Lucky you. Jesus, how can you be thinking of that guy up there. It feels so good, though. Damn, why does it feel so good? I wonder if Eddy has noticed me looking at him.* I surfaced and gasped. I slicked my hair back and pinched the water out of my nose. I felt better. But the damn song was still playing. Gliding on my back toward the ladder, I bumped into a soft leg. The guy's girlfriend. Then I heard the voice and saw the blue trunks as he pulled himself out of the water.

Abruptly, I got out and insisted to Eddy, "Hey, we've got

51

more important things to be doing. We shouldn't be at the pool with all the stuff going on at home." We returned home to Angela, who was putting a frozen pizza in the oven.

"Mother called. She said that we should fend for ourselves for dinner. They're eating at the hospital. Figured pizza would be the safest call. That okay with you both?" Angela tried to sound upbeat.

"Damn," I complained. "No real food for the second night in a row. We're gonna starve."

"Be that way, Yarrott. You ingrate. Make your own dinner." Angela continued to set the table in the breakfast room.

I drove to Green Hills Shopping Center and ordered a Big Mac from the new McDonald's. I sat by a window and watched the traffic on Hillsboro Road. I felt detached from the normal world and was getting angry. Now there was one more thing in my life that made me feel weird and different. *Look at all of the cars. They're all going somewhere, probably somewhere stupid. To eat their pizzas. Frozen, stupid pizzas. Wonder what Charley's eating tonight. What about Mother and Dad?* I felt a stab of regret that I had driven off to McDonald's.

"Mother and Dad called again, Yarrott." Angela met me at the back door. "They said Charley has started to bleed again. The headache's back and he's not very coherent. Something about the blood he received today not lasting. He's being given more of those platelets and they're waiting to see what happens."

The random platelets, administered to Charley early that morning, had been used up by his body and he was in dire need of more. Cross-matching for platelets was not a difficult process to accomplish in the blood bank, but it meant that several units of them should be readied in advance to avoid his spontaneous and dangerous bleeds. Each unit of random platelets would have a different response from Charley's system. Some were a closer match to his blood than others, increasing the length of their effectiveness. Red cells were easier to match, easier to find, and had a longer period of effectiveness.

Almost four decades later, John Sergent recounted to me

his helpless vigil with my parents as they watched Charley's condition deteriorate. Platelets that had been administered in the early evening had little effect. Dr. Sergent ordered a heavier dose of pain medication and Charley slipped into a prolonged sleep. The oozing from his gums increased to dripping. The cotton packs inside his nose were deep red and full. His body had become as fragile as a turgid, overripe tomato. Of even more concern, he had begun to demonstrate cerebral distress, flailing his arms in aimless pursuit of nothing. He had a persistent fever of unknown origin, indicating that his low white cell count had made him susceptible to a systemic infection.

A third infusion of random platelets was administered late in the night, with no apparent benefit. A fourth had just been administered. An X-ray of his skull had confirmed subcranial bleeding. The bone marrow biopsy had shown virtually no platelets or red cells, indicating a state of refractory pancytopenia, a critical shut-down of his marrow. His spleen was now enormously enlarged. At one o'clock A.M., Sunday morning, John Sergent approached my parents in the corridor outside Charley's room with the deafening conclusion of the house staff: "We have tried everything. I'm afraid there is nothing more we can do. We have to look at the possibility that Charley won't make it to morning."

Mother faced Dr. Sergent and quietly said, "My husband and I have been worried that would be the case. If it's unlikely that he'll pull through this, we want to take him home. To be with us there. To be in his bed." My father nodded his head, his eyes red and filling with tears.

TWELVE

Vials on a Plane

Against the odds, Charley hung on. After four units of random platelets failed to stop his bleeding, the fifth one worked. The nurse administering the small transparent bag could tell by the time the last of the gold-colored platelets ran through the tubes that Charley's clotting was suddenly improving. At four o'clock A.M., the doctors and staff took a deep breath of relief, but they knew that Charley was living on borrowed time. No one knew how long it would take for his body to use up the platelets. If it were anything like the day before, it would be a matter of hours. As things were stabilized for the moment, Mother and Dad decided that he was much better off remaining in the hospital, so they drove home in the early morning to change clothes and sleep.

They woke us up to talk about what had just happened at the hospital the night before, exhausted and gray from lack of sleep. The emotionally wrenching events of the weekend had flattened them. We sat at the breakfast table and Dad began grimly, "We've got to prepare ourselves for the fact that the blood bank's platelets can't keep Charley alive very long."

Eddy, Angela, and I stared straight ahead, trying to grasp what he had just said. In my mind I saw Charley's body as a dam holding back a lake of blood. The dam was bowing, about to burst, and all of us had our fingers in the leaks. Eddy broke the silence by asking complex medical questions. I couldn't bear them. His questions were irksomely scientific and seemed useless at this point. I felt myself standing outside of the situation. I could only hear Angela's occasional sighs and sniffing.

She put her arm around me and thought aloud, "I wonder if Charley knows what's going on...that he's so close to losing his life." Her eyes brimming, she stared straight ahead and whispered, "Do you think?"

That morning at eight o'clock, we heard the phone ringing in the house and everyone stiffened. "Oh, no," Angela said under her breath, thinking the worst. But it was John Sergent calling from Vanderbilt. Excited and breathless, he related to Mother and Dad a crucial turn of events. After forty-eight hours at the hospital, he had gone home at four-thirty that morning. The emotions of the night had been cycling through his mind, making it impossible for him to calm down. He opened the new *Journal of Experimental Medicine.* Flipping through it, he was startled to find an article describing a new technique for blood and organ donations from closely matching family members. The matches were made with unprecedented precision, and they worked particularly well for patients with aplastic anemia and leukemia! These matches were achieved by comparing a newly discovered natural component of the blood, called the human leukocyte antigen, or HLA. There, on the page in front of him, were patients with severe cases of aplastic anemia as bad as Charley's whose lives had been saved by this new procedure. The article was written by Dr. E. Donnell Thomas of the University of Washington in Seattle. Unable to sleep for the rest of the night, Sergent said he put a plan into action. At seven-thirty, he was on the phone to the head of hematology at Vanderbilt, Dr. John Flexner.

Beside himself with excitement, Sergent said, "Dr. Benz, if we can keep Charley alive long enough, we can then test your family and just possibly find someone that can donate the platelets he needs. I found a friend at National Institutes of Health in Bethesda who is working with Dr. Thomas in Seattle. My friend can do the testing there in Maryland. I think we can get the samples from the family up there by the late afternoon."

The arrangements were made to take blood samples from the entire family and get the vials on a midday plane to Maryland, where the tests could be run at NIH. Testing would start as soon as the blood reached the laboratories in Bethesda, and the results could be known by ten A.M. the following morning.

Mother and Dad immediately gathered us in their bedroom to explain what lay ahead that morning. Their nineteen-year-old son had been at death's door. Now, out of the blue, a potentially life-saving measure had been offered to him. Mother settled into in her wheelchair, parked next to her dresser. She gathered her thoughts and twisted her wedding ring. Angela and I sat on their high bed, our feet dangling, rocking slowly, and sitting on our hands. The air-conditioner in the window blocked out the humid summer noises beginning to stir in the big backyard. From the bed I could see the barn, the elm trees, and the barbecue pit in the distance. All seemed as it was the day before, the week before, and beyond. Yet nothing was the same. I could feel the change just as I could hear thunder on the horizon or see the sun being obscured by clouds.

Eddy sat in the armchair next to the window, waiting for our parents to begin. Dad entered from their dressing room, pulling on a clean shirt. "Last night, your brother came as close to death as I have ever seen someone come. Your mother and I stayed with him while he just bled away. He was awake for most of it, but I don't know how aware he was. I doubt he knew that he almost died."

Mother interrupted, "Right now the crisis is over, but only for a short while. He will start to bleed again, that's a certainty...in a matter of hours, possibly as long as a day or two."

Dad then repeated what Dr. Sergent had told him that morning about the experimental procedure that might save Charley's life. "The odds are not great for such a match in the family," he said, looking grim, "but it's worth trying, I think. Do you agree?"

In unison, my siblings and I responded, "Yes."

Dad gave us more details. There was a one in ten chance that one of the siblings would match closely enough that the platelets would help. The odds were much lower for the parents, and even worse for more distant relatives such as cousins. Nobody could predict how long this might help him, even if there were a good match. But it was this or allow Charley to die in the next days. To me, to us, there was never a question as to whether we should or should not try this procedure. It was the life of our brother at stake. Nothing else figured into the equation.

The five of us took two cars and sped to Vanderbilt. In the hematology lab, a technologist took several ounces of blood from each of us, filling three test tubes per person. The glass tubes were labeled with orange stickers, wrapped in paper, and placed in a Styrofoam cooler. Then all our faith was put in the hands of strangers as the samples traveled in the closet of a jetliner and were transferred by airline personnel during the change of planes in Atlanta. At the gate in Baltimore, a technologist from NIH accepted the samples and rushed them to the lab, thirty-five miles away in Bethesda. Eddy and I obsessively followed their path with our watches.

Charley's hospital room had been darkened to encourage him to sleep that afternoon. Mother sat in a big chair with her feet up, occupying herself with her sewing. Angela kept her company and read a paperback. Dad returned to his office to reschedule his surgeries for the next several days. Eddy and I took one of the cars and drove home, taking a long detour through Nashville. Aiming for downtown on Broad Street, we passed the derelict and deserted Union Station, a great limestone skull with Romanesque arches. By ourselves, Charley and I had climbed onto a train there as six- and nine-year-olds when we traveled to Popo's house in Kentucky. Despite our lack of tolerance for each other, I remembered the security I felt with my older brother. *He won't lose our tickets, he won't cry when we wave good-bye, he'll take care of me.* Farther downtown, we passed Tootsie's Orchid Lounge with its purple door. Charley and I had cracked the door once to gawk at the famous red-haired Tootsie. She had squinted at us in the daylight and frowned. Then she resumed wiping the bar with a wet rag. Tootsie's Orchid Lounge was closed this Sunday afternoon. Porno shop after porno shop along lower Broad Street seemed to throb in a sweet, foul odor off the hot sidewalks. We turned left and drove up the hill to our church, McKendree Methodist.

The new marble facade blazed white and brilliant in the sun. From the car I could see my family's stained-glass window in the facade, the middle window on the second floor. Mother and Dad had dedicated it to his parents four years earlier, a simple design of just two clasped hands. I glued my eyes to the hands as we drove by the church and held on to them as long as I could, until we turned right and drove down the hill. *Two clasped hands. Did they mean Grandmother and Grandfather?* There was the auditorium for the Grand Ole Opry, empty and quiet on this summer Sunday afternoon. We followed Franklin Road back to the southern end of the city, toward home. The multi-acre front lawns of the houses were bright green and lush from the frequent storms. I started counting the big white columns lining porches with antebellum pride. We turned right on Tyne Boulevard and drove the two winding miles to our house.

All this was Charley's map, too. It was just as full of his footprints and memories. I thought of our vials, the blood of my whole family flying to some northern destination so that maybe one of us could keep Charley alive a little longer. I could not bring myself to think of the times I had hated him and his damning of me. That seemed irrelevant today. Charley was no threat to me now. He was vulnerable and in trouble. In the past three days, he had become the focus of the family, something that glued us to a common goal. In my sixteen-year-old brain, I could not grasp, feel, or understand the very real possibility that he might not live beyond the next few days. He might never retrace his steps in this same world that I was riding through.

Once home, I picked up as many of the puppies as I could hold in my arms and smelled them, let them chew on my lips and nose. They smelled of milk. I kissed them on their velvet mouths and looked for the life in their flighty eyes. Gretel jumped on my leg and worriedly pawed at my knee. "Okay, sweet girl. I understand." I bent down and gave them back to her.

THIRTEEN

I Can Handle It

I concentrated on the puppies. Now that they were nine weeks old, it was time to sell them or give them away. "It will be an exercise in self will," I told myself. "I will not cry when I hand them over. I will not." That night they slept with me in bed. I took them to my room, spread out newspapers on the floor, and closed the door. For a time, their squirming stopped under the sheet as Gretel let them nurse, then I put them back on the floor so they wouldn't fall from the bed during my sleep. Gretel stayed by my side, however, until I drifted away.

When I awoke in the morning, I first remembered the puppies. They were whining, and Gretel looked up at me from the floor to take her outside. Then I remembered Charley in the hospital and my stomach sank. We were to hear the results of the HLA testing by ten. It was now seven-thirty.

Charley had been holding his own when I'd gone to bed the night before. I wondered how it had gone for him through the night. I hadn't heard any commotion in the house, so I guessed things were okay. I wanted get in touch with Draper and Natalie, who were at separate camps. They knew nothing of what had happened the past weekend. *Today is Tuesday. August 3. In four weeks school starts again and I will be back in my new element.* I looked at the white rabbit poster. *I'm finding my way, I'm finding my way. Finally.* Then I thought of the dark-blond guy at the Sequoia Club and felt the familiar knot in my stomach.

Mother's crutches came closer to my door and she tapped on it before cracking it open. "Honey, you up?"

"Not yet. How's Charley?"

"We were able to sleep here last night. Your father talked to the hospital this morning and they said he only had a little bleeding during the night. Charley's anxious, like we are, to know the results of the test. Let's take the pups out, okay? I'll have breakfast ready in a few minutes."

She pulled the door shut and I was left alone with my dogs in the room that meant my whole childhood to me. My entire sixteen years had been anchored to this room. The white rabbit presided over the diagonal morning light. *Keep your head.* I heard Angela's voice downstairs in the kitchen and kicked off the covers.

When the phone rang at eight-forty-five Mother answered it. John Sergent was on the other end. "You have the results, Dr. Sergent?" I ran to join everyone in the kitchen. "There is a match? And a close one? Yarrott?" Mom looked at me across the room and motioned to me to join her at the phone. I let loose with a yell from my gut, "I knew it! I knew I would match!" Dr. Sergent heard my scream over the phone and laughed.

Over the phone, Dr. Sergent told me that NIH had said our match was remarkably close, much closer than they ever imagined. It was the best possible match. I was to begin the first donation as soon as I could get to the hospital. He would be waiting for me in a room in the round wing. Since Charley had done well through the night, he wanted to bring him there, too, so he would know what was happening.

The room that Dr. Sergent had found for the procedure was light-filled, on an upper floor looking through the foliage of oak trees onto Vanderbilt's campus. A gurney was covered with a white sheet and an I.V. stand was next to it, along with a metal arm brace with a grip at one end. Two easy chairs were pushed against the white walls. On a counter next to the donor chair were several glass liter bottles of saline solution and an unopened boxed package from NIH containing the plastic tubing and bags for the procedure.

When we arrived, Charley was up and waiting for Mother and me and talking with Dr. Sergent and a young female lab technologist. With the help of an orderly, he had washed and dressed himself in a clean blue Oxford shirt and khakis. He had cleaned himself up but still looked awful, with gray hands and lips. His appearance shocked me. He extended his hand to congratulate me and I put my arms around him. I felt how much weight he had already lost and held him tightly. He returned the embrace and we stood there for a long moment, two brothers as different as night and day, light and dark. "Okay, guys, let's get to work." Dr. Sergent introduced us to Claudia, the blood bank technologist who was assisting. He explained the procedure and its octopus-like configuration of eight bags extending from one line of tubes. "We withdraw a pint of whole blood from Yarrott, disconnect it from the line into Yarrott's vein, spin it in a centrifuge down the hall, squeeze the top layer, the platelets, into the attached bag for Charley, then give Yarrott the remaining red cells left in the original bag. And we do that four times."

My head was spinning. The procedure sounded so complicated and so long. *How will I get through this? How will I not faint? How can I not look like a scared pussy?* I thought of the toboggan races on television the winter before. I thought of skiing at the lake. The object was to grab the bar in front of you and not fall off. *I will hold on. I will hold on.*

I laid down on the gurney and put my hand through the grip on the arm brace.

"Now, the needle might surprise you, Yarrott. Unfortunately, because we are withdrawing so much blood from you, we have to use one of the largest needles available, an eleven-gauge." I felt sick to my stomach when I saw what he was describing. It was the size of a large nail. "We could deaden the skin at the puncture, but I don't really think you'll need it."

"Holy cow, Yarrott. That thing's a monster. You want Novocaine or something?" Charley was suddenly protective.

"No, I can handle it." I felt a new sense of confidence, being at the center of attention. I was about to be punctured to save my brother. Inside I was glowing with my sudden value to the world. I looked over at Mother and Dad leaning against the wall, watching intently. Mother and I made eye contact and she beamed with her gorgeous smile. I felt invincible.

After my arm's vein was prepped with soap and iodine, I watched Claudia, the technologist, as she made circles around the spot like a target. She smiled at me, too. A quiet, brainy Ursula Andress. Dr. Sergent and she conferred quietly as they prepared for the first stick. Claudia tied the tourniquet around my upper arm and the vein stood out like a pale snake.

With all eyes on my vein, Dr. Sergent pulled the plastic cover off the needle and laid the point down on the skin. "Here goes. You're a real trooper, Yarrott," he said quietly as he shoved it in slowly. I wasn't expecting the excruciating stick and gripped the hand piece so hard I thought I would break it. He entered the vein and a burst of red swirls shot into the clear tubing. Then I felt a deeper stab of pain. "Oops, too far. Gotta pull it out a little. Sorry about that. Okay, now we have it." The needle was taped tightly in place. My first stick probably took a total of fifteen seconds, but it felt like fifteen minutes.

I looked at a worried-looking Charley, whose eyes were glued to the needle in my arm. He walked over to me and put his hand on my shoulder. "Hey, little brother, you hang in there."

"Now we wait while the first bag fills up. Yarrott, try to remember to pump your hand now and then to keep the vein pressure up. It will assist the blood flow." Meanwhile, Dr. Sergent continued to explain the origin of the procedure. "It is called a pheresis, which comes from the Greek word meaning *to separate*. This is a brand-new procedure—we are making history at Vanderbilt today."

After ten minutes, the first bag was filled and clamped off from the central line, and it, along with an empty secondary bag, was cut from the assembly. Claudia carried it to the blood bank, where it was spun to remove the platelets. While we waited, a liter bottle of saline was connected to the tubing to prevent clotting. I felt no different, other than slightly bloated from the saline. Thirty minutes later, she reappeared with two bags, one with my red cells and the other with my platelets for Charley. The bag of platelets appeared almost empty except for gold flecks swirling in pink fluid. "Truly, this is liquid gold, fellas," Dr. Sergent exclaimed while showing us the smaller bag. "It doesn't look like much, but, believe me, it is. And remember, there will be four of these bags for Charley."

My remaining red cells in the original bag were given back to me. As we waited for the bag to empty Dr. Sergent laid a large piece of gauze on the puncture site. Another ten minutes passed and the bag of red cells still had not emptied. My arm began to feel tight at the elbow, as if I were about to have a cramp in the joint. When Dr. Sergent removed the gauze, he burst out with "Yarrott, why didn't you tell us?" To the right of the puncture, a large mass had swelled. Blood that had been returned to me had missed the vein and instead had invaded the tissue next to the vein. Either the needle had gone through the other side of the vein or there was a hole in the vein, allowing the blood to escape. Dr. Sergent repositioned the needle by withdrawing it some, then taping it at a different angle. "I hope we can keep using this needle if we reposition it." I looked beyond the pain by focusing on Dr. Sergent's fingers tapping on my skin, the black hair on the top of his head, the downward perspective of his face from my position in the chair. Anything to take my mind off what was happening. I lost myself thinking about the guy at Sequoia. In those thoughts, I could float where I wouldn't hurt. After another ten minutes of prodding and realigning, Dr. Sergent and Claudia gave up.

"I'm afraid we're going to have to pull this one out and try another vein," he said as he wiped his forehead. He looked me in the eye and said again, with a nervous grin, "You're a real trouper, Yarrott."

After another stick in a second vein of the same arm, the procedure continued without problems and we harvested four good bags of platelets. This, the first pheresis, had taken almost six hours. I was slightly drowsy, but otherwise fine, not light-headed, in pain, or nauseous.

As Charley sat in one of the easy chairs, his arm was prepped for the infusion. His needle, a small twenty-gauge size, slipped in easily and the bags of platelets, one after another, were emptied into his vein. Within five minutes, Charley's coloring improved. "Ed, look at that. Look at that!" Mother grabbed Dad's hand and held back a tearful outburst. The oozing around Charley's teeth stopped completely. A pink tone replaced the gray in his face. The adults in the room stood along the walls with tears in their eyes. The dam that kept back the lake of blood had held firm.

FOURTEEN

From Gray to Pink

Having laid on my back for six hours the day before, punctured and prodded with a needle like no needle I had ever seen, by a handsome, smart doctor who had driven into my arm a pain greater than any I had ever known—well, I was on a high. I was stimulated, alert, and energized as never before in my life. My blood matched my brother's and he needed it. *What does this mean? What will I have to do? For how long?* I had been thrown an enormous weight of unknown proportions, for which I alone was responsible, and I had, at sixteen-years old, instantly and instinctively accepted it. *I can do this.*

In a matter of hours, Charley went from dying to living, from gray skin to pink, from an end to a beginning. The dichotomy of those two days, August 3 and August 4, swinging from despair to hope, made our heads spin. On one day, I was about to lose a brother. On the next, I had saved him.

And yet, despite the life and death drama unfolding around us, the day spent at the hospital was enjoyable, almost entertaining. I liked the people who did this thing to us. They were not formal or patronizing or off-putting. They were young and smart and they seemed to really like Charley and me. They were people I would want to have as friends. They spoke in medical lingo and were confident in their professions. They were conscientious in their efforts to help Charley by removing something from me, and they tried so hard to make it painless, but it was, unavoidably, a painful procedure.

There was a sense of huge accomplishment and even pride in the success of the pheresis. My platelets worked beautifully for Charley—even better than Dr. Sergent had expected or, as he said, had allowed himself to hope. I looked at Charley on August 4 and could not remember how bad he'd looked the day before.

He had improved so quickly that the hospital had decided to send him home at once. I, on the other hand, looked like the walking wounded. On August 4 I developed an enormous black bruise, wrapping around my elbow and extending down one side all the way to the wrist. It looked like my arm had been caught in the vice of a malevolent machine and nearly ripped off. It was stunning how large the bruise had grown since the lump had occurred at the hospital the afternoon before. But my arm did not throb or ache. It was fine except for the shocking bruise. At Sequoia Pool the next day, every stern-faced lifeguard offered sympathy to me, when before they hadn't even known my name. Male and female lifeguards cautiously strutted over like police officers in flip-flops, curious about the boy with the massive injuries. I had never had this kind of attention in my life and I really liked it.

I was squatting down at the side of the pool, ready to slide in the water, when the dark-blond guy approached me. "Wow, man, what happened to your arm?" He squinted in the sun at me.

"Well, I, uh, gavebloodtomybrotherandgotabruise. Itsnotasbadasitlooks," I spouted out so quickly I wasn't even sure what I said. My heart was pounding and my face reddened.

"Looks like it hurts. Hope it heals fast. Good luck there, eh?" He stood there waiting for me to say something but I didn't. I just froze and he returned to his girlfriend, who was sitting up in her chaise and grimacing at me, presumably in sympathy for my ugly injury.

I would think of that summer years later on a trip to Greece. Swimming in the Aegean Sea, I remembered the perfect warmth of that summer in 1970, the turquoise blues of the sky and water. All those healthy young bodies splashing at the Sequoia Club looked like ancient Greek statues. Just before my life changed. I thought of the one exchange the dark-blond guy and I had and how I was so stunned by the moment I couldn't participate in it.

FIFTEEN

Mondays and Thursdays

S afely stabilized, Charley came home from the hospital within a week, and all eyes watched him for changes in his condition. By the fourth pheresis, it appeared that my platelets seemed to work for about three or four days before his platelet counts began to drop precipitously. Dr. Sergent and Dr. Flexner decided that the procedure would be best performed on Mondays and Thursdays, allowing an even, twice-a-week spread that could be scheduled on a regular basis and coordinated with my school day. The location for the pheresis, however, had to be moved to a room that would not interfere with regular hospital functions, since the procedure required so many hours to complete. A windowless storage room was located down the hall from the hospital's blood bank, and a red leather 1950s gynecological examination chair, complete with chrome stirrups, was located to serve as the donor chair. A large upholstered armchair for Charley was borrowed from a hospital room and delivered there, along with boxes of necessary supplies, such as bottles of saline solution, gauze, iodine, and alcohol wipes. The specially designed donor bags were configured with four sets of twin bags attached to a single needle, and were packaged in large tin cans and sent in bulk from the manufacturer. I felt an anxious twinge when I first realized how many donor sessions would be necessary to use them up.

Because of all the materials piled up in the room, there was barely enough room to stand up and to perform the procedure. Though there was neither fresh air nor natural light, and despite how unpleasant it initially appeared, over time this room became an indispensable inner sanctum dedicated to Charley and me.

In the first month, Dr. Sergent, Claudia, Charley, and I found ourselves acclimating to the long hours of one another's company twice a week. I thank God for Dr. Sergent's voracious appetite for news and conversation. I grew to think of the hours as enlightening and stimulating sessions, where the four of us talked about life in general. One part cruise ship, one part doctor's office, one part talk show, and one part prison, the hours together quickly accumulated. In 1970, the war in Vietnam was burning a hole in the American conscience. We talked about that, all agreeing that the conflict was unnecessary and that we shouldn't be there. Then *Life* magazine put an openly homosexual man on its cover and we talked about that. Dr. Sergent's reaction was, "I don't see what all the fuss is about." It was the first time I had ever discussed the subject with another human being, and hearing a doctor express his dismay over the treatment of gay people gave me the first inkling that my attraction to the dark-blond guy at the pool might not be such a crime. Charley and I sat silently while Dr. Sergent explained himself. I think we were both shocked that someone was actually talking thoughtfully about what had been absolutely forbidden as a topic in our house. I was terrified that I might give myself away if I said too much, if I reacted in any way in particular. Charley's reaction was to shake his head and say, "Well, I don't know, Dr. Sergent. The thought of them gives me the creeps. Seems so unnatural."

Claudia, normally extremely quiet and focused on the procedure at hand, was agreeable to everyone's point of view, as if she knew firsthand the role of family peacemaker. She laughed at Charley's cynicism but also nodded in agreement with Dr. Sergent's more open-minded observations. Within the first few weeks, I learned many important details about her. She, like Dr. Sergent and my mother, was from Kentucky, a small town called Monticello in the eastern part of the state. She was a beautiful young woman of fascinating contradictions—part Appalachian and part urbane sophisticate. She had skipped three grades in school as a child and had started college at fifteen. She was a voracious reader, a brilliant student, polite to the point of self-sacrifice, and deferential to older people such as my parents to the point of obedience.

Across the corridor from the storage closet—overnight renamed "the donor room"—was the Vanderbilt medical student lounge, which was outfitted with a sink, a refrigerator, a black-and-white television, several vinyl couches, and a long bank of windows overlooking a courtyard. If we left the door to the donor room open, we could see the outdoors through the lounge, which was better than no daylight at all. The bedraggled, sleep-deprived students became familiar visitors in the room, often showing interest in Charley's case and my involvement. It was also there that I first saw the hierarchy in medicine, as the students in their early twenties would assume patronizing voices with the rest of us, technologist and patient alike. The blood bank personnel who were subjected to their arrogance simply rolled their eyes and, when the door was closed, referred to the tiresome "medical school syndrome" that seemed to be a universal problem at that nascent stage of every physician.

As smart as everyone was, *no one* could tell us what to expect in the future, near or far. What we *were* told was that Charley's condition could be temporary, but the longer it remained, the less likely it was that he would develop a remission. He was introduced to many chemical therapies and treatments to stimulate activity in his bone marrow. First androgens, a hormone derivative, were administered to stimulate production in the bone marrow. They did not work. Then there were many experimental drugs, and after each one we stood by anxiously for a response. We developed a rhythm of waiting. First in weeks, then in months.

SIXTEEN

The View of the Corridor

By the time autumn colors had swept across the front yards
of Nashville, Mother had become an expert nurse again.
Charley's weakened immune system required special care to
avoid opportunistic infections, so Mother washed every dish
by hand, and then machine-washed them with very hot water.
She changed his bed linens three times a week and insisted
that he wear his clothes only once before washing them. She
encouraged him to sleep late in the mornings after I had gone
to school. She watched our diets and insisted that we eat plenty
of iron-enriched vegetables, rare red meat, and drink lots of
milk, juice, and water. She made sure he took his medications
three times a day. Any cut, abrasion, scratch, or bruise was
checked out and treated by both Dad and her.

Because of the experimental hormone treatments trying to
stimulate his bone marrow, Charley was undergoing all sorts
of physical changes. His weight fluctuated dramatically. With
estrogen supplements, his beard disappeared into a black down.
With testosterone, it reappeared in whiskers. By Thanksgiving
of the first year, he had lost thirty pounds and had become very
gaunt, with dark circles under his eyes. A few months later he
had gained it all back and had become bloated. His face was
often inexplicably blossoming with acne, when he had never
had it before. The tip of his nose and the area below his mouth
were often red, swollen, and shining with Neosporin.

Initially, he complained that Mother was nagging him and
meddling in his life. He resisted, like any other nineteen-year-
old whose efforts at independence were being foiled by his

mother. By the time six months had passed, however, Charley had grown more patient and cooperative with her. On the afternoons of the pheresis, if either one of our red cell or hemoglobin counts came up low in our blood tests, he would call her from the hospital to let her know that we needed to eat red meat that evening. By the time we arrived home, the square wood steak plates were already on the table.

It did so happen that I became anemic within a few months. I was summarily instructed by Dr. Flexner to take an enormous iron pill with dinner every evening. I did not understand all the fuss about my anemia. I felt okay. I only noticed the pounding of my heart in my neck when I climbed stairs. But with the iron pills, I felt worse. My bowel movements turned black and began to burn so badly that without telling anyone I stopped the pills after a few months.

After the third or fourth month of the pheresis I was aware that I was no longer looking forward to going to the hospital. The excitement of the drama had passed and the long visits to the hospital had become routines through which I trudged twice a week. I was becoming a fixture on the hematology floor and now knew the names of everyone who worked in the blood bank and in Dr. Flexner's lab, and many of the know-it-alls congregating in the medical student lounge. As the curiosity of the situation wore off for everyone, fewer new people, smiling, upbeat, and dynamic, poked their heads in while Claudia and I sat there among the bags and tubes.

We settled into a routine. The tiny room served to corner us at times with occasional visitors. People like Georgia dropped in. She was one of the technologists now running my blood back and forth from the donor room to the centrifuge in the blood bank. Her long black hair was pulled back with a piece of colorful yarn, parted down the middle and tucked behind her ears. Her favorite fashions under her white lab coat included quilted granny dresses with short puffy sleeves. She was sweet-tempered in a Southern, countrified way, and the deep dimples on either side of her grin intensified that nature. While her speaking cadence had the gentle rise and fall of a spoken song, the words that came out of her mouth sometimes took my breath away. "My boys think you are one of the bravest young men they've ever heard of, Yarrott. They're only six and eight, but they've got good hearts in them. I've told them all about you and Charley."

I groaned to myself. Georgia was making me very nervous. Inside my seventeen-year-old self I knew very well that I was not who she thought I was. I knew that inside me there was some kind of sexual sea roiling. I heard my heart pounding in the locker room and felt the dampness of my palms when I saw muscles on the backs of other boys. I knew that these attractions were homosexual, but I was also hoping they would disappear like acne. It was becoming clear to me that I was something that the world ridiculed and that my family despised, but not one other person knew my true identity.

Giving blood to Charley gave me a pedestal from which I could rise above everyone else, and if I failed at all other pursuits in life I would have done at least one thing right, one thing in a truly superior fashion. I felt protected by what I was doing, but I also felt swamped by it. The responsibility was overwhelming.

Claudia left me alone to get snacks from the cafeteria for us. Georgia glided back into the donor room with the bag of my red cells. I heard her sandals flopping all the way down the corridor. The white lab coat contrasted brightly against her dark suntan. "You wouldn't have believed all the people at the lake this weekend, sweetie. It was packed. You would have loved it, with your love of waterskiing. I wish I could ski, but as you know, I don't swim."

Two men in clogs rushed down the corridor past the open donor room. One wore a bright blue T-shirt and khakis. The other wore a striped shirt and tight jeans. They both had clipboards in their arms. Georgia threw her hand on her hip and hissed. "Lord a-mighty, look at them, will you? Swishing like two ballerinas. Man, that's something I really can't stand. Queers, Yarrott, they make me sick." She stuck her head out the door and watched the men as they turned the corner, heading to the round wing. "Look at them. Just look at them." She sucked on the tip of her extra long Virginia Slims and let the smoke creep slowly out of her nose. She looked straight ahead with one of her plucked eyebrows raised.

"I couldn't see." My mouth turned dry and I tried to act uninterested.

"I've noticed them up here before. Believe it or not, I think they're med students. I'll tell you one thing: I'm never letting either one of them ever touch me. That's for sure."

"You sure they're...gay? I mean, a lot of guys are wearing clogs now, especially working in the hospital."

"Nah. I can tell. I can always tell. Those guys are fags. They're always together. Disgusting."

I thought of Draper and me, always together. Would Georgia say that about us?

Claudia returned with our snacks and passed out sticky buns. Since my arm was stuck with a needle, she opened mine for me, broke it into pieces and put it in my free hand. "What were you staring at, Georgia?" Claudia asked.

"Oh, two queers swishing down the hall. There ought to be a sign somewhere that says 'Queers Stay Away.' Don't you think?"

"Now, Georgia, what makes you think those men don't have the right to be here?"

"Oh, come on, Claudia. Think. The things those men do to each other...it's criminal, not to mention gross. Faggots are filthy. I want my children to enjoy life as God intended. I don't want my daughter being a queer! I don't want my son being a queer! It's not only unnatural...it's repulsive!"

I was sure that both women could see me turning red and withering in the donor chair.

SEVENTEEN

Insecticide

A cause for Charley's disease was never determined, but it was often said by the doctors that something environmental might have caused it. We always wondered about the paper mill across the river from Charley's dorm at UT and the nauseating fumes he complained about. We also wondered about the petroleum material he had used to blacktop the driveway on Tyne Boulevard the August before he left for college. It had given him headaches every day until he finished the job.

Nobody will ever know.

There was talk in the news about the dangers of everyday chemicals, such as household cleansers and pesticides, and what they can do to our air and our bodies. Photographs of the smog in New York City and Los Angeles were on the covers of *Time* and *Newsweek*. The chemical DDT had even wound up in the lyrics of "Big Yellow Taxi," the popular song by Joni Mitchell. Clearly, the world in the early seventies was beginning to worry about the cost of its conveniences.

Charley and I began to argue one afternoon in the car on the way home from the hospital. "What the hell is the matter with you, Yarrott? Why do spend so much time on the yard? I never had to when I did the grass. You spend, what, all day on Saturdays? I did the cutting in about four hours."

"That's because you left the yard looking like shit."

"What are you talking about? It looked great."

"No, it didn't. You didn't trim carefully. It looked like shit."

"Fuck you! You are so goddamn prissy and righteous. Not to mention so fussy it makes me sick."

"Thanks a lot, Charley. You asshole. After all I've done for you."

"Yeah, well, if I had anything to do with it, you wouldn't have to. Think I enjoy getting your blood? Of all people's? Yours?"

"Pull over. Now. I want to get out."

"Oh, yeah. I bet. Pussy."

"God, I hate your guts. Bastard."

Dinner that night was pork chops, cooked spinach, and boiled potatoes. Charley and I sat across from each other at the table in the breakfast room, still fuming. Mother and Dad frowned at us, disgusted with our inability to get along. The table was silent except for the sounds of chewing and swallowing and an occasional furious sawing at a pork chop.

"I don't know why you can't love each other," Mother muttered under her breath.

Without looking up, I answered into my plate, "Because he's a Neanderthal and I'm a Homo sapien."

"You mean homo *period,* don't you?" Charley quipped.

"There you go again, you pig."

"Stop it! Right this minute." Dad erupted and threw his fork on the table. "You two make me sick."

Leaving her half-eaten meal, Mother got up from the table, grabbed her crutches, and stormed off to their room. Dad followed her and ordered, "You two wash up. We don't want to have anything else to do with you."

"See what happens, Yarrott?"

"Don't blame me, asshole."

"Let's clean up this mess. I want to go to Joe's."

We gathered the dishes, glasses, and silverware and stacked them in the sink. I scraped the remains of the spinach and potatoes into Tupperware containers. Charley returned the milk to the refrigerator and emptied the pitcher of water into the sink. Without looking at me, he said, "Okay, I'm off. See

75

you later. Tell Mother and Dad I'm over at Joe's."

"The hell you are. We're not done with the kitchen. You can't leave me with it."

"You always do such a better job, Yarrott. You finish it," Charley answered sarcastically.

"Goddamn you!" I followed him down the back steps with the bottle of Ivory detergent in my hand.

"Right. See you, pussy boy."

I flung the detergent at him and it splattered down his back. He turned around and shot me a look that said he was going to tear me to pieces. I turned and started running, with him right behind me. Passing by the open cabinet under the sink, I grabbed the can of Raid wasp spray and flew out the front of the house onto the porch. There, he grabbed my shirt from the back and yanked me toward him. I felt his slug on my shoulder and it knocked the wind out of me. I turned around and faced him. "You goddamn asshole." I quickly raised the can of Raid to his face and sprayed. I wanted to hurt him badly. Charley screamed and covered his eyes.

Dad was standing in the doorway and saw what happened. He ran to me, grabbed the can out of my hands, and hit me hard in the face with a passion I had not seen in him before. He shouted, "Stop it! Stop it! Stop it!"

I caught my balance and stood on the porch with them. I could feel a searing pain across my cheek and realized I was crying hysterically. Looking my father in the eye, I screamed, "You asshole!"

Dad was stunned. He had spanked me as a child, but he had never hit me like this, nor had he ever received such a verbal blow from me. He tried to gather his wits and then said, with his voice shaking, "Yarrott, you could kill him with that stuff. Don't be stupid." Dad said nothing more to me and stood there, his whole body pulsing with his furious heartbeat. Finally, he raised his chin and peered through the lower part of his trifocals to examine Charley's eyes. "Let me look at you, son. It missed. You're okay."

EIGHTEEN

The Luck of Birth

"About time you showed up," I snapped at Charley as he breezed into the donor room. Still groggy, I held my arm over my head and pressed on the gauze pad taped over the wound. "We finished ten minutes ago. You might have called to say you'd be late."

"Oh, get over it, Yarrott," he brushed me off as he rolled up his sleeve and took his seat. "You're looking beautiful today, Claudia." He smiled at her and continued to ignore me.

The hostility that Charley and I felt for each other only grew as the platelet pheresis became our twice-weekly routine. I cannot imagine how difficult Claudia's job was, to safely perform the procedure while being caught in the middle of the two warring brothers. On top of that, alone with me in the tiny room, she had to keep me engaged—for hours on end, until we had gone through four cycles with the centrifuge. Consequently, she and I talked about almost everything in the world and became close companions in that chilly, ugly room. I felt fortunate to have such an open-minded, intelligent, and kind person caring for me.

She must have sensed my need to talk about this predicament, my imbroglio. When I was alone with her, we talked at times of spirituality and of miracles. Neither of us could stand the crazy and literal Bible talk of the occasional fundamentalist who strayed into the donor room to offer a prayer. But she must have known that after several months of the overwhelming routine at the hospital I needed to talk about the invisible things in the world that we do not understand.

I needed to place the fact of Charley's illness and my blood matching his into the context of something extraordinary, something magical, heroic, and divine. I could not swallow the idea that it was just something ordinary taking place. If this were mundane, I was trapped in stagnant water and there was going to be no end to it. I had to focus on the story's rarity and its drama, the diametric design of two brothers— one light and the other dark.

That fall, my high school junior year, I studied slavery and read William Styron's book *The Confessions of Nat Turner* in Mr. Roger's American History class. It was just occurring to me that my mother's family in Kentucky must have had a history of its own on that subject. The truth that I eventually learned was that my great-grandfather Yarrott McElroy owned a farm called Sugar Grove, and along with the house, barns, and enormous acreage, he also possessed seventy-five slaves. My great-grandfather—a man with my name—actually *owned* the rights of seventy-five human lives. It was a fact that settled like a leaf on a windowsill one hundred and fifty years ago—there for so long and so quiet it was hardly seen. For generations after the Civil War, my mother's family in Kentucky had acknowledged it without speaking of it directly. For example, Mother fondly referred to her favorite servants as a child, Big Wash and Mary. In my mother's memory, the two had always worked in the big white house on Harrison Street, their own histories and backgrounds intertwined with her own. But her memory was oddly limited.

"You're pressing!" Mother scolded me. "You have to stop asking me more than I can answer! Wash and Mary were always part of the household and always felt like part of my family. We treated them very, very well. I don't know any more than that!" I could hear an automatic defensiveness in her voice, a nervous and angry reaction that I do not believe she herself understood. I wondered if her own parents used the same tone when asked about the histories of their servants.

If I wanted to know more of the truth, it was up to me to search for details. I learned, through letters of the McElroys written during the Civil War, how difficult survival was at that time. The Kentucky farm was plundered first by Confederate soldiers, then by Union soldiers, who left it barely standing. The McElroy family was not alone. The cataclysm of war probably scarred every family surviving it. To speak about the biggest contributing factor to the war, and the very subject of which the family was guilty, was tacitly considered in bad taste.

Mr. Rogers, my history teacher, instructed us to write an essay on the subject of slavery after reading Styron's book. All I could think of was the role that *luck* played in that world. The luck of birth: who was born black versus who was born white. The nature of one's birth and the measure of luck in that was a paramount fixation of mine. Why was Charley the one of us who was hit with this illness? Why was I, of all people, the one who matched him? He and I could not have been more different. Eddy looked more like him—why didn't he match?

My paper "Slavery and the Luck of Birth" got an A+ and Mr. Rogers read it to the class, but it didn't keep the rest of my grades from sliding into the gutter. My straight A's from the year before were appearing to be a fluke, as my grades began a gradual descent as the junior year rolled along. I was not successfully reading much assigned material at home, because I could not concentrate on anything except sensational stories like *The Confessions of Nat Turner*. That was a story that slapped me in the face so loudly and painfully that it commanded me to read it. All else was futile. I sat with books for hours and moved my eyes along the lines of words, but could not take in images or meanings.

I depended upon class discussions and the summaries from Cliff's Notes to know what was occurring inside the books. To be truthful, I had difficulty concentrating long enough to comprehend even the Cliff's Notes. I followed the class discussions carefully and could enter them at times with great opinions. The subjects and themes of the materials were interesting and relevant enough and I wished that I had read the books firsthand. I berated myself for my lack of discipline. I had no idea that what was occurring elsewhere in my life left me unable to concentrate.

The more anxious and upset I became, the more I wanted to escape. The accumulated effect was that I was humiliating myself. In my eyes, I was becoming the quintessential confused teenager who could not stop dreaming. I was embarrassed by my anxiety so I tried hard to appear calm and all-knowing on the exterior. But all I wanted was to escape. God knows there was little to feel good about in my conscious world. The compliments I received about helping Charley made me feel worse than ever because they were made by people who invariably assumed I was a clean, straight, heterosexual boy. Those very people were often the ones who told me and the rest of the world that homosexuals were sick and wrong. To me, the one area of my life in which I was achieving approval was based on a lie.

My facial tics had migrated to other parts of my body by this time. I had learned to satisfy some of my anxiety by clenching my stomach muscles. It did not completely replace my facial twitching but it did succeed in reducing it. Only rarely did I hear anyone in my family comment on my *habits* anymore. But they were there, just under my shirt.

To give Charley and me space apart at home, I painted an empty room in the basement and moved my furniture downstairs. I believed that I could find peace of mind by moving as far away as I could while staying under the same roof. I painted the rock walls the same white I had painted my room upstairs. I tried my best to turn the dank, dark room into a cheerful retreat. The first night in my new place I felt as if I had moved to Mammoth Cave. The noises of the house were foreign, originating over my head instead of below. The smells were moldy, but I had succeeded in carving out a more private place.

The creative and zany friendship that had developed the year before with Draper was all the more vital to me our junior year at Peabody. It was my link back to a teenage life where the worst worries were about pimples, grades, and clothes. Neither Draper nor Natalie knew how to ask questions about the situation I was in, but I could tell they were concerned. The same was true of my teachers. They asked few questions, if any at all.

But Draper helped me breathe in the golden relief of humor. A talented and precocious child from the day he was born, he had cultivated a brilliant sense of humor. We met at the right time for humor to be the saving grace for both of us. We laughed that we were the only people we knew who could whip shit into gold.

ॐ

He called me one Friday afternoon, excited about a film he had just read about that morning in the library at school. I rolled my eyes, fearing it was another Barbra Streisand movie. Just a few weeks earlier we had seen *On a Clear Day* at the Belle Meade Theatre and I had just about slid off my seat with indifference. "And what's *this* one about?"

"Relax, Barbra's not in it. It's called *The Last Picture Show. The New York Times* says it's incredible. It's by this guy Peter Bogdanovich. Cybill Shepherd's in it."

"Uh-oh. This I gotta see." I had pictures of Cybill Shepherd taped up all over my bedroom.

Draper continued, "You know how you like that James Dean movie—*Rebel Without a Cause?* This sounds a lot like it. I think we should go see it tonight."

That night we settled into our seats in the smoking section of the Belcourt Cinema. We lit up our cigarettes before the previews were over. When the movie began, I did not like the bright black-and-white graininess. "Looks like a Marx Brothers movie," I whispered to Draper.

"Shh..."

"It's so—"

"Shhhhhh!"

Five minutes later, I was transfixed by the dry landscape of Texas, the prickly three-day beard of Timothy Bottoms, and the loping melodies of Hank Williams. I felt at home in the isolation of small-town 1950s Anarene, Texas. I felt at home inside the head of Sonny, the kid wandering from empty school to empty home to empty adulthood. Here in this movie, though, the emptiness felt beautiful, even heroic. When the film ended, Draper and I remained in our seats, silent, and smoked cigarettes until the theater cleared out.

"Want to see it again?" he broke the silence.

"Yeah. Do you?"
"It's kind of late."
"I don't care."
"Neither do I."

Over the next month, we saw *The Last Picture Show* enough times that we could recite some of the dialogue. At the coffee shop near the cinema, Draper reached across the table and patted my hand like Cloris Leachman does to Timothy Bottoms in the final scene. "Nevah yew mind, Sonny, nevah yew mind."

I gestured with the hamburger in my hand. "Ya wanna learn about monotony quick, girl, yew marry Duane."

On the way home in the car, we sang one of the Hank Williams songs from the soundtrack. "Why Don't You Love Me?" poured out in an earnest and mournful two-part harmony. It was effortless and pitch-perfect. "Damn, listen to us," I said, surprised.

"Yeah, really," Draper added. "Move over, Everly Brothers."

Part Two

NINETEEN

Pitch Black

We had a house full of guests during Christmas of 1971. Eddy and Angela were back from their schools. Uncle R.Y. and Aunt Jane drove up from Palm Beach, and Aunt Beck and Uncle Harry flew down from Groton, Connecticut. Charley moved into my room in the basement for a few days to make enough beds for everyone upstairs. It had been a difficult year and a half of Charley's illness and the company had converged on Nashville to give a moral boost to my mother. The tree Dad bought that year was the largest we ever had, leaving scrape marks in the ceiling of the living room and filling the entire space in front of the French doors. Mother asked Charley and me to decorate the humongous evergreen wreath, which we pulled up by rope to its usual hook on the second floor. That night we aimed the spotlight on it from a tree in the front yard.

In the South, the presentation of one's home was always a big deal, no matter the time of year. But at Christmas, people were driven into a fever pitch surrounding their homes' appearances. As I got older, I began to suspect that there was more attached to Christmas decor than glitter and light. It seemed to me there was a psychological phenomenon: the more troubled a household, the more decorated it was at Christmas. I could drive down the road and tell from the abundance of holiday lights who had the drunk father, the depressed mother, the bankruptcy, or, in our case, the sick son. To me, Christmas had become a time for compensating in light and color for the bleakness of the rest of the year.

While the decorator in me celebrated times like this,

Charley was not buying any of it. I accused him of being a downer and withholding joy from the rest of us. He chided me for the fakery of it all.

"It's only electric light, Yarrott. It doesn't make anything better, does it?"

"Why does it have to? Why can't decorations be just something cool to look at once in a while?"

"Because they're phony and a waste of time!"

I walked off and left him holding the empty boxes of lights. "Just leave them on the stack in the garage," I ordered. "I've got more important things to do than argue."

"Hey, Yarrott?"

"Yeah?"

"Screw you."

"Screw you, too, asshole."

While Mother was cooking a large turkey on Christmas Eve, several of us sat around the living room that evening drinking and listening to Perry Como's holiday album. Each of us wore something red, like a sweater, a skirt, or a tie. Uncle R.Y. and Charley were upstairs, looking at maps Charley had collected in his room. They had become great friends during Charley's illness. Despite his meteoric rise to rear admiral, Uncle R.Y. had been forced to leave the Navy a few years earlier for medical reasons and was living a prematurely retired life in Palm Beach. He was in his early fifties. Both he and Charley felt their lives had unfairly been put on hold. I wandered down the upstairs hall and heard them talking.

"Keep me out of that stuff, will you, old man?" Uncle R.Y. said under his breath.

"What, you mean booze?"

"That's right. White lightning. Hooch. I've been on the wagon now for two years. I intend to stay that way."

"Wow. You have a problem with it?"

"You didn't know, Charles? Yeah, *big* problem. Aunt Jane left me for a while because of it."

Charley sounded uncomfortable with the subject, as if it

were none of his business to be discussing this. He tried to gracefully change the subject. "It must have been hard to go from top banana to Citizen McElroy. You miss the Navy?"

"Sure do, boy. My life's mission has been taken away from me. I'm sort of floating around now. Now listen to me, Charley. I don't want the same to happen to you. You can't just float, no matter what the situation is. You hear me?"

"I'm not sure I understand, Uncle R.Y."

"I mean you have to stay on top of things, keep taking your classes, keep learning, keep thinking about the future, no matter what you're told by the doctors."

There was a long pause. I heard the maps rustling and being folded. Charley cleared his throat nervously and carefully asked, "Do you ever think that your life's over, I mean now that you're out of the Navy?"

"Hell, yes. That's what I'm saying, man. But you have to fight that feeling. You can't give up, Charles."

"Well, I have to admit, sometimes I feel like I've already given up. That there's nothing left. That death's just around the corner."

There was silence. No maps folding. No throat clearing. Then I realized I was biting my lip, standing there in the hallway, listening to them talking about death. What were they doing now? Did Uncle R.Y. throw his arms around Charley and hold him? Or did he just look straight ahead and freeze like a deer in headlights?

Their conversation abruptly ended when Uncle R.Y. said, "We better get back downstairs, boy. Your mother and Aunt Jane will tan our hides wondering where we've gone." On tiptoe, I hurried down the stairs in front of them, ran to the kitchen, and told Mother I would set the table.

Everyone was in bed by midnight. Down in my basement bedroom I turned off my desk lamp and crept across the cold floor in the darkness. Charley and I settled into the twin beds placed along the painted stone walls. The hissing of the furnace was the only sound as we lay down in darkness.

I put my hand out and felt the rough limestone six inches from my face. "You ever sleep down here before, Charley?"

"Never."

"I've gotten to like it. It was sort of creepy at first, but then I got used to it."

"Was it worth it to move down here?"

"Sure was." I was emphatic. "It's important to have some space."

"You're telling me. I guess I ought to thank you for leaving me the whole upstairs."

"Well, I did what I had to do."

"Except..."

"Except what?"

"I get lonely sometimes, Yarrott."

"You, lonely? Nah."

"You wouldn't believe how bad sometimes. To tell you the truth, I wouldn't mind you being back upstairs with me."

"All you have to do is ask me and I'll be up there in a flash."

"You mean, moving back into your old room?"

"No, just visiting. Anytime you want."

"Okay, I understand. That's groovy."

We lay silently in the darkness for several minutes, fully aware that we were both not falling asleep.

"Yarrott?"

"Yeah?"

"You've been really good to me. I just want to make sure I've said it to you."

"Thanks, but I think you would have done the same for me."

"But you'll never know for sure about me, will you? Not like I know about you."

"Whoa, Charley, don't go so deep there. Hey, you okay?"

There was another long pause when the furnace took its turn to whisper.

"No, I'm not," he slowly admitted.

"What's going on?"

"I dunno. I keep thinking about what must lie ahead."

"What do you mean? You mean with aplastic anemia?"

"With dying." He answered with a voice I did not recognize in the darkness, a voice that was gravelly and deep and tired and worried. I was suddenly afraid to know more, but felt that he needed me to ask, to get it out of him so he wouldn't be alone with his thoughts.

"Do you think about dying a lot, Charley?"

"More and more."

"Like taking your own life? Like suicide?"

"Sometimes that, yeah, but mostly it's about having a heart attack or bleeding to death."

"You afraid of it?"

"Shit, yeah, I'm afraid. I don't want to die. I'm too young. Wouldn't you be afraid, Yarrott? It's not fair. Fuck it. It's not fair."

"What are the images you have in your head when you think about your own death?"

"Darkness, Yarrott. I just feel darkness and a big, empty nothing. That and being completely alone."

I let myself fall into his picture and it made me cold and afraid. "Can I turn on the light, Charley? Would that bother you?"

"Go ahead."

I switched on the desk lamp and sat up in the bed. He had an arm draped over his head, covering his eyes.

"I heard you talking to Uncle R.Y. in your room this afternoon. Did it help any?"

"Sort of," he answered, not moving his arm. "It made me feel less alone. Except his problems are so different from mine. It's like he has so much life he doesn't know what to do with it. My problem is that my life is too small, too narrow and too short. I don't have enough of it to know what to do."

"I see what you mean." I said, not really understanding.

"But, Yarrott, it sure helps to know somebody cares. That alone helps more than anything."

"I will always care," I said automatically.

He lifted his arm and looked at me and smiled.

TWENTY

A Letter

The miniature Sony TV I brought from home produced tiny metallic voices from the afternoon soaps. Twice a week, I watched the shows religiously, to kill time and make the procedure go faster. It worked, too. On Mondays and Thursdays, I would leave cafeteria lunch and high school classes and friends, sports, and homework for the donor room. Then, from one until five-thirty or six P.M., I would lie down in the cramped little room under the huge fluorescent light and would get pinned on a gynecological chair like a pimply teenage bug.

Two hours into the pheresis procedure, I would feel bloated and tired. No wonder. By that time, I had already received a liter of saline solution in my veins, to keep the needle and tubes from clotting. Sometimes I found it difficult after that to follow conversations in the donor room between Claudia and the doctors. Sometimes it felt like the confusing haze after a long afternoon nap. I would suddenly have to pee and then the whole floor would know about it. Claudia would give me a clean urinal and usher everyone out of the room and shut the door, leaving me to stand up alone with the lines attached to eliminate into the opaque plastic jug with the turquoise lid. I would snap the top closed, open the heavy wood door, and call down the corridor, "Okay! I'm finished. Y'all can come back now!"

The haze I felt in the donor room followed me into the corridor, across the parking lot, and down the road to home. The worlds of my peers were spinning faster, while mine was slowing down. Draper and Natalie and Danny and Libby and all the others were making plans for college and their futures and setting goals, but neither I nor my parents—nor, for that matter, my teachers or doctors—were paying attention to *my* planet as its rotation slowed down and nearly came to a full stop. They were occupied with keeping Charley healthy, hoping to keep *his* planet spinning. They had presumed a tremendous lot about me.

I was caught in an emotional riptide, pulled out to sea with Charley. I drifted away from my friends and stopped seeing Natalie. I was angry that they all had such uncomplicated and satisfying lives. Teenagers don't know how to empathize with dire situations, and my situation was dire indeed. My friends avoided the subject of Charley's illness and the hospital when I desperately wanted to talk about it. I resented the freedom in their lives. They could focus on themselves, their studies, their interests, and their futures. I was stuck and did not know what to think.

Mother and Dad had, in effect, two children whose lives were critically compromised, not one. Charley, poor guy, had to deal with being told that he might not live more than a few months, a year maybe, no one knew. As for me, I was not told anything at all.

I was told nothing about how to plan a future when you don't know when the freedom for it might come. I was told nothing about how to cope with the emotional responsibility of providing a source of life to someone who would literally die without *my* blood. I was told nothing about how this might affect my concentration, my moods, my body, my self-esteem, my friendships, my grades, the relationships inside my family. I was told absolutely nothing by anyone. Instead, the single message I was given was *We know you can do it.* But there are things one needs to be provided with to be able *to do it,* such as psychological counseling, regular contact between parents and teachers, heart-to-heart discussions between doctors and the donor about how *he* is faring. As far as I know, there was not one meeting between my parents and the doctors or my teachers to discuss the emotional and physical state of Yarrott. *Yarrott is getting along fine. We don't have to worry about him. We know he can do it.*

God knows I wanted to prove them right. I wanted to prove to everyone, particularly the doctors, that I was one of the good guys like them. These men were considered the backbone of the medical community and were often Ivy League handsome to boot. They played handball during their lunch breaks and mixed and mingled socially, along with their wives, on the weekends. They sure as hell were not gay. Their pasts, presents, and futures were set permanently and handsomely in granite, impregnable, unaffected by the Vietnam War and the draft and the other traumas of the world. Psychologically sound and intellectually impressive, they set sail in their profession with the highest grades and board scores. Their self-confidence was as noticeable as their handsome ties under their white coats. These guys were so used to the sun shining brightly on them that they could not see anyone flailing about in the darkness right in front of them.

A letter was sent to me that suggested I might possibly have been one of those bright, successful guys. It was completely unexpected, perhaps a result of my one extraordinary year at Peabody, when I proved how well I could do in school; that sophomore year, that single year when I was free of sibling friction and free of Nashville's stifling social strata, and when I stunned myself by my capabilities. I'll never know who or what was responsible for the letter, but when I became a senior in high school—in the fall of 1971, when all my classmates were shopping for colleges—the letter came for me from the Harvard Club of Nashville. I had given little thought to college or what it might mean for me since I was committed to the pheresis for Charley. If pressed, I said I would go to Vanderbilt, because it was in Nashville and, after all, I could not leave town. I had not a clue how to put together the application package. I was not even aware that I had to ask teachers for recommendations. I did not have one meeting with a college counselor. I didn't know to ask for one, and no one approached me. I was drifting in my somnambulant haze, unaware that my world's rotation was coming to a full stop.

In February, well after the deadlines for the submission of college applications, I found the letter in an opened envelope addressed to me, on the table in the front hall. It was printed on expensive bond paper embossed with a red crest. It read:

Dear Mr. Benz,

Because you have demonstrated outstanding scholarship and citizenship in your school, your name has come to us highly recommended and thus you are cordially invited to attend a gathering of The Harvard Club of Nashville on November 30, 1971. We would like to answer any questions you may have about our alma mater and to get to know us. Will you kindly write or phone us of your acceptance?

Best regards,

The Harvard Club of Nashville

It was now February 1972, but the letter had just appeared on the table, opened. I yelled and screamed and kicked the front door with my foot. Normally, Mother would have appeared at such an outburst, but nobody came down the hall. She was in the kitchen with the door closed. I was exploding with disappointment that I had missed a date that could have been a pivotal moment for me. I was not too young to know that. On top of that, I was embarrassed, too, that I had not even replied.

Or had someone done that for me?

My head began to spin in a cold panic when it occurred to me what must have happened. Mother and Dad had retrieved the letter before I could see it. They made sure Harvard could not complicate the program in place to keep Charley alive.

I felt so trapped by my burden that I could not breathe. I heard myself repeating in short breaths the same phrase, "*What am I going to do? What am I going to do? What am I going to do?*"

Then I screamed at the top of my lungs, "SOMEBODY GET ME OUT OF THIS!"

TWENTY-ONE

Demon Tongue

I could be mean with my mouth, no doubt about it. Being the youngest and smallest child, I learned that if I had to fight I would do it with my tongue. I honed the talent like a sharp knife. Every once in a while I would take it out and use it.

On a Saturday afternoon, Charley and I were carrying lawn furniture together across the backyard to be stored in the barn. Earlier that day, I had visited a hairstylist and pointed to a picture torn from a magazine. Draper had mailed me a copy of Andy Warhol's *Interview* magazine on one of his visits to New York. The guy in the picture was very sexy, with a handsome face surrounded by shaggy hair. *Maybe if my hair were shaggy, too, it would make my face look better somehow.* The problem was that the guy in the picture was Dino Martin, a chiseled blond hunk, and I was, well, me.

Carrying his end of the table and walking backward, Charley looked me up and down with disgust. "Jesus, you look queer," he said. "Even more than usual."

We were next to the barn. I stopped in my tracks and dropped my end of the table. "Well, at least I don't look like Eleanor Roosevelt in a work shirt. Like *you* do."

Unfortunately, with his weight loss, sick color, and bad skin, Charley was a toothy scarecrow every bit as homely as the late first lady. It was a cruel comparison because it had a nasty truth to it. I knew the comment would jab at his ego, stick deep into his self-esteem.

Charley slowly walked over to me. Then, in a flare of male pride, he grabbed my shoulder and jerked me into a chokehold.

I felt his hot breath on my neck as he whispered in my ear. "You? Why *you?* Why the fuck did it have to be *you?*"

"Let me go. You...crazy...fucker. Let me go!" I wriggled in his hold, but he just gripped me tighter. "What the fuck are you doing?"

He threw me to the ground against the wooden fence and stood over me. I was trapped. "Don't get any ideas about telling Mom and Dad about this. And you're not gonna hold this over me either." He stepped closer and twisted his body like he was about to kick me in the stomach. Then he stopped himself. "You deserve it. With your mouth, Yarrott, you're lucky I don't do worse. You goddamn pussy." His anger echoed in my ears as I grabbed a fence rail and pulled myself up.

I sneered back at him, "Yeah, you know, that's a good question. Why the hell *did* it have to be me? Why can't I just have my own life back? Why the fuck did my goddamn blood have to match yours? You stupid, ugly bastard!"

I saw Charley grab something shiny off a hook and then its glint tumbled toward my head in an arc. I shielded myself with my hands and ducked. The impact was hard and cut deep into my left hand, striking bone between two knuckles. The serrated jaw of the plumber's wrench ripped open the skin and the wound bled fast, all over me. Charley stood frozen. My hand throbbed. He suddenly looked sorry.

"Happy now?" I was lightheaded and getting nauseous. I shoved my bloody hand in front of his face. "Is this what you wanted?"

"Yarrott, God, Jesus, I didn't mean to do it." He stepped toward me and I shot around him.

"You stupid animal! You sick loser! Why couldn't you have died three years ago?" I screamed, running toward the house. He stood frozen, with his mouth open.

I hid behind Dad in the kitchen, glaring at Charley and holding my hand in a towel. Dad was furious. Saliva shot out his mouth as he yelled, "Why the hell can't you two get along?" I had never seen him so disgusted with us. His white hair was pulled in clumps over his red face like messy cotton. "You're going with us to the hospital, Charley. You're going right now to help me sew up your brother. You did this to him and, by God, you're going to look at what you've done."

TWENTY-TWO

.22 Magnum

Brushing my teeth in the bathroom on the top floor, I heard the television in Charley's room down the hall. I had no idea what he was watching. *Bonanza, Gunsmoke, Mannix, It Takes a Thief*—all the late-night reruns sounded alike through the walls, with the male voices rhythmic, hollow thuds and the voices of women piercing and metallic. I cracked the door open and poked my head in to say good night. I found him slumped in the big easy chair with his legs stretched out on a stool. Staring blankly into the black-and-white screen, he rested his chin on a fist.

"Good night, Charley," I said softly. I heard no response. "Hey, you okay?"

He replied without turning around to me, "Yeah. Sure. 'Night, Yarrott."

Climbing down the stairs, I heard another television in Mother and Dad's room, and as I passed it on my way to the basement, a blue light twitched under their door. They had fallen asleep again with the TV on. In my white painted hideaway room behind the furnace, I curled up on the bed with an old *Life* magazine. Overhead, the televisions were muffled. I strained my eyes to see the Lennart Nilsson photo essay of fetuses. *How did he take pictures of these unborn things? Were they still alive?* I was drawn to their colors, orange and pink, like exotic fruit. *What does that little shrimp thing sucking his thumb look like, if he's still alive seven years later?*

The miniature Sony that I took to the hospital twice a week sat squarely on my desk. Sticking out beneath the television was my half-finished application to Vanderbilt University. I checked the clock: ten twenty-five. Johnny Carson starts in five minutes. *Who's on? It doesn't matter who's on, I'll watch it anyway. It's a way to kill time on a school night.*

The boom from upstairs suddenly exploded through the quiet of the room. My heart jumped in my rib cage. *Holy shit! What the hell was that?* The dogs were barking hysterically. I heard Mother's voice upstairs shrieking, "Ed? Was that a gun? Charley! Charley!" followed by Dad's footsteps running up the stairs. I froze on the bed, knowing immediately that the gunshot came from Charley's room. I was afraid to know more. *What did that bastard just do? Oh, no. Did he...did he shoot himself? Or is he now aiming it at Dad? What do I do?* Mother's crutches clicked hurriedly up the steps after Dad.

Suddenly seized with concern for my parents, I threw the magazine on the floor and ran upstairs. Turning the corner to Charley's room, I smelled the gun smoke in the air. The room was weirdly quiet and the only sound was my parents' TV chattering in the distance downstairs. Dad sat on the bed with his hands in his lap. Mother was leaning on the back of the big arm chair, her hands softly stroking Charley's head as he slumped, looking just as I'd seen him last, but now holding his .22 rifle. The television tube in front of him was cracked and a large black hole in it was emitting white smoke.

Was Charley crying? Is that what I saw? Charley, the tough and the terrible, crying? His face was red, wet with tears, and he seemed broken-down and defenseless. It was such a private, naked moment that I immediately turned from him. Dad gestured nervously with his hands for me to stay, gently took the rifle from Charley's grasp and gave it to me. He looked at me with intense, almost angry eyes and mouthed that I must go hide it somewhere.

I quietly ran to the garage, hid it behind the hoes and the rakes leaning against the wall, and remained in the dark there, my heart pounding, light-headed, relieved that Charley had blown a hole through the television and not through himself.

Back upstairs, his door was closed and I heard the warm, reassuring waves of my parents' voices as they stayed with him.

I listened from the steps while he yelled and beat on the chair with his fists. Then he bellowed, "All I do is watch the goddamn TV. Everybody else has a life. Not me. I watch TV. *This* is my life!"

"Don't say that, Charley. Don't say that." Dad's voice trembled. It was clear how much he was hurting, too.

"Goddamn it, Dad. I feel like I'm disappearing. Truth is, and you know it, I have no future. Just now, I had a choice. It had to be one of us, either me or the TV. I came so close...."

Dad's voice tightened on two anxious words and barely got them out, "I know...I know...I know."

TWENTY-THREE

The Fix

In August, the sweet, humid air made the evening twilight delectable on the terrace. The long shadows poured across the backyard like syrup and an orange fire slowly faded through the black silhouettes of the elm trees. Through the living room doors, I noticed Mother sitting alone with a drink at the wrought iron table in front of her. Her posture, leaning forward against the table with her head cast down, caught my attention. *Oh, no. Is she crying?*

She took a long sip from the squat, elegant glass and returned it carefully to the raised wet circle on the napkin. Dad was not yet home from the office and it was already eight o'clock. Mother continued to stare into her lap. I opened the French doors and called to her from the top step.

"Mother?"

She quickly lifted her head and straightened in the iron chair. "Yes? Oh, honey. Whaddya know?"

"Oh, I was just wondering when we were going to eat." I held open one of the screen doors.

She continued to stare ahead. "In a bit, Yarrott. We're waiting for Daddy. He called with an emergency late this afternoon. If you're hungry, do, go ahead and eat. I'll wait for your father."

"Mom?"

"Yes?" she answered wearily.

"You okay?"

"Don't be silly. Of course I am." She continued to face the darkening yard.

"Well, you seem sad or something."

She remained quiet for a moment and slowly relaxed in her seat, dropping her head again. I drew up a chair next to her and put my hand on her shoulder. She took a few deep breaths and sighed. I was mortified.

She faced me. "No, I'm not okay."

"Gosh, what's wrong? Can I do anything?"

"No, Yarrott."

"Well, what's happened? What's wrong?"

"Oh, Yarrott. I can't tell you. For gosh sakes."

"Is anything wrong with Dad? With you? Come on, please tell me."

She turned around to face me and said, "Honey, listen, you won't understand this, but I was crying...for *you*."

"Ma'am?" My heart stopped. *What did I do wrong?*

"For *you*, honey. Don't you see? Can't you possibly see that?" I smelled the familiar smell of scotch on her breath. She squeezed my wrist with her cool fingers, just lifted from the glass. "You can't possibly understand, can you?"

She was right. I did not understand. Not a word.

"This is a terrible fix you're in. You don't deserve it. No one does."

I froze in my tracks at this declaration. She meant about Charley and me, his illness, my blood, our dilemma, our *fix*.

"I was crying for *you*, honey."

TWENTY-FOUR

Entrance Test

The trees climbed upward like black fractures against the white January sky. Nashville was bleak and I was restless. My last semester as a high school senior had begun and for English class I was reading Alan Silito's *The Loneliness of the Long Distance Runner*. For some reason, the words were sticking when my eyes passed over them. And I liked it. I liked the main character, Colin, and his recollections of a rebellious, aimless life, the life he had had before he found his talent in running. I was jealous of Colin's discovery. He had learned that he had some strengths after all, that he could be the best in something. *Damn, I want to be like that...and aim for something. I am burning to do something, but I don't know what that is. Art is easy for me. Is that what it is? I've got good grades in English, too...but I don't know...I'd rather make things with my hands. That's when I feel most satisfied.*

The application to Vanderbilt University sat on my desk for two months, collecting creases and stains. I would read it through, nervously twitch my head left and right, then put the application down. I was supposed to write a description of myself. I would start a paragraph, twitch, then put the pen down. *If they saw my habits, my tics, I'd be rejected for sure. Shit, what can I write about myself that's any good?* I picked up the pen and chewed the tip. *If I wrote the truth, that I'm only applying to Vanderbilt because it's in Nashville and I have to stay in Nashville because of my brother, what would they think? Ha! They'd say get*

the fuck outta here, buddy. Outta here, you twitching freak. I put the pen down again.

Driving to school in the white Impala, I thought about the question: Who the hell am I? *I make platelets and keep a brother alive who thinks I'm a piece of shit. I go out with girls but I crave the hairy guys I see in the locker room. I make A's, teachers get all excited, and then I make C's and D's and the teachers act all sad and disappointed. Does that mean I'm complex? Does complex mean I am smart? Or talented? Or just fucked up?*

I finally filled out my one college application. With a terse description of who I am, I stuffed the application into a manila envelope, shoved it into the mailbox at home, and raised the little red flag.

The week before Easter, I received a crisply polite rejection letter from Vanderbilt University, the alma mater of my father, my mother, and my oldest brother. Quietly, I sat in my room in the basement and twitched myself into a headache. I thought things through. I backed up and realized I had done this application thing all wrong. *They have to give me another chance.*

"Hello, I'd like to make an appointment with the Director of Admissions, Mr. Walton, please." I heard myself talking firmly to a receptionist on the other end. "Yes, my name is Yarrott Benz and I would like to speak to him about my application."

The uninterested drawl on the other end asked, "Have you received an answer from the university, sir?"

"I have. I was rejected."

"Well, there's nothing Mr. Walton can do for you, sir."

"Miss, you don't understand. My situation is completely unique, and I am the son of two alumni and the brother of another. I think he should see me."

"One minute, sir." She put me on hold. I stared at my desk in my room behind the furnace and blinked. My head did not twitch. My whole body felt poised to leap on something. The receptionist returned. "All right, Mr. Benz. He'll see you. Can you be on campus tomorrow at three P.M.?"

"Yes, I will be there. And thank you."

෨

The admissions office was located in an ivy-covered bungalow, once faculty housing, framed by mature magnolia trees. Ironically, I could see the roof of the hospital from the front door. *I practically grew up here.*

I was relieved to meet Mr. Walton, the director of admissions. He was young, probably Eddy's age, and immediately sympathetic when I explained my situation with Charley and my platelet donations. "Well, I can see why you would need to go to Vanderbilt. Your grades are scattered, but you really show promise. You have what I call a *precocious* academic history."

I was defensive and gripped the arms of the chair. "That sounds like you mean childish or something."

"Oh, no. I don't mean childish. I mean that your developmental timing seems a bit out of whack. Like those magnolias outside the window. Sometimes they produce leaves at the wrong time of year and their fruit ripens early. Your skills and your talents are scattered and their development is uneven. You are way ahead in your development in some areas and way behind in others. I definitely do not mean you are childish."

"Well, two things I know, Mr. Walton. One is that I can't leave Nashville to go to college. Vanderbilt would ordinarily not be my choice, but given that I have to stay in Nashville—and this is my second point—it is now the only suitable college for me. There's Peabody, but that's a teachers' college. I don't want to be a teacher. Since I have been connected to Vanderbilt one way or another for my entire life, I ask you to look at my situation here in Nashville and reconsider the rejection. I am asking you to let me in." I was as red as a beet and I did not care.

Mr. Walton continued to look at me with a faint smile on his face. He was mute. I think he was a little shocked by my insistence. I kept thinking that I had nothing to lose.

Finally, he said quietly, "Thank you for letting us know more about you, Yarrott. Yes, I will look into your file and will let you know our answer in about a week. Will that be acceptable to you?"

I took a deep breath and thanked him. I had been heard and something I said triggered a reaction of respect or maybe just plain kindness. Later that week, the university reconsidered my application and I received a letter of acceptance. I had taken one step, on my own, toward some kind of a future.

TWENTY-FIVE

Tune It Out

Two months into my first semester at Vanderbilt, Mother and I stood, not speaking, side by side at the kitchen sink. She shoved the wet pot in my hands and I dried it perfunctorily, resentfully. Charley was nowhere to be seen, which was usual after dinner. Was he outside on the porch smoking something? Down at the barn in the tack room cleaning his shotgun? Dad was watching television in their bedroom, probably a formulaic sitcom, perhaps *Sanford and Son*, his favorite manner of escape. *Sad. Phi Beta Kappa and wasting such a great mind like his in front of stupid nonsense. How pathetic is that?*

The tension in the house was palpable. And from what? I had stayed out late the night before with my friend Danny and came in at four. *So damn what? I'm an adult. I'm almost nineteen years old. I can smoke if I want to, get drunk, take the car, skip class, flunk a course, and most of all I can fuck, yes fuck, anybody I want to, girl or guy. I can go to a gay bar if I want! And I don't have to tell them a damn thing about it. Hell, I don't want to live in this house. If they don't like me here, then let me move out!*

But really? My biggest problem is that I'm not screwing anybody. The rest of the world is screwing someone every Saturday night, but not me. Who'd want to do it with me, anyway? Look at this face, I'm one ugly sonofabitch. Last night at The Other Side, my first time to a gay bar, and I just stood around like a stupid coat rack with all those hot guys eyeing one another, but not a single one looking at me. I'm invisible.

"You certainly are silent. Feeling guilty about something?" Mother's superior tone was as abrupt and cold as a bucket of ice. She jabbed another pot in my hands.

"I certainly do *not* feel guilty about anything," I replied flatly. "I just hate living here. I hate living with all of you. That's it."

"Well, little man, if you want to move out, you're certainly going to have to prove you're ready for it. And staying out until four a.m. is no way to prove it." She sprayed the sink and watched it drain. "And what's more, your grades are absolutely horrible. You think your father is going to trust you on your own? What if you flunk out? What *then?*"

All I could think of was the strong handsome faces in the bar last night and the tight jeans contouring their muscular asses. The more I heard Mother's ice-cold voice, the more I thought of the warmth of those bodies cruising next to me and how all that warmth eluded me. *A warm-blooded life is out of my reach as long as I stand here with this crippled old woman... and she's just one of my balls and chains. God help me. Somebody save me.*

"We have enough problems without you adding to them. You are one of our biggest disappointments right now. Look at our other worries, will you?" She shook out Comet along the sides of the sink and quickly, efficiently made tiny circles with the wet sponge. "You have one more chance. If you repeat what you did last night, you may not use our car. Do you understand me, little man?"

"Then I'll get my own car."

"No, you won't."

"Try to stop me."

"Don't you *dare* talk to me like that, Yarrott!"

"Oh, would you *please* just go to hell?" At that, Mother threw the sponge in the sink, turned around, and slapped me hard in the face.

"I said DON'T talk to your mother like that! Now, look what you've made me do. I've busted a vessel in my hand. Damn you, Yarrott!"

"Too late, Mother, I'm already damned. I'm already *very* damned." I felt a welt rise and realized she had caught the corner of my eyelid with her ring. Man, that woman could slap. Mother limped out of the kitchen angrily and I remained there, floating in space, numb, disassociating myself from the very moment. It was like hallucinating or hyperventilating. *I can't stand around here like this—I've got to study for those two big tests tomorrow. But, I can't even think, much less read the material I've ignored.* I was right. I could not read. I could not focus on the words or hold on to the meaning of the words. I felt a cold panic rising inside me, beads of sweat inching down my forehead. *Christ, German II. Ich bin ein dumkopf. Oder ist es dumbkopff? Und dann ich habe Baroque und Renaissance Architektur!*

Having never met the adviser assigned to me at Vanderbilt freshman year, I signed myself up for all the wrong classes, with no logic whatsoever to my choices or to their level of difficulty. Renaissance and Baroque Architecture was my first art history class. I had not taken the prerequisite survey class—I just thought the sound of Renaissance and Baroque Architecture was appealing. These lapses of judgment haunted me from the first day at Vanderbilt. I had convinced myself that school did not matter, that what I got or did not get from college was irrelevant to my life. I was separate and apart from all the other students, so why would I have to play by the same rules? But at times, like this particular Sunday night, the rooster came home to roost. I had to take the tests like everyone else tomorrow and the result of my confused thinking was unavoidable. *The truth is that I am a fool, a stupid fool.*

Then it entered my head. Dying. My death—not Charley's death, but mine. *I'm not living, so I must be dying instead. Yeah, dying. That sounds good. It gives me a weird pleasure to think about it. Roll my tongue over the word like they say you do a sip of brandy. It feels good. My own death. The end to everything. No more of the weight of the world on my shoulders. They would like it upstairs. No, they wouldn't. They'd all panic about Charley. Well, good. That feels even better, to know they'd suffer.*

But Charley wouldn't suffer one bit. Yeah, he'd die himself soon after if I died, but he wouldn't grieve for a millisecond. I might even do him a favor—getting him out of the stinking mess he's in. Yes, the world now is a trap for us and I can get both of us out of it. Death. Death. Death. It feels like such a relief to say it.

I pulled out from my backpack the pint bottle of Crawford's

Scotch that I had bought last night with Danny and took as much as I could in one gulp. *Tune it out, Yarrott. Tune out Alberti and Wittkower and German and subjunctive and humanism and all those concepts and words that don't relate to my trap of a life. Tune out Mother and Charley and Dad. Tune it all out.* The burning down my throat hurt deliciously. I took another and another. Finally, the heavy, iron-like weight of the schoolwork piling on me started to lighten. I lay on the bed and watched the candle flame throw its twitching, manic shadows across the walls, and I settled into myself with comfort, shutting a door to the outside, where a nervous wind beat and scraped. Within myself I was safe.

TWENTY-SIX

Reward

I was alone in the house. Mother and Dad were at a Surgical Society event. Charley had gone camping for the weekend. It was a Friday night, the school week was over, and the house was quiet. *Just the dogs and me. The fraternities at school are partying like crazy tonight. Damn. I made an A on the German paper. I did something right this week. I deserve something.*

I pulled out a tall bottle of scotch from Dad's liquor cabinet and poured an inch and a half into a squat glass with a ladybug painted on it. *Let's see how much I can drink down in one gulp. Not bad. Now try it again. More this time. Feels warm. Nice.*

I refilled the ladybug. *Man, I like this. It's making everything feel smooth, like a steamroller's flattening my bumpy road. Ladybug's thirsty again. Give her some more. That's it. Nice.*

Hey there, Gretel, little girl. Come back here. Where'd she go? Gimme some love. Damn. Room's spinning. Bed feels good. Hold the pillow. Keep one hand on the floor. It'll stop spinning if I touch something. I don't believe this. I'm gonna puke.

TWENTY-SEVEN

Just Like Us

The gray pigeon spent several days building her nest on the window ledge of the fine arts library. The early spring sky was blustery, the wind cold, with stripes of clouds passing overhead in quick succession. People on the Vanderbilt campus ran quickly from building to building. I had been hiding out in this part of the library ever since I stumbled across it by accident in the fall. I could always count on few students, if any, being in the stacks or studying around the green tables. This was a place to be alone with myself and safe from the constant insecurities I felt being among the other students. More times than I could count, I had passed my time here, not studying the material from my classes, but absorbing old journals like *Architectural Record* from 1895 to 1910, bound collections of the magazine that had sat untouched for decades. I loved my secret entry into American life long before my parents were born.

This corner of the library drew few students, if any at all. There were surely no fraternity jock types, the most conservative and therefore most threatening kind of student to me, full of testosterone, muscle, and sideburns, like Charley used to be. This was a place I carved out for myself among the dark metal shelves and dividers, a hidden cave of compelling material that did not make demands on me.

As I sat near a window, balancing my chin on the back of my hand as I read, the cooing sounds from the window ledge caught my attention. The pigeon's nest was growing, just behind a gothic parapet, a foot and a half from the windowpane.

The female was completely unaware of my watching behind the glass.

I returned for several days, to watch the nest grow more defined. Finally, I found the pigeon sitting contently, facing away from the window with her belly nestled in the mass of sticks and leaves. It seemed an awfully agreeable domestic scene, although I never caught sight of any male accompanying her. When the female finally left the nest for a moment, I slowly opened the window and leaned out to find four scrawny hatchlings, quivering, purple, and veiny, like congealed blood. *Look at that! Four offspring, just like us at home.* The mother flapped back to the ledge, hopped over to the nest, and stretched open her beak, wide like a stew pot. The babies poked their huge triangular beaks deep into the back of her throat.

After a few days of this, the clutch of four had grown quickly, developing downy feathers and holding their heads more steadily. They seemed to be observing the world while soaking in a bathtub, blinking their eyes in occasional astonishment. After two weeks, their collective skin and feathers poured over the sides of the nest.

East Asian History class began very early on a dark Friday morning, just as a heavy downpour began, with screaming winds and thunder crashes. The black branches of the gigantic magnolias on the Vanderbilt campus bent low to the brick sidewalks. As soon as class ended, I ran across the lawn in the wind to the fine arts library and leapt three steps at a time up the four stories to my corner. When I got to the window, the glass was covered with bits of twigs, dirt, leaves, and small feathers. An inch of standing water filled the ledge and the nest was battered into pieces. My birds were gone.

A dark, solitary world became darker. While the rest of campus was excited about the Grateful Dead concert that weekend, I was obsessed with the lost family of pigeons. I transferred the tragic image onto the impossible dilemma of my mother and her sons. Perhaps my poor mother felt as panicked at times as the pigeon must now, as dumbfounded by nature and as overwhelmed. *Does that make me one of the hatchlings swallowed up in nature?* The awful demise of the birds had opened up a hole in the ground that widened quickly into a crater. I felt sick to my stomach at the implications. Around me on campus, the many good-looking young people were enjoying this time in their lives. This was their very own safe, exciting, narcissistic moment, and they were as many miles from me now as the country of China. Crossing campus with my books, their bodies to me disintegrated into a jumble of blurred streaks, a tangle of murmurs and echoes. The nausea intensified and I realized that I had been seized emotionally by something very strange. I found my car and drove around the neighboring streets, trying hard to decide what to do and where to go.

I knew something was wrong but I had no idea where I could find help. The doctors I knew did not seem like the types to understand this abrupt and flawed emotion in me. They were older versions of the same good-looking students I saw all around me, for whom I was developing contempt and of whom I was deeply envious. No, I could not go to the doctors I knew.

What about Dad's office? Maybe. If he's there. I need somebody to steady me. I feel like I am on the deck of a boat in the middle of a churning ocean. One big wave is going to come knock me off into the dark place I've always been afraid of going. Maybe Dad can help me.

Dad was there, but Mrs. Buford said he was with a patient. Did I want to wait in his office? *No, I'll wait in the little lab between his office and Uncle Louis's.* I drank a Coke from their refrigerator under the counter. I could hear Dad calmly talking to his patient down the hall, explaining how to change the bandages, being careful with the sutures. The lady's voice was high and anxious. Dad's was soothing. I sat on the high stool facing the chrome sterilizer. His assistant Elise passed through to retrieve a syringe.

"Hi, Elise. School's great, thanks. I'm fine. You? That's good. See you."

The shelves in front of me were stocked with unfamiliar items with Latin names, drugs I had never heard of and equipment I had never seen. My father's knowledge was wide and impressive. It made me feel small. I could put him in the same company as the many confident students and my other doctors. *Do I really think he can help me? No, I don't. I should go.*

Just then Dad rushed into the little lab. "Wunnerful! Always a treat to see my boy. But don't you have class now? Something wrong? You okay? Yarrott? Let's go have a seat in my office."

I described to Dad my confusion, my thinking that felt fast, blurred, and chaotic, my utter and complete feeling of bleakness. Sitting across from me, he put his knees in front of mine and looked me in the eyes as I spoke. He was frowning, but he seemed empathetic.

"Golly, Yarrott, I can see you're not feeling good. What can I do for you? Maybe this will help for now." He gave me two small pills, sedatives, and told me to drive home immediately and take them once I got home. They would calm me down.

I felt the roiling ocean settling just looking into Dad's hazel eyes. I immediately felt that he had extended a rope to me. All I had to do was hold on to it and pull myself through the fog closing in on me.

Gripping the steering wheel tightly and focusing straight ahead, I drove up 21st Avenue, the asphalt wet and slippery, while the small shops of Hillsboro Village passed by the car, then all the big stores and traffic and blinking lights in Green Hills Shopping Center. I followed the cars in front of me obediently, carefully, slowly. I turned through the stone gates at home and continued to the edge of the driveway, then jerked the car into park.

The rain was starting up again so I sat for a while in the front seat of the white Impala with the wipers slapping. The two pills stuck in my throat as I swallowed them dry and I waited impatiently for their effect to come over me. Through the smearing rain on the windshield, I noticed a shadowy, bird-like movement on the front porch. *Mother? Yes, I see her silver head over the long brown arms of her raincoat.* In slow motion,

Mother was waving her arms to me, broadly, like she was flapping her wings. I lowered the window and stuck my head into the rain and could see her mouthing something. "Yarrott?" she seemed to be saying. "Yarrott, are you okay? Honey, why don't you come in?"

I continued to sit in the car in the rain at the side of the driveway, sure that I was about to break open and that my gelatinous interior would spill all over the floor mats. But I did not. Somehow, through some remarkable fight in me or perhaps some kind of surrender, I did not break apart. My eggshell remained intact in the storm.

TWENTY-EIGHT

Psychiatrist

On my Sony TV, Rachel and Mac were fighting again on *Another World* and I was hypnotized by it, oblivious to what else was happening in the donor room. A small bit of my blood was coagulating in long strings inside the tubes and Sandra the technologist was on her knees squeezing silver pliers along the tube to coax the clot into a syringe. This was nothing unusual in the course of the procedure.

Suddenly, Dr. Flexner, the head of hematology, stuck his head in and got my attention with his loud bark. "Yarrott, your father called me." He reminded me of Darren McGavin in *The Night Stalker*. His big voice matched his big personality. I turned off the TV and gave him my full attention. "Your dad says you're not feeling well. Sorry to hear that, son. I have somebody you should talk to. His name is Ferris Miller and he's an old friend of mine. He's a good guy and a helluva racquetball player. You'll like him."

Just like that? Well, okay. I gotta talk to somebody so it might as well be this Dr. Miller guy. I've got to get this stuff out of my head. It's driving me crazy. All this about other guys that I'm feeling. All this stuff about sex I'm not having. All this stuff about hating college. I'm going out of my mind. I'm so lonely. I've got to talk to somebody. I'll feel better getting this out of my head.

The next afternoon, I found Dr. Miller's office in the bowels of the oldest part of Vanderbilt Hospital, in one of those long white corridors with heavy wooden doors. Below his name on the door, it said *Psychiatrist*. I knocked lightly and got no response, then I knocked harder a second time.

Through the door I heard him, muffled. "Yes, one minute, please. I'm on the phone."

I stood at the door in front of the word Psychiatrist and wanted to hide. *Oh, shit, here come three med students. Hurry up and open the door.*

Finally, I heard movement in the room and the door swung open. "Yarrott, is it? I'm Dr. Miller. Sorry to keep you waiting. I had an important call."

I sat in a chair opposite his desk and gripped the metal armrests. I was nervous and had no idea what to expect from the meeting. Dr. Miller smiled faintly and kept eye contact with me as he circled his desk and sat down. He seemed confident, like a handsome, middle-aged teacher.

He said, "I understand you're in a very unusual situation at home with your brother. Can you tell me about it?"

I explained the twice-weekly platelet pheresis and that we had been doing it for three years. I described how different Charley and I had always been.

"It must be hard living with someone who is so ill, huh?" he said with a sympathetic smile.

"Well, yes, it is, but..."

"I know that watching someone so sick is a terrible burden," he continued, "and that burden accumulates."

"But it's more than..." I tried to squeeze in.

"And when the burden accumulates, it does things to your thinking." He leaned back in his chair and put his hands behind his head. He maintained eye contact while he kept talking. "It can cause severe depression."

I clammed shut. *That certainly sounds right. Maybe I'm in a severe depression, like he said. But I think I should also be talking about the other stuff, like why the hell I'm thinking about guys so much. Why do I feel so lonely? I've got to get that off my chest!*

"How's everything else going in your life, Yarrott?"

"You mean, school?"

"Yeah. How're your grades? You playing on any teams? What's your social life like? You know, got a girlfriend? That stuff."

Oh, shit. He's a jock. He's going to think I'm such a loser.

I tapped the chair's arm frantically with my index finger. I clenched my stomach muscles and gritted my teeth to keep from twitching my head.

"And how's your sex life?"

I thought I would pass out. *Did he just ask about my sex life? What do I say? That I go out with girls occasionally, but I dream about guys? That I don't have a sex life? What the fuck do I say? He'll think I'm such a loser, a loner, a goddamn misfit.*

I finally answered him. "About like anybody else's my age."

He paused for a moment and just looked at me, waiting for me to say more. I did not. Finally, he changed the subject back to Charley. "Does it get you down being around somebody who's so sick?"

"I'm used to it by now. It's been three years." I tapped on the armrest. *I need to talk about me. Please help me talk about me.*

Dr. Miller looked at me quietly for a moment, then reached across his walnut desk and picked up a book, already opened and face down. "You might be interested in this, Yarrott. *On Death and Dying.* Have you ever heard of Elisabeth Kübler-Ross?"

"No, I haven't."

"There's a whole layered process about dealing with death that she discovered. This can be about your own death or someone else's. There are several stages. The first is denial, then comes anger, then something called bargaining, then depression, then finally, acceptance. Everybody goes through these same stages. Maybe that's what's going on with you. Maybe you're depressed or even angry about your brother's illness... and his death in the near future. What do you think? Does that sound likely?"

Did he just say Charley was going to die? That's right, Charley is going to die and that's the important thing that's happening here. I'm feeling sorry for myself when it's Charley I should be thinking about. I am such an asshole. Charley's the one we need to think about.

"Since our hour is almost up, was there anything else you wanted to talk about, Yarrott?"

"No, sir. That's about it. Thanks."

"Don't mention it. I'm glad I could be of some help."

I wandered back to the parking lot through the corridors, past skinny old people in the clinics, past dying children in the pediatric wing, past broken arms and legs. *God, am I lucky. I've got a body that works, a strong heart, and lots of good blood. I've got a life ahead of me. Stop acting crazy.*

TWENTY-NINE

New Odds

By the spring of 1973, most of the original cast at the hospital had left. Dr. Sergent had moved to a position in New York City. Claudia had taken a job in Florida. Our brother Eddy had taken a post at the Mayo Clinic in Minnesota. Most of my high school friends had left Nashville, too. Draper wrote me from Brooklyn about his wild and stimulating new life at the Pratt Institute. The world seemed full, rich, and fun outside the dark little donor room.

Inside, however, it was the same tight, claustrophobic cube. I showed up, punctual as always, like the chimes of Big Ben, every Monday and Thursday from one until six, affable as always, ready to smile and to bleed.

On the other side of the door, unknown to me, some big things were cooking. One afternoon, Dr. Flexner rushed into the donor room with his black hair flying over his ears and asked, "How'd you like to visit Seattle, Yarrott?"

"I...don't know. Why?"

"Well, your time in the chair here might be over, boy. Where's your brother?" He looked behind the door for Charley. "Not here, huh? Come down to my office as soon as he gets in, okay?" He suddenly turned and disappeared.

I looked at Annelle, the technologist newly in charge of the platelet pheresis. "What's all that about? He's excited about something."

"Well, I don't really know, sugar," she said sweetly as she monitored my tubes.

Later, after I had finished with my donation and Charley

had received it, we knocked on Dr. Flexner's door, settled into the leather chairs parked at his desk, and waited for him to look up from his writing.

He lowered his reading glasses and smiled. "We have some good news, fellas. You know Dr. Thomas in Seattle, E. Donnell Thomas? The man who has been developing bone marrow transplants? His clinic at the University of Washington just let me know that they are ready to take you if you're interested."

"Take us?" Charley asked. "What do you mean *take us?*"

"For a bone marrow, son. A bone marrow transplant. From Yarrott to you."

"Holy cow," Charley said under his breath. "I thought those things were risky."

"They are, but they've made some real progress. It would mean that you'd be free from Yarrott. And, of course, vice versa."

I had a grin on my face but I stayed quiet.

"When do we have to let them know?" Charley asked.

"By next week. Go on home and discuss it with your parents. Let's talk more on Thursday. This could be the break both of you have been hoping for." Dr. Flexner pushed his hair off his face and slid his reading glasses back up his nose. "Let's talk more later, guys. Okay?"

Mother, Dad, Charley, and I poked at our dinners as we talked about Seattle. "Don't feel any pressure to do this, Charley," Dad said earnestly. "The survival rate is still not good. Please think long and hard about it."

"What exactly are the odds? Do you know, Dad?" Charley looked at him with some fear in his eyes.

Dad took a sip from his water and swallowed. He put the glass down slowly as he collected his thoughts. "I won't sweeten it up for you. The odds are good that you will not survive. You would only have a fifteen percent chance of success. That means, think about it, if one hundred people start out sick, only fifteen of them will be alive at the end of the bone marrow transplant. I hate even thinking about it."

Mother added, "Honey, don't feel pressured into doing it. Okay? Just try to be as calm as you can while you decide."

I finally said something. "Don't do it for me, Charley. Your own life is more important than my freedom, as awful as this gets at times." What I said sounded good and brave. It sounded like I knew what I was saying. I said what came natural to someone growing up a child at McKendree Methodist Church. *Think of others before you think of yourself.*

"Thanks, Yarrott. I appreciate that." Charley tapped his knife on the cloth place mat.

The weather was finally warming up in Nashville. My first spring on a college campus was invigorating, with mowed lawns and blossoms everywhere. The jocks wore torn basketball jerseys, cut-off jeans, and flip-flops. The freaks wore tie-dyed T-shirts with their frizzy hair in ponytails. The frat boys would not put away their Oxford shirts for anything. I stood somewhere between all of them. Not one of them. Not any of them. I was nowhere and everywhere in my personal style. But something was afoot on Tyne Boulevard that would put the trivial vanities of campus life into a more worldly perspective.

THIRTY

Connie's Concert

Every so often new people would wander into my path who would give me a glimpse of life in the bigger world. From them, I would know that there would be something waiting for me in the future if I could just survive the present. A serious and extraordinary violinist, my friend Connie was such a person.

Although she was a year behind me at our high school, Peabody, I felt that I had a lot to learn from watching her. Connie was easily the most disciplined friend I had, practicing daily and performing on a regular basis at seventeen. She had already studied with the best of the Juilliard teachers in the summer program in Aspen and was being groomed to continue with the violin in New York. This was a crucial time for her. Both Sarah Lawrence and Juilliard wanted her for the following year. It meant choosing between a focus on music or a wider range of subjects in liberal arts. She said it was not an easy decision. My respect for her outshone my jealousy.

The day before we flew to Seattle for the bone marrow transplant, I asked Connie if she would come to the house that night to play something as a send-off for Mother, Dad, Charley, and me. My parents and I had regretted missing her recital in Nashville earlier in the week. She agreed. "Sure, if you think everybody will enjoy my program. It's pretty intense."

Mother, Dad, Charley, and I sat comfortably around the living room, grinning expectantly at one another as Connie readied herself in front of the fireplace. She explained the program of Beethoven, Scarlatti, and Hindemith and then solemnly looked at Charley. "May this small program be dedicated to success awaiting you in Seattle."

Over the next hour, she transformed our unexceptional room with blue furniture and yellow carpet into a glorious concert hall. Dad and Mother, at one time students of music themselves, were acquainted with all the pieces and smiled with their heads tilted and their eyes closed. For Charley and me, who were new to most of the works, the moment was electric. Charley watched Connie's movements intently, as if she were an athlete. At one point his mouth hung slightly open in disbelief. She played magnificently, whipping her bow across the strings boldly and emotionally. It was almost shocking to me how she was willing to strip away her personal shell to expose herself like this. When it was over, we all stood clapping and embracing her. Connie's face was beaming. It was flushed and wet.

Afterward, as I was driving her back to her parents' house, we took a detour into the hills to see the lights of downtown Nashville in the distance. She was suddenly very quiet. I pulled the car over so we could talk. In the light of the dashboard, I could see that she was holding her hand over her mouth and trembling.

"Hey, Miss Cornelia, are you alright?"

"Yeah. I am. Sorry. I don't know why I'm crying."

"Was it too much for you, playing for us?"

"No, on the contrary. This has been a really important night. More important for me than for your family, I'm afraid."

"I don't know what you mean. Everyone loved it." I scooted across the vinyl seat and put my arm around her. "I hope you know how much Charley enjoyed it. And, of course, my parents. And, God knows, I sure did. It was a beautiful send-off for tomorrow." I added earnestly, "Man, music really touches the soul, doesn't it?"

She looked into the swarm of lights in the distance. "I just can't imagine what is going through your brother's mind now. I'm glad the music gave him a break. I guess I'm just emotional from playing. It's intense performing in front of just four people like that."

"I can only imagine. You really gave it everything, too." I squeezed her shoulder.

"Wish I had some water to splash on my face." She shook her hands out and then patted her face. "Let's have a cigarette." She passed her Marlboros to me and we both lit up.

She took my hand. "Yarrott, do you think he's afraid of dying?"

I felt the firmness of her grip, its warmth and compassion. I could sense the fear she had for Charley. Her question made me think carefully. I wanted to answer her truthfully, not give a stock brave answer, making him into a comic book martyr. *Is he afraid of dying?* I had not asked Charley that question in years, since the night in my room in the basement.

"Truth is, I don't know, Connie. I can't say if he's worrying much about it. To me, he's kind of got blindfolds on. I think he's walking toward the transplant without thinking about it. That's the way it looks to me. Listen, I know he wants to be free from me. Maybe as much as I want to be free from him."

"But his survival chances are so slim," I heard Connie repeat.

I thought about the question again. *Is he afraid of dying?* It stunned me how I had blocked myself from thinking about his position in the transplant. I had considered only myself and my leap toward freedom. *Of course he must be afraid.*

THIRTY-ONE

Seattle

We changed planes at Chicago's O'Hare Airport. Mother, Dad, Charley, and I walked onto the orange, navy blue, and white 747 and found our two rows of seats on the right side of the aircraft. I was fidgeting so much on the world's biggest plane that I had knots in my stomach. To the others, this plane was no different from any other jet, except larger and more spacious. It was 1973, but I felt like Keir Dullea in *2001: A Space Odyssey*. Okay, we were on Northwest Orient, not Pan Am, like in the film. I had never heard of Northwest Orient before, but that didn't matter. The mystique and glamour of air travel were still bound up in the experience. The aroma was not just of coffee—it was the airborne coffee of a 747.

I was shaking my head and twitching off the wide cabin's plastic walls. The purpose of our destination had wound me up to the point of hysteria. The University of Washington in Seattle had agreed to perform a bone marrow transplant and I was finally going to get my freedom from Charley. The Siamese Benz Twins could finally be cut apart. I was excited to the point of manic overdrive, obsessing on every detail of the airplane, from the shape of the lights in the wall panels to the typography of the seat pocket's emergency card. As we barreled down the runway, I swiveled around in my seat to Mother and Dad behind us and insisted that we four hold hands as the plane's front end lifted up and roared into the air. Mother and Dad smiled agreeably and let me go on in my dramatics. Even normally undemonstrative Charley grabbed my hand and held firm for a long moment. We ordered white wine and made a toast to Charley's fine, healthy future ahead as the thunder-heads outside the window shook the plane. Somewhere in the big belly below us, our dozen pieces of luggage rocked and bounced. We had brought enough clothes for three months: April, May, and June.

Dad planned to return to Nashville in about ten days, after Charley's total body irradiation had been completed. My bone marrow would be administered shortly after that. Then we would sit tight and wait to see if it took. The most dangerous phase would be the two months while we waited. Charley could reject my marrow in host versus graft disease, which would leave him without any defenses for survival. Or my marrow could attack him in graft versus host disease. Or he could take my marrow and do well, recovering and finding a longer life span in front of him. There was only a fifteen percent chance of success, but Charley was willing to take it. Whatever it meant for him, it meant I would finally be free, after three years of pheresis twice a week. I could go to art school in the Northeast! Or maybe journalism school in Chicago! Or film school in California! I could fly away as far as this 747 jetliner could fly! I was euphoric. I felt my time had finally come, or was just about to come. In my twitching head, this trip was mostly about me. It was not about Charley.

Upon finally reaching a small apartment in the Beacon Hill neighborhood of Seattle, Dad parked the rented car while the rest of us tried to find space inside for our luggage. Immediately, I smelled an unfamiliar odor, which felt wrong, like mildew or mold, but was both sweet and acidic. The apartment was leased by the hospital for the families of transplant patients and was furnished in early-sixties dinette. The walls were stained plywood paneling, the carpet brown as dirt. Except for the beautiful green views of the nearby hills, the apartment was depressing, a difficult place to spend a difficult time. Something felt wrong to me the instant I entered it. When I mentioned my dislike of the place, Dad became irate, blamed my increasingly snobbish tastes and my lack of tolerance for anything new. I did not disagree. I, too, blamed myself. Nevertheless, I felt something wrong. I could taste it in my mouth.

The first morning, after an argumentative, difficult sleep on a sofa bed shared with Charley, we immediately headed to the hospital to meet a woman named Kris, the administrator in charge of settling families into their long stays in Seattle. She was our charming hostess for the day. She introduced us to Charley's doctor, E. Donnall Thomas, a name well-known to us from Dr. Flexner and also from *Time* magazine, where we had read a glowing article on the eminent physician. Bearded and somewhat formal, like Czar Nicholas II or Captain Smith of the *Titanic,* he was pleasant enough but detached, seeming more like a scientist than a physician. At first, he did not recognize Charley's case and needed prompting by Kris. "You remember, Dr. Thomas, the Benzes from Nashville? The two brothers undergoing platelet pheresis for several years?"

"Oh, of course," Dr. Thomas nodded. "We have some questions. May I see you by yourself, Charles?" The two went into an office with exposed brick walls and a view of the hills and closed the door. Mother, Dad, and I, a bit confused, quickly followed Kris through a pair of double doors into the transplant wing for a tour of the facilities. After a half hour, Charley returned as Kris was introducing us to three men in their twenties—Thomas, Win, and Billy, who had each received marrow transplants within the past two months. All three slumped in their wheelchairs, bald, yellow, and thin.

Winn grinned broadly at Charley and whispered, "We've been expecting you guys. Don't let the stories of Seattle's rain scare you."

Charley stepped toward Winn respectfully and said, "How are you doing? I mean, really, how *are* you...you know, after the transplant?"

Winn tried to make his voice louder, but only strained. "So far, so good, buddy. When is your transplant scheduled? Charley, is it?"

"I'm not sure. I guess in the next day or two."

"Listen, you hang in there, okay? The first part, the radiation, is scary. You'll get nauseous and all that, but you'll get through it fine. What comes next is a different story. It's the tough part."

"What do you mean?" Charley knelt down to Winn's chair.

"Well, everybody's sitting around waiting for the bad stuff. You know, rejection. It's pretty hairy."

Charley looked nervous and asked, "When'd you have your transplant?"

"About a month ago," he whispered. "From my big sister. She's already gone back home to Wichita. She's a nursing student."

"I'm getting mine from my brother here." Charley smiled and motioned my way. "I hope he can stay the whole three months with me."

The other two patients, Thomas and Billy, listened passively. When Winn introduced them, they lifted their hands from their wheelchairs and nodded their heads like two tired eggs. After we said good-bye and were led down the corridor by Kris, I wondered who of the three would survive. Even that would be thirty-three percent, though, and one person's chances were still just half of that.

After eating lunch in the hospital cafeteria, Kris suggested that we take the rest of the afternoon to explore Seattle. We tried to keep our minds occupied by driving around the university campus and into the lovely residential neighborhoods of Beacon Hill. Seattle was beautiful in the warm late March sun. Despite advance warnings about its rain, the skies were cloudless. Flowers were in bloom by the millions, many of them exotic types I had never seen. Asian-looking gardeners were clipping and digging everywhere, even on the grounds of our modest apartment complex. Many people wore shirtsleeves and sunglasses. With the large numbers of Asian people in our neighborhood, I wondered if it might resemble Japan.

Charley was to be admitted the next morning, and he would be given a series of blood tests and a bone marrow biopsy that first morning. Later in the day he would be prepped for the irradiation procedure. He was calm about all of it, excited to try something new, and after talking with the three patients he no longer seemed nervous about the dangers that lay ahead. He was determined that he would be a member of the fifteen percent club, the lucky few who survived.

Mother threw together an early dinner for us of toast, scrambled eggs, and bacon, with the utensils found in the kitchen cabinets. As we were finishing, the phone rang. It was Kris asking how our afternoon had gone. She said that Dr. Thomas would be calling us within a half hour and she asked us to remain near the phone.

Mom returned to the table and said, "I wonder what Dr. Thomas wants? Kris sounded so high-strung."

"Probably just last-minute details for tomorrow, reminders like fasting after midnight." Dad took his plate into the kitchen and began washing. Charley and I went outside to smoke a cigarette. We laughed that perhaps he'd be quitting the habit for good after his transplant. I swore I would if he would, and we walked around the complex slowly in order to smoke two apiece.

When we came through the front door, we could hear Dad on the phone. "I see. Yes, certainly. That is very disappointing. They will be crushed, but I'm sure they will see your point. Of course. Goodbye."

"Ed, what is it? What did Dr. Thomas say?" Mother was already reacting to the distress on Dad's ashen face.

"I'm so sorry, boys. This is hard to say, but Charley is disqualified from the transplant."

Charley and I froze. Did we hear him correctly? "He said that Yarrott is no longer considered a viable match because of his long history of platelet donations. By now, Charley has probably built antibodies to Yarrott's bone marrow. He also said—and this is very important to hear, boys—that Charley is in excellent condition, given his illness, and that his slim chances of surviving the transplant cannot justify the risk. He could have many more years ahead of him just doing what we're doing."

I felt a heavy black blanket drop on top of me, shutting out light and cutting off my air. I yelled, "'Doing what we're doing' is what he said? *'DOING WHAT WE'RE DOING?'*" I stormed out of the apartment and ran down the hill into the neighborhood, hoping I would get lost or hit by a car, hoping they would never find me. I can only imagine what went through Charley's mind hearing the news. Perhaps a bit of relief, but mostly, I would guess, intense disappointment. But, I confess, I did not think of Charley or his predicament as I ran. I only knew I hated him, hated Mother and Dad, and most of all hated my life and the heavy dark blanket on top of it.

THIRTY-TWO

The Waterfall

We returned to our life in Nashville as Siamese twins. The disappointment in Seattle was so big that Charley and I could not talk about it. The blood bank personnel at the hospital tiptoed in and out of the donor room, careful not to interfere with the soaps on the little TV. I began to sleep through the entire pheresis, waking up in time to press the square of gauze on the needle hole and raise my arm over my head. Charley and I entered a state of mindlessness, buoyed by smoking grass and drinking beer. I doubled my cigarettes to two packs a day. My face broke out. I lost more weight. My grades at Vanderbilt plummeted. At the end of my freshman year, I wandered into a summer break that felt pointless. To make some money and to get out of the house, I mowed neighbors' lawns and manicured their yards. At least I found some gratification in that.

Two months after the Seattle trip, we received a card from Kris, our hostess in Seattle. Mother had sent her a silver tray to thank her for all her help. In her card, Kris wrote that Thomas, Win, and Billy, the young patients we had met there, had all died. They lost their lives through rejections of one kind or another just weeks after we talked to them. The tragic news flattened Charley and he disappeared into his room with his door shut. But the next afternoon, he burst out of the house and went off to buy a used red Jeep with his savings. He had always wanted a Jeep and damn it, with all the recent bummers and downers, he was going to get one—no matter what.

The rugged, open-air vehicle looked like fun but ultimately provided anything but. My parents wanted to find the weasel salesman and have him arrested. They couldn't understand how the man could sell a lemon to someone whose skin was so gray and who was obviously sick. Within a week of buying it, the Jeep's clutch failed. Then the ignition. Then the transmission. Between the ignition and the transmission problems, Charley and I made plans for camping on Brushy Mountain, one of the most remote places in the South, so remote that a maximum-security prison is located there.

Charley, his friend Joe, and I cruised down I-40 with the canvas top removed. I hung onto the roll bar in the back, both hands gripping with white knuckles. It was July, eight weeks before I would begin my sophomore year at Vanderbilt. The three of us were heading to the mountains in East Tennessee to camp out, and I seriously questioned if we would ever get there. As I faced backward with my little round sunglasses, my hair whipped my eyes in the wind the entire way. I could have used a headband or a rubber band, but I was too uptight to wear anything that could draw the word *faggot* from the minds of these guys. Charley drove like a madman, weaving in between heavy trucks and leaving us vulnerable to their easy mistakes. I held on and concentrated on the Allman Brothers, whose voices I could only hear in their highest shrills. The rusty exhaust pipe had a hole in it and the fumes we were inhaling were hot, just like the air off the highway.

But, like a fool, I was in urgent need of their approval and I would go anywhere with Joe and Charley. Their avowed disgust for gay people meant that I could never let on who I was. But I still found being with Charley and his beautiful best friend exciting. Damn, if my brother didn't have the best-looking friends. To me, they all embodied the type of man I wanted to become. Or more truthfully, the man I *wanted*. I would do anything to spend time with these guys under the dark skies. With scruffy hair, a three-day growth of beard, a prominent nose, and a strong, sharp chin, Joe was the epitome of the mid-seventies sexy rocker, a Rod Stewart on horseback.

They had been best friends since high school and had gone to the University of Tennessee in Knoxville together. Despite their über-masculine dispositions, they were so familiar with each other that they could get to snapping and bitching, especially if one of them was suffering a hangover. I don't remember Robert Redford bitching at Paul Newman in *Butch Cassidy and the Sundance Kid*, but then those cowboys probably got more sleep than these two did.

Charley had been grouchy from the moment we drove through the gate leaving home that morning. We were several hours late leaving. Joe and he had had an argument while smoking grass the night before and were still sore with each other, and I was in the middle trying to placate. We had planned to set up camp near a waterfall they had found on a map, and we had intended to spend a day there doing nothing but hiking, swimming, eating, drinking, and smoking dope. There was nobody around but the three of us. Well, in my mind, the *two* of us. Joe and me. It would suit me just fine if Charley remained the impossible old fuck and insisted on being on his own. That would give me time to find the waterfall with Joe and get naked and lose myself in the wilds of East Tennessee.

Each of us was nursing a headache by the time we found the exit. We still had several hours further into the mountains to drive. The exhaust was nauseating, but we continued up through the hills and dense scrub, up past overlooks, hemlock forests, and creek crossings, up into the primeval wilderness that plays host to some of the nation's most dangerous felons. We were four hours later than we'd planned, and by the time we entered the state park it was already getting dark. Joe and I were fine with pulling over and setting camp right then and there, close to the entrance. But Charley said no, "I'm sure there's something better up a ways."

Darkness descended rapidly in the woods while crickets and other night sounds grew. In moments, we couldn't see anything in front of us so Charley pulled over and said, "This is it. We're here."

Joe sneered back, "And where exactly is *here*? I can't see *here*."

"Oh, fuck you, asshole," shot back Charley.

I dropped the tailgate and stepped into six inches of mud. "Hey, Charley, you better move the Jeep so we don't get stuck."

"Fuck. Shit." Charley started the Jeep and slowly stepped on the gas. Both back wheels spun and the Jeep sunk several inches farther into the mud.

Joe laughed. "Hey, way to go, Mario Andretti."

"I'll leave the lights on long enough for us to set up tent. No point in trying to move until daylight tomorrow."

"Just don't drain the battery for us, huh?" Joe was pissed.

"And just don't worry so much, *huh?*"

I carried a couple of bags in my arms through the mud, heard my footsteps hit a drier area, and set the things down. "Over here. I think this is a good spot."

Just then I noticed an odd sound, like lots of little leaves shaking, and Charley yelled out "Hey, what is *that?*" He pulled his flashlight from his jeans and pointed it under the scrub for a quick second, then shut it off. "Holy fuck! Holy, holy fuck! Baby rattlers...a bunch of 'em. Joe, get me the ax. Quick!"

I backed up into the mud and stood still. Charley told me to aim the flashlight while he struck with the ax over and over until the rattling stopped. I could feel the pounding of my heart in my ears.

Joe rummaged with a stick through the dead snakes. "Shit, Chuck, you can kick ass when you want to. Look what's left of these little fuckers."

"One nest now extinct. Rest in peace," Charley crowed.

"Where's the mother?" I asked.

"Mother? Shit, that's a good question. I don't know. We didn't get her."

I asked, "Don't they say that where there are babies, the mother is close by?"

"Maybe the mother packed her bags and flew the coop. She heard Chuck was on his way, the big, tough dragon slayer."

"Oh, fuck you, Joe Boy. We're gonna have to keep our ears open for her. We'll kill her as soon as we find her."

Great. I felt the hair on my neck rise and really just wanted to run back to the Jeep and sleep there for the night. Tell me again, why are we here? That waterfall better be the most beautiful waterfall in the whole fucking world. It better be worth what we're going through tonight. Then something else occurred to me: the mother pigeon. The idea of killing a mother, even a mother rattlesnake, felt wrong to me. Very wrong. We can't go around killing mothers.

Raising a tent was out of the question, so we cleared ourselves a little dry circle ten feet wide, where we could unroll our sleeping bags and sleep there in the open. Eating a hot meal was too complicated, so we passed around uncooked hotdogs and white buns and ate them raw, washing them down with cans of Coke. Joe lit a joint and passed it to Charley. I was too scared to smoke. Somebody had to stay sober. What if the adult rattler came back?

And sleeping? Just how *does* one sleep next to a nest of dead baby rattlers? Almost not at all. Not zipped all the way up in a hot sleeping bag all night.

I woke up a little past daybreak to a popping sound, Charley frying eggs in an iron skillet. Joe was propped up next to a tree chewing on a piece of crisp bacon. They already had coffee in mugs and seemed perfectly at home in this hellhole. "Hey big shot, roll over any snakes last night?" Joe joked.

"Just the mother. Got her right here." In the sleeping bag I pulled off my cloth belt and threw it in his face. "Ha, ha, you flinched, you wuss!" I yelled, aping their cool.

The three of us packed up and left our things in the Jeep and hiked along the trail. After a mile or so we heard the sound of water rushing quietly in the distance. As we walked toward it, the sound grew until it filled the air around us and we had to shout to be heard. Through the dense woods we could see a bright clearing. The trees opened up, the ground dropped, and we found ourselves at the bank of an oval pool. Water fell in a white curtain from a ledge sixty feet above us. We looked at one another and began laughing hysterically. Joe and Charley stripped in seconds and ran like mad into the foamy water.

For the rest of the morning we swam in circles, crouched under the falls, and floated spread-eagle on our backs. It was pure joy. The fumes, the snakes, and the lack of sleep were all worth it for us to find this extraordinary world, a paradise really, and to have it all to ourselves. Charley and I caught each other's eye and smiled. This was what he wanted more than anything.

As we skinny-dipped, I could see that Charley's shoulder blades were now protruding and that his ribs were showing in the front and the back. He had lost so much weight that his ass was flat and scrawny. By far the worst part of his appearance, though, was his skin color, which was grayer than ever. After so many red cell transfusions, iron deposits had been left behind, giving his skin a dark gray pallor. Joe, of course, was lean and sexy, toned in the right places and tan all over, except for his white, muscular ass. His proximity to Charley just made Charley look worse. But Joe was careful. He watched his remarks and said nothing that would be demeaning about Charley's appearance. It was heartrending looking at the two of them together and wishing things were different for my brother. It was not much easier looking at myself naked. I had been swimming regularly at Vanderbilt's big pool, so my shoulders and legs had grown a bit, but I still felt, alongside someone like Joe, a rather bland specimen. *God, when am I going to outgrow this and grow into something better?*

For a while at least, I put aside my self-consciousness and enjoyed the murky water under the waterfall, and after we finally pulled our clothes back on we ate lunch at the side of the water. The hike back to the Jeep was slowly paced, in the insufferable humidity and with the sun blazing down on us. Charley backed the Jeep out of the mud, stiffer than the night before. It was a relief to be back inside the moving vehicle, with the wind to blow the flies and mosquitoes off of us. Driving westward toward Nashville two hundred and fifty miles away, the Jeep began lurching with a crunching noise when Charley tried to shift gears. "You motherfucker. It can't be the clutch. I already had that replaced. Now what?"

We pulled off the highway and parked on the shoulder. The transmission was shot. We were suddenly stuck on the east side of Knoxville, still four hours away from home. Joe waved down a truck and got a ride to a gas station, where he called some friends from University of Tennessee to help us. A tow truck arrived within an hour to pull us to Knoxville and we found ourselves staying for the night with friends of Joe's in an overgrown bungalow occupied by three tall, beefy dudes in cut-offs and flip-flops. One of them, Nick, froze on the porch with his mouth stupidly agape, until we got close.

"My man Joe!" bellowed Nick on the porch, so loud it shook the air.

"God. I can't seem to escape this town," Charley groaned under his breath. He was tired. The other two housemates swaggered onto the porch, greeted Joe with tight little grins and macho shoulder swipes, then saw Charley and me in the yard and offered us lukewarm handshakes. I noticed Nick and Jamie size up Charley and then look at each other askance, as if asking *What's with him?*

Jamie, Nick, and Ray were broad-shouldered jocks, but had become serious potheads over the course of their college years. The three studs, still undergraduates in their mid-twenties, each wore an impressive example of facial hair—like a Fu Manchu mustache or mutton chop sideburns—and a hip accessory, like a military dog tag, dark aviator glasses worn inside as well as out, or an olive-green GI cap with someone else's name stenciled on the front.

I disliked them instantly. My facial hair was still downy blond stuff. What were they, three years older than me, four at most, and I still looked like a damn kid.

We dragged our packs up the front steps and there was an immediate smell of pot coming from the house. A continuous party atmosphere filled the first floor. Jimi Hendrix tortured and wrung out his electric guitar in the background, while in the kitchen two girls gyrated among piles of dirty dishes, washing dishes and cooking up some brownies at the same time. Joe showed us where we could sleep that night. He would stay in Nick's room, Charley on the couch in the living room, and I on a broken cot in the basement room next to the broken ping pong table. Everywhere was piled with stuff, dirty clothes, books and magazines, and bicycles. Everything was damp with mildew in the wet Knoxville August.

THIRTY-THREE

Tina and Terri

Despite Charley's intense moodiness, many of his childhood friends maintained their ties to him after he became ill, visiting him often and involving him in their lives. Wilson was one of those friends. He was also the scoundrel heartthrob of the neighborhood. He was Michelangelo's David and *Leave It to Beaver*'s Eddy Haskell in one. Wilson was a scoundrel, all right, but he had a big heart and was patient with Charley's testiness in a way that I could not fathom.

Well into the fourth year of the disease, on a Sunday afternoon not long after our camping trip to East Tennessee, Wilson careened up the driveway on his chopped-up Harley with his latest girlfriend, Terri, hanging onto him with a grin, her curly hair a mop in the wind. Mother stood frozen on the back stoop, staring at Wilson, anxious about who in the neighborhood might be watching this arrival of Easy Rider. The dachshunds barked furiously at her feet. Wilson could charm blood from a stone and in a matter of seconds had Mother sitting on the long leather seat and gunning the gas with her grip.

Terri, stood by laughing, completely enthralled by Mother's mix of Southern lady and tomboy. When Charley came down the back steps, he immediately liked Terri. Later, alone in the kitchen with Wilson and me, he said, "She's great-looking, she's got a solid head on her shoulders. She's funny—look at her out there with Mom. Hey, Wilson, don't blow it, huh?"

Coming from a surgeon's family in Pittsburgh, Terri immediately felt comfortable with us, and over the course of the next year and a half, long after she and Wilson had broken up, she spent a lot of time at our house. She and I harmonized immediately and found a real magic in our friendship, a mix of hilarity and seriousness. I was impressed with her dedication to her studies in psychology and her determination to live a colorful life. She seemed responsible in all the important ways, like studying and having a job, but also seemed to absolutely love risky new experiences in life. She was, after all, a smart Northern girl who decided to go to college in the South. That alone said she was looking for an interesting journey in her life.

One night Terri made a big dinner at her house on Kapers Avenue. The crowd sat around the floor on her big turquoise and red oriental rug, eating chicken curry with Elton John playing in the background. Across the rug from Charley was Terri's best friend, Tina, a student in special education. She was small and shapely in her faded jeans and camisole. "So what do you do, Mr. Charley?" Tina asked across the room with a musical lilt.

I cringed at the question. Oh, God. Everybody knows how sick Charley is. How is he going to answer her? The whole room waited for his answer.

He took his time, turned a little red, scratched his head, and let a mischievous grin cross his face. "Well, *Miss* Tina, you might say I'm a student of the world. I watch and I listen."

Bravo, Charley. There was a collective sigh.

"And I bet you've learned a hell of a lot," Tina said and smiled at him. "I can tell."

You sweet girl, I already like you. Charley was not his usual bungler with her. She had put him at ease at once with her warmth and her big almond eyes. By the time Terri brought out her apple pie, Charley had moved to Tina's diamond on the rug and the two were laughing together. I saw Terri spot them from the kitchen and giggle to herself.

Later, I heard Tina say, "And because of that you don't even want to try?" She looked at Charley with a kind and empathic face.

Oh, try, Charley. Go ahead and try. Whatever it is. Try.

Tina knew of Charley's illness. Everybody did.

༽

Within a few weeks, he was dropping by Tina's little house near the Vanderbilt campus and staying later and later into the night. I was shocked when he said one day to me at the hospital, "Man, Yarrott, I never knew how painful waterbeds were. Knock, knock, knock, who's that knockin' against your nuts. Ouch!"

"That means, uh, you slept with Tina?"

"Well, damn, of course it does. Why? Shouldn't I?"

"Oh, don't get me wrong, Charley, I think it's great. I think *she's* really great. I'm glad for you. I'm just a little surprised, that's all." *Why am I sounding so damn wistful? I should be jumping up and down for him. The truth is that I'm jealous and scared shitless. He's as sick as a person could be, yet he's having sex. I'm as healthy as a person could be and I'm not. I'm still a goddamn virgin at nineteen. What's wrong with ME?*

For the first two months after meeting Tina, Charley always came home to sleep, afraid he would upset Mother and Dad if he didn't. That ended one winter night when he did not return. The next morning Dad drove by Tina's house on 29th Avenue on his way to the hospital. He passed the house slowly and found Charley's red Jeep parked halfway down the block, then called Mother from the office. She was standing in the kitchen with her arms crossed when Charley returned home around noon.

"What do you mean by this, Charley?"

"Oh, Mom, please don't make a big deal over it!"

"Don't make a big deal over it? You have disappointed us terribly! Do you hear me?"

"I'm sorry you're hurt by this somehow, Mom, but it's time for me now. It's time for me."

"That young girl over there doesn't know what she's getting into. It's not fair to her!" Mother started to cry.

"Stop it, Mom. It's not fair to *me*."

Despite my parents' initial hand-wringing, Tina became a welcome fixture at our house. Somehow she knew how to draw laughs out of both Mother and Dad. Angela and I liked Tina immediately and we felt a close bond with her. What her attention did for Charley was incalculable. So much seemed to change about him, from his clothing to his posture. He suddenly appeared more confident, humorous, and kind. At Tina's insistence, he smoked pot less often. He was suddenly absent from Tyne Boulevard much more often than he was present. An adult life, a life with companionship and stimulation had come out of nowhere for him.

He signed up for classes in electrical engineering at Nashville Tech, a community trade college, and began to stitch together some ideas for making a living for himself. He finally felt independence and a sense of responsibility, because of Tina. She didn't cure his illness, which still loomed over him, but she stimulated him back to living.

In fact, medically, Charley was gradually declining. At this point, four years into his disease, he was often on the verge of serious systemic infections. The oozing of his gums had returned with a vengeance. He had several prolonged periods of severely racing heartbeats, called tachycardia, twice while hiking and once while having sex. His body was simply struggling to keep up with him. He was by far the longest living person in medical history with his acute level of aplastic anemia. Certainly, no other person had received donor platelets for four years. Despite all this, his relationship with Tina seemed to flourish. There was much to enjoy.

Tina's apartment was more than a college student's simple digs. She had an uncanny eye for valuable junk found in Goodwill stores, flea markets, and street corners. I was amused by many of her oddball treasures, such as a white enamel-top kitchen table, trimmed in red, with tubular chrome legs. She had an appreciation for imperfect stuff and could polish the shine back into anything. I began to feel as if she had done the same thing with Charley. The resurrection of his self-worth had an enriching effect on me as well. I felt lighter, as if I had dropped a constant, nagging, worrying guilt for having a healthy life in front of me while Charley's life was stolen. Not so! Charley was thoroughly enjoying himself and I could start living my own life. God knows I was drowning in self-pity about my pathetic first two years of college.

THIRTY-FOUR

Wise Old Women

With Tina and Charley off together, Terri and I became closer. We'd had an instant rapport. She knew I was miserable at Vanderbilt while living at home and suggested that I get a job. There was an opening for a line cook at the same restaurant where she worked as a weekend bartender. Spats was a popular restaurant and bar near Vanderbilt, down the street from Terri's house on Kapers Avenue. It took its nostalgic 1930s theme from the movie *The Sting*, which had been popular the year before. Terri was a fabulous bartender. No matter the customer, she maintained her charismatic and unflappable poise.

Terri talked to her boss and I found myself working on the weekends, just around the bar from Terri, spooning up ramekins of slaw and beans to serve on platters of smoked ribs. The job offered me a precious escape from home. Every Friday and Saturday night, after the restaurant had closed, I drank, smoked, and laughed with new friends from work until two or three o'clock in the morning. I usually managed to slip back into the house without waking my parents.

I developed an unlikely friendship with Mason, the owner and manager of the restaurant. Ten years older than I, and having grown up in Los Angeles, he seemed to be adrift in Nashville. He was suave and darkly handsome. He shared no interest in the city's country music culture or in Southern history. It was as if he had been driving cross-country and decided to stop for no other reason except that he was tired. Initially, as my boss, he was a brusque, terse taskmaster. With Ray

Charles on the jukebox, Mason would pass behind me on the line mouthing the words to "Georgia on My Mind." He coolly ignored me, or worse, carped that I was giving out too much slaw. He was a man who never smiled, never joked, whose life seemed focused entirely on work.

Terri's brick bungalow down the street on Kapers Avenue was the last surviving house on the block, the others having been torn down earlier in the year as part of Vanderbilt's endless expansion plan. Her house was marked for demolition, too, but the wrecking crew agreed to wait until she had finished her lease in six months. Meanwhile, she enjoyed absurdly spacious views outside her windows, and no neighbors. It was a perfect place for her to concentrate on the schoolwork of her senior year and enjoy a quiet, almost rural life in the middle of the city. Right down the road from Spats.

After we closed the restaurant, Terri and I, along with a few others from the restaurant, often gathered on her porch and drank Tequila Sunrises until our eyes could not focus. I began to understand why people liked to drink. I enjoyed the new confidence I felt and the humor that came with it. I learned I could make people laugh. I could move my body and dance. I could say things that sounded rich and colorful.

One night Mason came along with us to Terri's house. Nervous, Terri took me aside, worried that Mason might be planning on making an unwanted move on her. "Make sure he isn't left here alone with me, will you?"

Mason was quiet, but when he began to drink he gradually opened up to the rest of us. He showed a side of himself that was literary and opinionated. He was passionate about avant-garde films and books. When he asked me who I enjoyed reading, I thought about answering with some of the heady novels assigned to me in my literature classes. Instead, I told him the truth. I had heard playwright Lillian Hellman interviewed by Bill Moyers on television and she had seemed really cool for an old lady. I had watched the entire interview, and then had driven to a bookstore to buy her memoir, called *Pentimento*.

Mason was listening intently. "Pimento? Really?"

"No, not pimento. *Pentimento*. It's an Italian word for what happens to oil paint as it ages. The picture becomes transparent and allows old images to come through the newer layers."

He swayed with his drink and stared at me. "I see. Like life. Looking at the past through accumulated years."

"Yeah. Something like that. But what I liked about the book was Lillian Hellman's incredible sense of adventure. She wasn't just a wonderful writer. She put her money where her mouth was. She got vocal about American politics, tried to help during the Spanish Civil War. She refused to name names during the McCarthy trials. To me, she has lived an exciting life. A creative life. A good and true life. I wish I could, too."

Mason put his hand on my shoulder and said, "Goddamn, Yarrott, I had no idea you would be interested in reading something like that. I'm really surprised."

"Well, the book's been important to me. I've given it to people close to me to read. I've asked them to sign it, like some kind of ritual."

"You know, I have to say, I really like older ladies. I like listening to them. They seem to be the ones who really know what's going on in the world. Forget the old men...it's the old women." He continued to sway and stare into my face. Then he perked up suddenly and said, "You know who I saw on Dick Cavett last week? An old opera singer named Lili Pons. She was an incredible old dame, still singing like a bird, even those high C's."

Mason and I outdrank everyone and then continued our drinking in the darkest, most secluded place we could find, the abandoned train station in downtown Nashville. We pulled up a loose panel of plywood covering the main doorway and slipped through. We showed each other dance moves, laughed about movies, knocked against each other when we walked. I spoke as poetically as I could, grandiloquently quoting my writing teachers and even things I had written. Mason seemed to love it and listened intently. My heart was pounding through my shirt.

When the sky began to glow, I knew I had stayed out too late. It was almost six o'clock. My parents would be freaking out, maybe even have called the police. I had to make a beeline home. Mason and I stood in the empty parking lot of Union Station and held a long, belabored handshake.

"As I said, Yarrott, I am surprised to learn who you are. You're a guy who keeps everybody guessing."

"You want to read *Pentimento*?" I looked him in the eyes.

He paused for a second and must have seen me turn red. "I'd love to."

Driving home, I repeatedly played the night over in my head. I was obsessed with reliving it, with not letting it fade from my mind. My heart had calmed down, but my brain had slipped into overdrive. The surprising connection I felt with Mason was something very new, like a new taste or smell, and I had no idea what to make of it. *Jeez, what will it be like at work next Friday night? He's not the cold stiff that I thought he was.* I pulled into the driveway and parked as the sun was already casting long shadows across the front yard. I quietly opened the back door and found nobody awake and waiting for me. Mother and Dad were still asleep. To them, it would be another Sunday morning in April. To me, it felt like a new century.

In May, Tina and Terri's graduation was held on the great lawn, under magnolia trees and a flawless blue sky. Both of their families came to Nashville for the event and spent time with my parents at the house on Tyne Boulevard. Tina's mother was divorced and lived in Gainesville, Florida, working as a court stenographer. She was proud of her dynamic and personable daughter but was understandably concerned about Tina's relationship with Charley, whose illness hung over his head like the blade of a guillotine. It was a bittersweet dinner in which Mother and Dad sat at the table with Tina's mother and the rest of us. To our parents, the lady was charming and effervescent. To Charley, she was hesitant and guarded.

Tina was confused about her own future, about whether to go to a graduate program in Colorado or to remain in Nashville, get a teaching job, and live with Charley. Charley had given her his one and only opinion and even before graduation he had become strident about it: His illness must not influence her future. Tina must leave. They must break up. Tina's mother was naturally protective of her daughter and, as cold as it appeared, agreed with Charley.

Tina was devastated. Her relationship with Charley was paramount to her, but he convinced her that it was not paramount to him. He told her that he did not want her attention anymore and that he now found it suffocating. Alone with me, he admitted that he was lying and that he really loved being with her. But he could not see standing in the way of her future. He could not see his future at all. I felt for him and his painful choice.

During the first weekend in June, Angela, Terri, and I helped a weeping, inconsolable Tina pack up her car and take her remaining furniture to Goodwill. Charley kept his distance. When the car was full and the apartment empty, Tina stayed her last night with Terri on Kapers Avenue. The next morning she rose early and stopped by Tyne Boulevard on the way to the interstate to begin her drive to her mother's house in Florida. She was ashen-faced and exhausted as she summoned a big grin for Mother and hugged her tightly. "I've thought of you like my own mother, Mrs. Benz. This past year with Charley was wonderful. Thank you, guys. I love you all."

As her little car disappeared down the road, Mother said, "Damn it. Encouraging this break-up was so hard to do. You know Daddy and I really thought a lot of her, too, but it's better this way. For both of them."

THIRTY-FIVE

Dear Ms. Hellman

It seemed a tide of change was sweeping through our lives in Nashville. Having said good-bye to Tina, now Terri was planning her departure. She would continue working at Spats until the end of July. My stimulating little world that I had found in the winter would not hold together through the summer.

One month later, I was stoically waving good-bye to Terri as she drove off in her green Pinto with the orange plates of Pennsylvania. I stood in the middle of the empty street, my eyes fixed on the bulldozer parked down at the end. My car was the only one on the street. Terri's wooden porch stood empty except for a broken paper kite hanging between two posts. She had left all the doors unlocked and the windows open. With the house's life over, there was no reason to secure it. It no longer had any value. The bulldozer was waiting. With a slight summer breeze passing through it, however, it still seemed to be breathing. The kite frame tapped on the railing. Terri's smells still drifted through the windows. A knife twisted deeply into my nineteen-year-old gut.

Mason and I took a drive by ourselves one night after work, to a serene rural valley south of town by twenty miles. We hiked to the top of a hill under the full moon, to breathe in the view and to sit together, drunk, careful not to touch. I was imagining to myself how life would be if Mason and I got naked together and had sex. What would happen if we became lovers and made our meals together and wove our lives together? I was looking away from him as my mind wrote the story. Just then, he spoke. "You know, Yarrott, I've decided to sell my part of the restaurant and move back to Los Angeles. I need to go back. I've got unfinished business there."

My stomach sank into the ground. *No, not him, too! What did I just say or think to cause him to up and leave?* I concealed my deep disappointment and left exposed just a modest level of sadness between us—just two parting buddies, just a bummer, not the devastation of one man desperately hungry for the other. "Hey, what will be left here without you to boss me around?"

Yes, what will be left?

"By the way," Mason touched my shoulder and it occurred to me he might be about to kiss me. The first time kissing a guy in my life. My heart jumped. But he just continued with, "I need to give you back your copy of *Pentimento*. I loved it. Like I said, there's nothing like the perspective of an old woman."

I immediately felt abandoned by my friends and all the more trapped in my circumstances. Three people I had grown to love were leaving at the same time and what was left was a feeling of isolation, inertia, and Charley's dependence on me. I climbed down the hill to the car a much smaller person that the one who arrived there earlier.

I continued my shifts at Spats until Mason left Nashville in August, and then I quit. Afterward, I fell into the habit of driving by his former house on my way to classes at Vanderbilt. It was a squat, ugly place with three windows diagonally set in the front door. Funny, if it had been the front door of anybody else, I would not have overlooked such a tacky feature. But with Mason I ignored it. What else had I ignored? Each time I passed Mason's little house on the way to class, I chastised myself and swore not to drive by it again. It was not worth the small pang, but each time I forgot to make a detour until it was too late. Each time I nagged myself with the same pointless question: what if I had just had the guts to push open that ugly door?

Insomnia kept me awake many nights of the late summer. My stomach had a continual knot in it and I lost my appetite. Waking early in the morning, often before the sun, I found Dad in the kitchen making his breakfast. We often sat together at the table or outdoors in the side yard to watch the sunrise.

"Dad, I feel stuck in the ground. Like a stick. I feel left behind. I don't know how to catch up in the world and replace the people who have just disappeared."

"It's hard for you to see it now, but you'll fill the hole they leave."

"But I don't know what's going to happen with Charley! This could go on for my lifetime. It's already been five years!"

Dad put his hand on my shoulder. "It won't last your lifetime, Yarrott. His body won't hold out. You won't be at home forever, either. Try to make the most of your time here."

"But you don't understand, Dad." I tried putting into words the feelings of incompleteness and dissatisfaction coming from so many angles. I only alluded to the sadness I felt with Mason moving away. "There is so much on top of me here. I can't breathe."

"Oh, you've just got a bad case of wanderlust. You'll get over it. I have surgery at nine o'clock, Yarrott. Don't you have class or something?" He squeezed my knee and went back into the house. The sunlight glistened on the wet grass and I felt the oppressive humidity of another late summer day climbing like kudzu all over me.

Wanderlust, indeed.

By the time the fall semester of my junior year had begun, I had lost almost twenty-five pounds, which, on my narrow frame, constituted a stark, shocking change. I was confused. I was angry. For a few months, I had tasted an independent adult life with layered adult relationships and suddenly, in a matter of weeks, it was gone. The world had seemed for those months expansive and exciting. But just as quickly as it had opened up to me, it had closed.

Hoping for inspiration, I read *Pentimento* again, but I now saw Lillian Hellman's life with nothing but envy. She was no longer an old lady bravely nearing the end of her life; she was some kind of cold conqueror, a champion bitch who had grabbed the best of everything in the world for herself. Her work was admired. She had traveled extensively. She had known the creative giants of her time. She had received the love of another artist for twenty years. She had absorbed the world and reassembled it to her liking on paper. More than just privileged and accomplished, she was to me beyond human. She was not of the same dull flesh as the rest of us. I was jealous as hell.

I thought of my situation—being tethered to Charley, stifled, living at home, unable to learn anything at the college I hated—and I felt certain that my fate was sealed: I would never escape the trap. The artist I was meant to be would never be born.

As much as I resented her, I enjoyed the fact that Hellman was a child of the South, raised partly in New Orleans. But she had no drawl. In fact, she reminded me of Mrs. Hitchcock in my tenth grade at Peabody. Tough as nails and schooled in New York City. I had somehow related to Mrs. Hitchcock and she had liked me. Perhaps Lillian Hellman, too, would like me. I decided to write her a letter. Not a fan letter, but a letter written from my particular, unique viewpoint. A letter from an artist who will never *be* because of his circumstances. A letter from an artist who will never be to one who has been and still is. A letter from prison to the outside.

In my letter, I wrote that, as a young man caught in certain circumstances, I envied her "magnificently free and gloriously selfish life." Why I insisted to myself I had to use the word *selfish* I still do not understand. I was aware that it sounded critical, overly familiar, even emotionally off-keel, but I used it anyway. In my unrealistic mind, I half expected her to write back in agreement with my fearless honesty, asking to meet me, this oddly courageous boy. I now cannot imagine what Lillian Hellman thought when she read it, as surely she must have. I mailed it to her house on Martha's Vineyard and the letter was never returned.

I wonder how long she held it in her hands before she sucked on her cigarette, wadded the letter up, and tossed it in her wastebasket.

THIRTY-SIX

Clear Water

All during their childhoods, Charley and Angela were accustomed to being around horses, whether at our relatives' farms or at their summer camps. Riding together provided them times of intense friendship. As long as they were each in a saddle, they could meet on equal and neutral ground. This continued to be true even after Angela moved away to college and then returned to Nashville to live in her own apartment. The two of them continued to ride together. Charley seemed to forget the complexities and disappointments of life once he was on a horse. He could forget that he was too old to be living at home. He could even forget that he was ill.

When it came to horses, Angela and Charley were close enough to read each other's minds. When saddling up to ride at Aunt Dorothea's farm, one would toss the saddle, the other would grab the belly strap and yank. With the mad recklessness born in their childhoods, they would race each other in full gallop, with such a fast and powerful fierceness I would be scared to death to follow them. I could ride, but nothing like how they could ride. On horseback, I remained steadfastly cautious, still proving the appropriateness of White Cloud as my childhood name. Keep up with Geronimo and Pocahontas? Impossible. I had to cough and gag in their trail of dust.

Together, in October 1974, they bought two quarter horse mares and then begged Mother and Dad to keep them in the backyard, where there was a stable barn and a fenced-in lot. They named the older horse Maude and the younger one Culleoka, a Cherokee name meaning "clear water." Charley had found the name among his many books on Native American history and it had jumped out at him. He said to Angela, "I like how simple it is, but it's loaded with meaning."

Mother and Dad agreed to let the horses stay at Tyne Boulevard. They believed Charley's caring for them would occupy his time in a constructive way. He was still recovering from his breakup with Tina. Up to this point, he had been on such a roller coaster, of indescribable depths and highs, bad news and good news, optimism followed by pessimism. He deserved to have his time filled with something he enjoyed. Angela was his perfect accomplice.

To Mother and Dad's chagrin, the entire back of the property was ruined within a month. The lawn was turned into a mud field with ankle-deep pits everywhere you stepped. Still, our parents tolerated the ruination of the lawn. They were desperate for Charley to feel good about something, even if it meant this.

Looking out the kitchen window at the backyard, Mother sighed to me, "Look at that. It used to look like a golf course. Now? I just can't believe it."

"At least I don't have to mow it anymore." I laughed weakly.

"It's depressing to look at it. The yard's a swamp now. It's terrible. Can you imagine what the Lefferts must think next door? This is awful."

"Well, can't you tell Angela and Charley to move their horses somewhere else?"

"No, honey. This is all Charley's got right now. We have to just live through it."

Despite what was happening to the yard, the interior of the barn was beautifully organized for a change. The barn had not been in use for twenty years or more and now Charley was proving its purpose. Every tool had its spot on the wall, from curry brush to shoe hook. The saddles and bridles were kept oiled and cleaned and looked like fine furniture on their indoor perches. Up the ladder in the loft, hay bales filled the space with neat stacks. This was Charley's new territory, a working horse barn, and his satisfaction was obvious in the way he managed it. There was a sense of adult order in the place we messed around in as children.

"No, we just have to live through it." Mother repeated under her breath.

For six months the mares seemed to thrive in the suburban landscape. Charley and Angela exercised them in a ring of fences and jumps, and took them for longer runs through the bridal paths down the road. As the ground began to freeze in December, however, the horses were exercised less and less. Their stagnant life in a lot that was much too small began to take its toll on their humors. Maude had begun to limp after being kicked by Culleoka.

Each time I looked out the windows to the backyard, I saw the two horses standing apart in far corners, getting fatter.

"Charley says they're depressed," Mom said as she passed through the living room.

"Because of the cold?" I asked.

"Heavens, no. Because they're cramped back there." She stood at the window. "There isn't enough space for them. This is no yard to keep horses."

"They seem to be gaining a lot of weight, too."

"Well, having two horses here is too much for him."

"So what can he do?"

"Find another place to keep them." Quite a different Mother now held her ground.

The Ralphs, who lived outside Nashville in Goodletsville, had been friends of our family and we had ridden on their farm many times when I was in high school. They had heard of Charley's difficulty with the two mares and offered to keep them at their farm, where they would be in the company of other horses and would be ridden more frequently. Charley and Angela quickly accepted their offer and arranged to have the horses moved. The barn in our backyard was suddenly deserted and left encircled by deep hoof prints gradually filling up with grass.

The Ralphs' land included several hundred rolling acres of spectacular land on which primeval limestone hills rose like pyramids above red clay fields. At times, the open views seemed to recall more the high deserts of New Mexico than the glades of middle Tennessee. Much of the land looked barren. The predominant trees were tall, scrawny cedars that grew in homely, close-knit families. The hills were spare and rocky, so everyone had to be careful not to run the horses along the paths and slip.

Charley made the hour's drive by himself twice a week to ride Culleoka, whom he now considered his own. His attachment to the horse only grew stronger once she was taken to the countryside, and the attachment was mutual. Culleoka could recognize the sound of the old Jeep approaching along Long Hollow Pike and she would appear at the barn by the time Charley had parked and hiked up the hill with an apple in his hand.

The autumn of 1975 was wet, with black clouds filling the skies for weeks. More tornadoes than usual had taken down old trees, barns, and trailers across the state. The red clay and limestone hills of the Ralphs' farm had turned slick with mud, making serious riding impossible. On one visit, Charley had taken Culleoka out for a short ride when thunder struck nearby. She reared back and threw him onto a brush of cedar and sumac. He landed on his arm and he heard the bone snap in his wrist, sounding like a pencil breaking. Culleoka galloped away until she heard his calls, then returned to him. He knew his wrist was broken. He checked the rest of his body and found no other wounds or cuts. He could hear what his doctors would say. "No more horseback riding, Charley. Not for you. Not anymore."

"That's what you think," he said to himself as he walked the horse back to the barn.

Charley stayed home with the cast on his arm and out of the rain until Mr. Ralph called one afternoon. "We have a problem with Culleoka, Charley. She's down and can't seem to get back on her feet. Don't have any idea what's the matter. You better come out to look at her."

Charley was out the door in ten minutes. Angela met him at the farm. They climbed a hill in the rain with Mr. Ralph to find the unthinkable on the other side. Culleoka was lying on her side halfway down the hill. She was exhausted from kicking and thrashing on the wet ground, unable to get herself up in the mud. As Charley and Angela approached, she began to kick and thrash again.

"Stop, girl! Oh, my God, please *stop!*" Charley screamed as Culleoka's massive bulk slid a few feet further down the hill.

Angela grabbed his arm. "Back off, Charley. You're stirring her up. We can't get any closer."

"Look at her eyes," Charley called. "They're terrified. Look at those whites. I've never seen anything like it. Fuck, what can we do?"

"We can't get any closer, that's for sure," Angela said, assessing the situation. "If she kicks one of us, wow. With your cast, you shouldn't even be out here."

"I'm sure as hell not going anywhere."

"I hear you, but don't try to be a hero. You're too vulnerable. Let's call a vet."

❧

Within an hour a horse doctor had arrived. "No, sir, people. You can't assist a downed horse," he cautioned. "Not unless you want to know what it feels like to get trampled. No, sir. Y'all best keep a distance from her."

By looking at her from ten feet away, the veterinarian diagnosed leptospirosis, a bacterial infection. It was spread through the mud from other infected animals. Culleoka's case was dire. The whites of her eyes were yellow, proof that she already suffered serious liver damage. Stuck on a hillside, she could not be moved. No one could reach her to give her injections of antibiotics, because her thrashing was so violent.

Nobody could help her.

"If y'all need me to help put her down, let me know. She really doesn't have much hope, I have to tell ya."

For several more days, she periodically squirmed and kicked, sliding further in the mud. She was left completely exposed to the rain and lightning. She reared her head in terror as the fireworks exploded around her. Charley, Angela, and Mr. Ralph stood by, helpless.

"I can't stand it," Charley cried to Angela. "We've got to put her down. I don't want her suffering anymore. Let's call the vet back."

"You sure? Completely sure?"

"Jesus Christ, Angela!"

"Well, I just don't want us making a mistake. This is Culleoka we're talking about!" Angela angrily slapped her folded umbrella onto the hood of the car and put her face in her hands.

Charley put his arm around her and said, "Listen. We've got to think of *her*, what's best for her. She's lost it. She's out of her head. She hasn't eaten in a week. She's pissing on herself every time it thunders. Look, she's slid in the goddamn mud all the way down to the creek bed. Think of her. Wouldn't you rather be dead?"

Angela grabbed his hand and held it. "You're right, Charley. I know you're right."

"Know something else, Angela?" he continued with a subdued face. "Something tells me it's a beautiful thing."

"What is?"

"To help an animal out of her agony. A beautiful thing. We're helping Culleoka get out of her trap. We're helping her get to a...I don't know, a better place or a goddamn state of *grace* or something."

"Come on. What are you, a preacher?" Angela suddenly grinned through her tears.

"No, really. We're helping her to surrender and to quit struggling. Hey, isn't that why they sing "Amazing Grace" at funerals?"

❧

The doctor leaned a rifle against the red Jeep. "I brought two ways we can do it. Bullet or injection. If we shoot her, do you need me to do it or do you want me to show you what to do? It'd be pretty awkward with your cast."

"Can we do the injection?" Charley asked. "She's so weak now, I think we can get close enough to do it."

"Gun's faster. It's more efficient."

"No. Let's inject her. There's no way in hell I can let anybody shoot her."

❧

Angela and Charley and the veterinarian cautiously made their way down the hill in the mud toward Culleoka, on her side, taking small, quick breaths. Their voices echoed softly off the wet hillside. She heard them approach and snorted, flaring her nostrils. Charley knelt behind her and stroked the long shallow channel between her eyes that ran to her nostrils. She smelled his hand. He bent over and his right hand disappeared in the mud. He rubbed his face on hers. Angela crouched down in the mud behind him and watched. The veterinarian felt along the horse's thick neck, found the vein and looked over at Charley.

"Okay, do it, doc. Do it now."

Culleoka did not make a sound as the point of the needle disappeared under her fur and two bottles of barbiturate emptied into her vein. Her fast breathing slowed down and finally stopped. Her back legs twitched. Her eyes rolled back slightly, her lids remained open. Charley peered into them, keeping her company until she was gone.

They stood over Culleoka's body and regained their footing on the muddy slope. Charley tried earnestly to sing the first line of "Amazing Grace" but quit after he couldn't remember the words. His voice cracking, he blurted out, "Why does that damn song always show up? Nobody knows the words." Angela put her arm around him. They wobbled for a moment in the mud and then climbed back up the hill in silence.

THIRTY-SEVEN

Noon with a Dying Brother

Before the fall semester of my junior year in college had started, Angela helped me gain long-overdue independence from my family on Tyne Boulevard. One Sunday afternoon, Dad and I had argued angrily over my frustration that I was still living at home.

"Goddamn it, you old man! Don't you have any idea what it's like for me now? I can't keep living here. It's making me... RETARDED!"

"Don't talk to me like that, Yarrott. I'm your father, remember!"

"Oh, I remember, alright. Hell, I'd like to forget!"

Still fuming, I called Angela at her apartment. Convinced by her own experience that I was right, she drove out to the house to talk to Dad alone. The following morning, Dad passed me in the hall. "You know, you are lucky to have Angela as your sister. She really supports you."

"I know she does. I don't know what I'd do without her."

"She came over here yesterday to talk to me about you."

"About *me*?"

"Sure did. She changed my mind, too. I understand that you really need to move out. So, look, go find your own place and I'll help you out. Whatever you need."

"Oh, Dad!" I hugged him.

"Just one thing," he pulled away from me to look into my eyes. "You must not forget to take care of your health. You are responsible for Charley's life, too. Do you understand?"

෪

At the same time, I had met two young women, Beth and Susan, who had graduated from college the year before and were beginning graduate work at Vanderbilt. Among the three of us, we pulled together enough old beds, tables, and chairs to furnish a rented house near the university. Both women had been art history majors in college and were committed to working in the arts. They quickly became cohorts with whom I could talk about anything, particularly the subjects at school that intrigued me. They also were attractive, smart, and sociable women who knew lots of interesting people.

While making a home with these women, I crossed a bridge into a new kind of world for myself. I learned to shop for food and to cook. I did my own laundry for the first time and figured out the hard way that I must separate the whites from the colors. With Beth and Susan, I shone some light on my sexuality by talking about it out loud and I felt the relief that comes with honesty. My trips to the hospital twice a week for the platelet pheresis became compartmentalized. I did my job in the donor room, and then came home to my own life, leaving the hospital at the hospital. I crossed paths cordially with Charley only when he arrived at the end of the procedure. My grades started out high and remained high. After two months, I noticed a startling change in myself: the satisfaction that I felt in the tenth grade at Peabody was returning to me.

As soon as I moved out of my parents' house, I regained an appetite for learning. I was curious to know what was on the page and I could read again, retaining the information. At this time, I had also finished all my core subject requirements at Vanderbilt, as well as the prerequisite classes in my new major, art history. I could take more specialized classes and, by God, I was actually prepared for them. I signed up for topics I found genuinely stimulating: History of Modern Architecture, Early Christian and Byzantine Art, Classical Architecture, Italian Language, History of Opera, Filmmaking, Sculpture, Painting, Printmaking, Southern Literature. Hesitantly, I signed up for Advanced Poetry Writing, to follow an unsatisfying attempt at poetry writing the year before.

Before the teacher arrived for the first class, I looked around the room assigned to us. I figured to myself, *Here we go again, my junior year and another Narcissus who has no interest in his students.* The room was full of scattered chairs and desks, no order given to it yet. There were too many jocks and pretty girls with hair parted down the middle. *They're looking for easy grades. Aren't there any serious writers in this school?* The guys were beefy. Their thick, hard necks jutted out of their rugby stripes like columns of stone.

The teacher strolled in, a woman, a *young* woman in blue jeans and wire-rim glasses. She scanned the students and smiled. I instantly felt hopeful. *Maybe I'll like this one.* She introduced herself as Melissa Cannon and then said, "Please call me Melissa."

She said that she had just arrived from the University of Pennsylvania, where she had received her PhD. She was twenty-seven, and she had published a book of poems and had a play produced on PBS called *Between Two Stools.* She seemed like a focused, professional person, responding calmly and evenly to each one of us. She asked us to think about what kind of experience we wanted to get out of her class and then called on us to answer that question. I was impressed. *She actually wants to hear from us!*

She asked to read samples of our earlier-written pieces so she could gauge our interests. I gave her a poem called "Noon With a Dying Brother."

> As clouds waved sunlight
> And threw their arms out
> Over the dried barns
> Your mare leapt away
> A gnat in the sun
> Down the hill and gone.
>
> I galloped through wind
> That stumbled over

161

Grass and walls and the
Wind moaned and suffered
Through the bending trees
In a voice like yours.

Your mare leapt away
A red flea twisting
In the valley's lap
As moving clouds thickened
And dripped in your eye
That a twig kept open.

As the class was emptying the following Wednesday morning, Melissa waved me over to her. "Yarrott, I would love to discuss your poem with you. The imagery intrigues me. Can you come by my office this afternoon?"

Later that day, I sat on the edge of the chair in her office and waited for her to talk about the poem. Melissa rummaged through her leather backpack and pulled out a manila file with my poem in it.

"You have a powerful way with natural images, Yarrott. I love the use of the gnat in the sun, and then as it moves farther away it becomes a flea in the lap. What a great way to describe the movement of a horse out of control. What's the inspiration for the poem?"

"Something that happened to my brother. He has a serious bone marrow disease and he was recently thrown off a horse while riding."

"My God, was he hurt?"

I was touched by her concern. "He broke his wrist, but otherwise he wasn't hurt."

"And the title?" She tilted her head and looked me in the eye.

"Oh, I dunno. His disease was supposed to kill him several years ago and we're always waiting for something bad to happen. So he's been dying for years." My head twitched and I nervously rubbed my eyes. "The title sounds casual, I know, like I'm getting used to the idea of him dying. I know it's vague. I guess I just liked the sound of it. It sucks, I know."

Melissa touched my arm. "No, it doesn't suck. I think the

title works. I'm just curious, that's all. How long has he been ill, your brother?"

"Now? About four and a half years."

"And you said the doctors don't have much hope for him?"

"Well, if it weren't for my blood, he would have died four and a half years ago."

"*Your* blood?"

Melissa carefully laid my poem on the desk while I explained to her about our platelet pheresis routine. She looked upset.

"And nobody else's blood can work for your brother?"

"Nobody's."

"Well, what about *you?* That's an awfully lot to carry. Do you have a support system? You know, family and friends who understand?"

I sat stunned. I did not know how to answer that question. *Do I have people I can turn to? Do I feel support?* I thought of Mother's tirades about my staying out late and about my facial tics. I thought about when Charley threw a wrench at me and split open my hand. I thought of how I absolutely hated my other classes. I said, "No, I guess I don't."

"Well, then, maybe writing can be helpful to you. Write things down as you feel them. Keep a journal on a daily basis. I like your imagery and I'll bet there will be some interesting things to come."

"Can I show you something I wrote for my last writing class?" I pulled out a page about a dream I had where an Indian pins me down and shoots me with arrows, repeatedly, first in my arms, then in my neck, finally in my eyes. I frowned and added, "The professor read it to the class and called it homoerotic."

"Here, let me read it." Melissa went over it line for line, moving her lips as she read. She finally looked up and said, "And so what if it's homoerotic?"

"Do you think it is?" I asked, nervously propping myself on one arm.

"Sure, it can be read as such, but so what? It's also powerful and it's scary. That's what affects me the most. After you told me about your situation with your brother, it makes perfect sense. Listen," she put the page down and looked at me, "in my class I want you to feel safe about writing anything, as long as you feel it's honest. As far as sexual imagery goes, there is nothing—I repeat, *nothing*—that could shock me. Okay?"

"Melissa, can I trust you with something?" I decided to take advantage of the sudden swell of respect and safety I felt at that moment.

"Of course. I want you to know that."

"I think I'm probably gay." My hands were shaking.

Melissa looked straight ahead for a moment as she thought. She tucked her hair around her ears, sniffed loudly, then smiled. "Well, I'm glad you told me, Yarrott. Isn't that something? We have quite a lot in common. I'm gay, too."

We both began laughing and grabbed each other's hands. At that moment, my education suddenly sped into fourth gear. Having struggled with so much in my life that did not make sense, where I felt shamefully out of place and inferior, suddenly I saw the picture of myself in a new frame. Not only was I accepted, but I felt honored, as if I had something unique and powerful to say.

After that morning's discussion, my college experience suddenly lifted up on its toes, spun to face the other way, and started off in a new direction. Now school began to seem relevant and exciting. Someone was out there who would finally listen to what I had to say. I was vitalized with a new self-worth. I had the ear of the coolest teacher in the most august department at Vanderbilt University. Not only that, but we shared something important that set us apart from most of the other teachers and students. Our being homosexual, I believed, gave us a particular insight into the human condition, because of the hidden turmoil that comes with it. It is simply harder to live as a homosexual, and since we were surviving it, we were all the stronger for it. I walked a little straighter and I asserted my raised hand a little higher in my other classes thanks to Melissa. I had two more years of school, and all at once two years did not seem like a long time. I had work to do and I felt hungry to learn.

THIRTY-EIGHT

Heart Like a Wheel

In my Southern Literature class, I sat behind a tall, handsome guy named Jack, a senior, whose deep and languorous voice seemed to rise off a page of Faulkner. I found myself intrigued with his clear and astute comments in the class and noticed, too, that from my seat, his shoulders and neck rose squarely into his beautifully shaped head. His hands, with long fingers lightly coated with copper hair, seemed intelligent and nimble. Whenever he turned around to talk to me, he smiled warmly. He was from Mississippi and when he made observations about Flannery O'Connor or Eudora Welty, they seemed from an authentic, personal perspective. He became more impressive and more handsome each time I sat behind him.

To prepare for our midterm exam, the teacher suggested that we study in pairs. Jack turned around and grinned, "You interested in being my study partner?"

I quickly replied, "Yeah, that'd really help me out. Thanks! But I'm not the greatest student, just so you know. It'd probably do more good for me than you, I'm afraid." I noticed my mouth was dry.

Jack ignored what I said and grinned. "Well, hey, good, that's great. I'm glad you're free." His grin widened. "Want to come to my room tonight? About six o'clock? I live in Carmichael Towers—you know, the senior dorm—so I can fix us something to eat in my suite."

I took the elevator to Jack's floor and I could smell the thick sirloin steak searing in a pan the moment the elevator doors opened on twelve. The door to the suite was cracked for ventilation and Jack had his back to the door while he stood over the steaks in the narrow kitchen. He heard me and called out, "Why, a fine evening to you, Mr. Benz." He turned to grip my hand hard and dropped the other arm over my shoulder. I smelled his Right Guard deodorant. "Figured we needed to have some good brain food before we study. You eat meat, I hope, sir?" He took my coat and threw it over his desk. "Like a drink? I've already started one." The substantial alcohol on his breath had a refreshing immediacy to it.

"Please. Do you have any scotch?" I repeated my parents' favorite choice, which was becoming mine, too.

"Dang, I'm sorry. I only have bourbon."

"Oh, that'll be fine."

Jack's hands shook as he poured my glass and handed it to me. *Wow. Is he as nervous as I am?* I gulped down the bourbon and set the glass on his desk. He refilled it and I drank that down quickly, too.

The cinder block walls were painted institutional off-white. The furniture and doors of the suite were modern, heavy oak, built to withstand the battering of college students. In the dim light of Jack's steel floor lamp, I saw he had a poster of The Doors taped on the wall, alongside one of Monet's *Rouen Cathedral*. His room was tidy. He was not one to beat up the furniture.

By the time the steaks were ready, my eyes were out of focus and I noticed that we were laughing over anything that crossed our minds. How would we study for the exam tomorrow? We talked for three hours about where we grew up, about our interest in art and our time at Vanderbilt. We took long detours around the subjects of girlfriends and sex. Suddenly worried, I said, "Fine study partners we are. Look at us. We're drunk. Damn, what are we going do about the exam?"

"Listen," he said, passing a few stapled sheets of paper to me, "this is my study guide. Just read it before the test. I made you a copy. You'll do fine." He had simplified all the authors, books, and themes in vertical columns. He had broken the themes down to defining phrases accompanied by examples.

I looked over the notes. "But you've done all the work,

Jack. This is supposed to be a mutual study thing, not a tutoring session. It's not fair to you."

"Well, you can pay me back sometime. Maybe cook dinner for me."

"Sure, yeah. That's an easy trade." I raced through my mind's calendar to Saturday. I had no plans and both Susan and Beth would be out of town. The house would be quiet and Jack and I could be alone. "What are you doing Saturday night?"

"Supper with you, I reckon," Jack said slowly with his broad grin.

The next day, Jack sat in front of me as usual in Southern Literature. Despite my pounding headache, it felt good to see him and he was as friendly as the night before. The midterm exam was comprehensive and difficult, but Jack sailed through it and finished early. He winked to me after he dropped the test on the professor's table and slipped out of the room. I stayed on, my head twitching, trying to remember in my own words the thematic concepts of the fiction we had read. Despite how much I enjoyed reading Southern Literature, I did not enjoy the actual study of it. I finally finished the test and reluctantly left it on the table. Wriggling my shoulders into my coat, I turned the corner in the corridor to find Jack leaning against the wall.

"Just wanted to see how you did," he said shyly.

"I think I did okay. Not great, but okay. You?"

"Oh, fair to middling."

"Right. I bet you made an A+."

He shrugged. "Want to get coffee?"

"Sorry, I can't. I've got another class starting right now. See you tomorrow night, my place?"

"Not even a quick cup?" He seemed genuinely disappointed.

I shrugged my shoulders and smiled as I picked up my step and left him on the landing. I floated to the next building knowing how eager he was to spend time with me.

Jack arrived at eight o'clock with a handful of tulips. "Thought you might want them on the table, since you're such an artist," he said sheepishly, looking down at the floor. He was shy on my turf and was even deferential toward the old, rented house. He was terribly nervous, even more than I was. I poured him a glass of the bourbon I had just bought that afternoon and put on Linda Ronstadt's album, *Heart Like a Wheel*. He relaxed quickly.

"I love these songs," Jack said, closing his eyes and mouthing the words. "Glad to know you do, too."

"Yeah, they're sad and they're beautiful." I stood next to him holding my scotch and soda, feeling awkward. "Sad and beautiful."

Jack looked at me and paused for a second. He seemed like he was about to say something, but silenced himself. I led him into the kitchen, where I had the water boiling on the stove for spaghetti. I broke the noodles in half and dropped them into the pot. I had made the sauce that afternoon from canned tomatoes, chopped onions, garlic, and ground beef. I had also burned the sauce in the thin enamel pot. Not knowing any better, I served it anyway, thinking the burned flavor would not be so noticeable.

By the time the Linda Rondstadt had finished and been replaced by Van Cliburn performing the Emperor Concerto, we were already drunk. We sat down to eat and neither of us had much appetite for the blackened spaghetti sauce. We went straight to the salad of lettuce and store-bought Roquefort dressing with Pepperidge Farm croutons. I suggested that we go into the living room and start a fire in the fireplace. My head was spinning at this point, but I did not want to stop the momentum of the evening. We took the bottle of red wine with us and knelt down in front of the fireplace, stuffing newspaper under the logs. The fire blazed quickly and the room heated up. "Man, it's warm all of a sudden. I'm getting rid of this sweater," Jack said, raising both arms over his head.

"Me, too," I said.

We sat on the wood floor facing the fire, not talking. A drunk tension was in the air and neither of us knew what to do next. I gulped down another glass of wine and turned around to him. I found myself leaning into him and closed my eyes. I just aimed with my face until I felt his breathing. I felt a sudden sandpaper of whiskers surrounding the soft, damp warmth of his lips and then it was finally happening: I was kissing another guy. And he was kissing me back. For a while we just took off on what might be called a flight to somewhere, our hearts pounding while opening each other's shirts. It was the first time I felt another guy's chest, neck, face, and mouth. I wanted to remember how the topography and texture of his body were different from a girl's. Everything on Jack was firmer and tighter and his smell was salty instead of sweet. It was as if I were tasting and smelling meat instead of a flower.

Rolling over the warm hardwood, we knocked down the broom leaning against the fireplace. I sat up and the flight ended for me as my head began to spin. I wanted to be doing this so much I was crazy and yet the wine, which had made the whole thing possible in the first place, yanked me back to a nauseating reality. I started to feel sick.

"I gotta stop. I'm feeling shitty."

Jack sat up quickly and pulled his shirt together. "Yeah, sure," he said defensively. "Don't worry about it."

"Don't get me wrong, Jack, this is great. I just drank too much too fast."

"You're not freaking out about what we're doing?"

"God, no. But I'm drunk and about to puke, though." I scrambled to my feet and ran to the bathroom. I heard Jack whistling something and putting Linda Ronstadt back on the stereo. I heaved a couple of times into the toilet, wiped my face with a cold cloth and my nausea passed. Jack was lying on the floor when I returned, his arm across his chest, asleep.

I lay down across the couch and watched Jack's torso on the floor move with his breathing, his eyes closed and his head twisted hard to the left, pulling the skin tightly across his Adam's apple and his prominent chin. He had pulled together his shirt and buttoned the wrong buttons, leaving open several at the top. Now that I had finally physically touched another guy, I was not sure what I could do or wanted to do next. Or when. I wanted Jack to wake up and go home, to let us ruminate a bit before seeing each other again. I wanted to be alone.

"Hey, Jack. Gotta get up, okay?"

He stirred a little but did not wake up. I left him on the warm floor and weaved down the hall to my room, stepped out of my clothes and climbed into the twin bed. After tossing and turning uncomfortably, I drifted off to sleep. I was cold in my underwear and a headache was pounding when I heard footsteps in the room. Jack paused at the foot of the bed and I heard him scrape his belt buckle on the floor. "Do you have room for me?" He pulled back the cover and I smelled his Right Guard coming closer as he sidled in next to me.

The great feminist poets of the seventies, such as Denise Levertov, Adrienne Rich, and Kate Millet, were celebrating sexual images with a flourish, those metaphors of licking, rutting, and penetrating. In Melissa Cannon's poetry writing class, I found myself writing about those same raw things, and I was so happy to finally be experiencing some of that myself. With very proud faces, classmates male and female seriously considered the words to describe the taste and feel of sex. Bitter, salty, sweet? This was the perfume of naked bodies and I was relieved to participate, finally, with firsthand knowledge, in any discussion about it.

THIRTY-NINE

Friends?

"Yarrott, I think I've fallen for you. Yeah, that's the truth." On the phone, Jack sounded worried, even scared. What he was saying sounded like a confession of something bad rather than an announcement of something good.

"Well, Jack, I don't know what to say. I'm pretty damn flattered." *Hell. Why does this have to happen?* The idea of his having a crush on me made me nervous.

"Do you feel the same thing?" Now there was desperation in Jack's voice. *God, I hate that tone.*

I said nothing. My stomach tightened. I wanted to get off the phone so I would not have to complete another sentence. I ran my hand through my hair. Finally, I said, "No. I'm sorry, Jack, but I don't feel that. Maybe I just need to be on my own. Do you know what I mean? You're a really handsome and smart guy, but I'm not ready for anything with anyone."

"Good Lord, Yarrott. You know, you've really led me on."

"What? No, I didn't, Jack." My mind raced over the short time we were together. *Did I do that? Did I lead him on?*

"You've really hurt me. I just want you to know that."

I felt horrible. Maybe he's right. Maybe it's my fault. Maybe I just didn't want something after I got it. Wait a second! Wait a second! Maybe I just don't want more pressure on me. I've got enough people on my back now. The idea of another person depending on me makes me sick to my stomach. I took a deep breath and said, "Jack, I know what it is now. You're vulnerable and I'm not a person who can deal with it."

The receiver was wet from my nervous hand. Waiting for

Jack's response felt interminable. *What's he going to say? God, what's he going to do?*

Jack was resigned. "Well, if that's the way you feel, there's nothing I can do about it, is there?"

"I think you're right. But maybe we can be friends."

"Yeah, right. Friends. Listen, Yarrott, I've gotta get off the phone now and study. See you around campus." With the click came relief, but also a cold, lonely feeling, like I had just jumped out of a moving car on a dirt road...a long way from the nearest house.

FORTY

Dinner with Angela

"You're not around much. Even though you live in town, I never see you." I handed the plate of spaghetti to Angela as I talked. We headed into the living room of my house, with its windows onto the front yard. A yellow autumn had come to the oak trees. It was late Sunday afternoon.

She dropped down heavily on the couch, annoyed, and took a gulp of wine. "I've got stuff going on in my life, too, Yarrott. Look, you and Charley are not the only people with problems."

"Oh, lots of people are caught in the bind we find ourselves in, are they?" I asked sarcastically.

"I have problems, too, but they never get looked at. By anybody."

"Like what?"

"Like everything. I hate my life. I hate Nashville. I hate the way Mother and Dad talk to me. I hate trying to please them, especially when it's no use. I'm not their golden daughter, and I never will be. I'm a clerk at the hospital. I'm not a doctor's wife."

Angela nestled back into the couch with her plate of spaghetti in her lap. Emphatically, as if to claim her territory, she swung her feet up on the coffee table, a dark cherry Chippendale thing I had just bought at a flea market the weekend before.

"Do you mind, Angela? It's new."

"Hell, Yarrott, you're as bad as they are."

"Yeah, well, I didn't buy it so you could ruin it." We stared at each other for a second, anticipating a climbing series of insults, but they never came. We had more important stuff to discuss.

I broke the ice. "Okay, so you were saying...you hate your life."

"I do. I'm not aiming toward anything here. I mean, why am I here in Nashville, anyway?"

"That's a question both of us could ask."

"Anybody could understand *your* predicament, Yarrott. You have no choice. I'm sorry about that, too. But, me? I'm here because I've fallen asleep at the wheel."

I thought this might be a good time to broach the subject I wanted to talk to Angela about, why I'd invited her to eat with me tonight.

"You know, there's something I've wanted to bring up, but have been too chicken-shit to do it."

"Really, Yarrott? Gosh, I thought we could tell each other everything."

"Well, in theory, maybe, but the family has not exactly been the most accepting of my, my...let's call them idiosyncrasies, and you know it. What did you used to call my nervous tics? My habits? As if I could turn them off and on at will? What were you all thinking?"

"Okay, I apologize about it, but we were young and stupid then."

"Mother and Dad weren't young," I said flatly.

"No, they weren't. I can't give excuses for them. They should have known better. So do you think you've got a nervous disorder or something?"

"That's exactly what I think," I said. "And since I've come to that conclusion, I feel a whole lot better. It's amazing when you get things out in the open how much lighter you feel."

Angela stopped mid-chew and held her fork in the air. She was thinking. "That sounds good, Yarrott. I've got something going on I want to talk to you about, too. In that same vein of getting things out in the open." She took a sip of wine and put the glass down slowly while she gathered her words. "You know my roommate who Mother can't stand? Marsha?"

"Yeah, Mother calls her The Slob."

"I know. Well, Marsha and I...this is hard to finally get out..."

"Just say it, Angela."

"We're lovers."

"Huh?"

"I'm gay." Angela looked at me, waiting for a response.

But that's just what I wanted to tell her! I wiped my lips with the napkin and folded it neatly, just like Mother would do. I could not think of a single thing to say, positive or negative, good or bad; I was so surprised. The silent pause continued as my mind started to fill up with pictures of Angela looking miserable in white gloves, expertly tossing the football to Charley across the backyard, standing over me in a powerful display of authority. I finally said, "You sure?"

"Yep."

"That makes sense, Angela. I think that's great. Know something?"

"What?"

"I am, too." My mind was racing, suddenly free to be honest with someone from my family I had feared for so long.

"I thought so, but wasn't sure," she replied politely.

There was a moment of thought digestion and we did not say anything. Immediately, I was disturbed to know that two of the family were gay. It felt weird, deformed, and wrong. This was way above the reputed national average of one out of every ten people. What was up with our family, anyway? Then I realized what a great thing it might be to have a gay sister. There would be someone who would understand my life now. I would not have to be so humiliated not to fit the image of the typical straight male. Now there was someone in the family who would understand. And she was there all along. Our laughter and giggling erupted. We jumped up from the couch and hugged for a long time.

"Yarrott?" Angela said soberly in my ear.

"Yes?"

"I promise, from this point on, to be your friend. Whatever, whenever, I'll be there for you."

"And, Angela, I promise the same."

175

FORTY-ONE

Dinner with Charley

Looking over his shoulder at me and frowning, Charley said, "Something's up with Angela." He was in Mother's kitchen, cutting apart a chicken to barbeque on the grill. Our parents were visiting relatives in Kentucky until Tuesday. Joe was watching the Sunday evening news in the study. "Want a toke while I cook this, Yarrott?"

"No, thanks." I lay the joint down in the ashtray. "I've got to drive back to my apartment after dinner and study for a test tomorrow."

"Suit yourself, hero." He called across the house to Joe, "Yo in there! Want some dope?"

Joe answered, "Nah, Chuck. I'll wait." The glow from the TV flickered at the doorway of the study. A somber rumbling of televised voices filled the background. The world seemed tense.

"So, you said something about Angela," I reminded him.

"Yeah. She's acting pretty weird. She seems angry about something. I know she hates her dead-end job at the hospital. I don't blame her. I mean, can you see her as an admitting clerk? But it's more than that. We really had it out the other day. I thought she was gonna slug me."

"What about?"

"I told her she ought to shave her legs. I said she'd never get a man like that."

Oh, no. I don't want to get into this with him.

"Why'd you do that, Charley? It's her business."

"Come on, Yarrott. She's starting to look like crap. She

dresses like a farmer. So do her friends. What's up with all those women, anyway?"

I've gotta change the subject quick. He's getting way too close.

"Well, think of what they're responding to. Oppression, like what Mother grew up under. Can you see Angela becoming a Southern belle?"

"C'mon, Yarrott. It's way more than that. What a stupid argument."

"Is it? First, Mother had to endure it as a young woman in Kentucky. Look, she wanted more than the life of a Southern lady. So she became a nurse. Then she married Dad and her short-term independence ended. She became a doctor's wife. But she can't see what she's now doing to her own daughter! Just like the society that she bucked, Mother tries to squeeze Angela into a hole she can't fit into. You know, round hole, square peg. Angela's always been a tomboy. Let me ask you, Charley, why does it upset you so much?"

"Because it's embarrassing. Isn't that enough?"

"God, I can't believe what you're saying. You're such a goddamn snob."

"Listen, Yarrott. Look at Eddy. He's a nerdy brain, but he's still cool. He's into popular music. He dresses himself like he knows what's in style or not. He's hot for women, sometimes too much so. But at least you know where he stands."

"And your point is?"

"You, too. You know how to dress, how to look good. Sometimes you make a mistake and go off looking pretty fagotty, but most of the time you look pretty cool."

"Charley, what the hell are you trying to say?"

"I guess I mean that Angela dresses and acts like she has no idea how the world operates. It's like she refuses to play the man and woman game, so she's in a world of one."

"Okay, I agree. She could look a lot better. But why is it so important to you that she looks like a dressed-up girl?"

"Because, for Christ's sake, I worry about her! That's why!"

"Yeah, but your worry comes off sounding like anger. Like you disapprove of her. Which is it? Anger or worry?"

He stopped for a minute and gathered the pieces of

chicken on a plate. "Hell, that's a good question." He headed for the terrace and turned to me. "I don't know."

At the French doors in the living room, he stopped and yelled to Joe, "Hey, shitface. Get your sorry butt out here and help, will you?"

Part Three

FORTY-TWO

The Machine at the Red Cross

Eddy shoved his chair under the breakfast table impatiently. "Dad, I don't understand why they haven't bought one yet. I just don't get it."

Dad tried to calm him down, "You don't understand, Eddy. The hospital can't buy an expensive machine for just one patient. They don't have that sort of resources."

"That's bullshit," Eddy yelled. "They'll buy one if it makes them look good."

Mother turned around to them from the other end of the kitchen and scolded Eddy, "Don't talk like that in this house. You can talk like that in your apartment in New York, but you can't come down here and talk that way."

"Mother, you're forgetting the purpose of this argument. There's a machine out there that can cut Yarrott's time down to two hours. It's outrageous Vanderbilt hasn't already bought one. It's absolutely inexcusable. It wouldn't just benefit Yarrott. It's a brand-new technology that would eventually help a lot of people."

"Still, you don't have to be crude," Mother said as she continued filling the dishwasher. Eddy rolled his eyes and followed Dad into the living room, where I was playing on the rug with the dachshunds.

I had heard them talking about me. "What's this about a machine?" I asked.

"It's called a continuous-flow centrifuge and it's being marketed nationally now. We already have one in New York." Eddy had moved that year from the Mayo Clinic in Minnesota to a post at Albert Einstein College of Medicine in the Bronx.

I rubbed Gretel's belly. "How's it work?"

"Basically, instead of using plastic bags, you bleed directly into a closed centrifuge from one arm, it spins off your platelets, then it gives you everything else back in the other arm. It's much more efficient, the platelet yield is higher, and it takes about a third of the time."

I patted the dogs away from me and sat up straight. "Wait a second. You're telling me this thing has been on the market for a while but Vanderbilt has decided not to buy one?"

"That's right," Eddy said while glaring at Dad.

"Oh, come on," Dad tried to reason with him. "They don't have it in their budget."

"For Christ's sake, Dad, that's because they *choose* not to put it in their budget."

"Eddy, for crying out loud, you're talking about a machine that costs $15,000! It's not *nothing*."

I interrupted, "Come on, stop arguing."

Eddy looked at me and calmly stated his point. "Wouldn't you like to be doing something else on your two afternoons a week, Yarrott? It makes me sick that you're still tied down like you are." He turned to Dad and continued. "Listen, if nobody else is going to do it, I'm going to see what *I* can do to do get the money together."

"You would do that, Eddy? For me?"

"You're damn right."

That afternoon, Eddy called the former headmaster of Battle Ground Academy, the prep school from which both he and Charley had graduated. As an exceptional high school student, Eddy had developed a cordial friendship with Mr. Reddick that had continued for many years. Recently, the former headmaster had delivered an alumni speech describing Charley's and my situation as an illustration of fine family values. It was a brilliant idea to ask Mr. Reddick to help, and it was an idea that succeeded. Within three months, the $15,000 had been raised through alumni at BGA to buy the continuous flow centrifuge, a Haemonetics 30.

The problem was that the administrators at Vanderbilt Hospital felt the machine would be better used somewhere else, such as the Nashville Red Cross, where more patients throughout middle Tennessee would be served. I was angry as hell with Dr. Flexner. Why couldn't we continue to do the procedure at Vanderbilt? Why couldn't we use the new machine there? These people in the blood bank had become my friends and I did not want to leave them. I knew nothing about the Red Cross or the people who worked there.

A new pheresis center was made by joining three rooms at the Red Cross. In the summer of 1975, five years after the first pheresis at Vanderbilt, I said good-bye to my friends in the blood bank of Vanderbilt. When I finished the manual bag procedure for the last time and Charley had received his platelets, the blood bank staff crammed into the tiny room with us, carrying a spongy vanilla cake with white sugar icing. Thin red loops of icing around the top of the cake spelled out "Good-bye, Yarrott and Charley. We love you." I remember hugging each staff member and thanking them for their special care. In all of the years, for 520 afternoons, there was never one moment when a serious mistake occurred. Despite the crude appearance of the donor room, the professional performance of the staff was flawless. I had been cared for as if I had been one of their own.

After that day, the donor room, which had become my personal inner sanctum, returned to its prior function as a storage closet. The walls were soon painted beige and the heavy wooden door to the corridor was locked.

My first procedure at the Red Cross was scheduled for one o'clock on a hot summer day. I parked in the visitor's lot and gritted my teeth. I did not know what to expect.

"You'll be fine, little brother," Charley had said earlier that day on the phone. "I bet it'll even be fun on a new machine. Kind of space-age. I'll show up around three o'clock and you can tell me how it went."

The Pheresis Center at the Red Cross was named in honor of Murl Whitson, a woman who had died of leukemia. Her family had given the money to outfit the room with attractive wood cabinets and cheerful furniture. There were four fancy, rust-red motorized donor chairs, the type that reclined and even heated up. Standing along one wall was the new machine,

183

a Model 30 from the Haemonetics Corporation. It looked like a white bar refrigerator on wheels, with a clear Lucite window on its top looking inside and a chrome IV stand rising above that. Under its window was a round white cavity with a clear plastic disposable tub. This was the spinning device that would fill with my blood. A few black dials and switches were arranged on the flat surface around the window.

Two nurses in navy-blue uniforms stood by the machine when I walked through the door. The older woman, Dot, about fifty, was friendly and laughed easily. She seemed a little nervous and chewed gum to relieve her tension. The other woman, Barbara, was in her late twenties and seemed efficient and attractive, like a flight attendant. Making myself comfortable on the donor chair, I felt as if I were settling into my seat for a long flight. As with the first pheresis done five years earlier, I did not know what to expect. But this time, I was starting a procedure by myself, without my parents standing against the wall protectively watching over me. I was now twenty-one years old, after all. *I can do this. I can do this.*

The preparation for sticking both arms was the same. Three little vials of soap, iodine, and finally alcohol were broken open and applied to the skin in circular patterns, turning the puncture site into a sterilized target. The needles were the same fifteen-gauge that the manual pheresis eventually used. The stick pinched and stung like always. Dot pushed a button and a soft whirring sound began, like a finely tuned spin cycle on a washing machine. She took a clamp off the tube connecting my arm to the machine, and my blood shot down the tube as if something were sucking it.

"Holy cow, look at that stuff go," Dot exclaimed. "There must be a vacuum in the centrifuge. Incredible!"

Losing so much blood so quickly, I expected to feel light-headed, but I didn't. The procedure went smoothly. I praised the women for their expert handling of the brand-new machine and said, "You know, this reminds me of the supersonic Concorde, that new plane everyone's talking about. It cuts down the time from New York to Paris to a couple of hours. Hey, it's sort of like this, isn't it?"

That afternoon, around three o'clock, after Charley had arrived to get his yield of platelets, I drove back to my apartment and called Eddy in New York. "Damn, that thing is incredible. Have I said thank you?"

"Hey, don't. Really, I had to do something when I saw there was a better route for you. I just hope it makes your life easier. Let me know how it goes, okay?"

"You got it, Eddy. I'll tell you, it's gonna take me a while to get used to having these afternoons back."

"Oh, Yarrott? Wait a second. There's one thing you could do. Would you write Mr. Reddick and thank him? He's the one who got the money together. He's the one who made it possible."

Throughout my senior year at Vanderbilt, I would race over to the Red Cross twice a week, spend two quick hours on the machine with Dot and Barbara, and then would speed back to my afternoon classes. Yes, the experience was efficient, but the women with whom I spent my time were also warm, personable, and fun. Charley and I eventually met Dot's children, and we both attended Barbara's wedding. I continued to miss my friends at Vanderbilt hospital, but the Red Cross provided a new chapter to the story. There's a lot you can know about someone by repeatedly sharing time together. Friendships can develop in unlikely places.

As the technology for matching patients with the human leukocyte antigen became ever more efficient, the pheresis procedure became a wider phenomenon. I was not the only person in the world doing this for a brother or, for that matter, a stranger. Eventually, the Red Cross bought a second continuous-flow centrifuge, and there were often other people in the donor chairs across the room from me. However, one fact remained: There was never another donor who continued to give beyond a few months. It seemed that either the recipient died or a bone marrow transplant was performed elsewhere. Regardless of the space-age technology, I continued to be the one ever-present face in the donor room.

FORTY-THREE

The Announcement

"Hello, Yarrott?" It was Angela. I could tell in those four syllables that something had happened.

"Hi, Angela. Beautiful Sunday afternoon. Do I detect something wrong?"

"God. The shit has really hit the fan at home. I need some support. Are you in the middle of anything? Can you come over to the house right away?"

"Sure. But what happened?"

"I came out to Mom and Dad. And to Charley, too. It's not good."

"Jesus Christ. I can't believe it. One of us finally did it. How'd you do it? What did you say?" I was awed.

"Mom and Dad were watching a football game on the TV in their bedroom. They had been nagging me this morning about where I went last night, who I was with, why I was out so late, I couldn't take it anymore. I just walked up to the TV, stood there between it and them, and turned it off. I said, 'Okay. You want so badly to know where I've been going every night? I'll tell you. I'm gay and I'm seeing a woman. I'm a lesbian.' And they just sat there staring blankly at me. Even Charley. He was in the back of the room doing something. He stopped and just stood there looking at me."

"Well, what did they say? How'd they react?" My heart was pounding with the news. One half of our secret was now out. It meant either war or peace.

"Dad spoke first. He asked me if I was happy. I told him not at the moment. Then he asked if I needed help. I said, 'You mean money?' And he said no, he meant *mental*. 'Do you need mental, psychiatric help? Will you agree to see someone?'"

"As if you, we, Angela, are mentally ill for being gay?" I asked.

"Yep. That's the implication," she replied.

"Well, I guess offering help is a generous reaction, given what it could have been. What did you say?"

"I got angry and claimed they didn't understand homosexuality. I refused. But Dad insisted that I see somebody for an outside point of view, like Dr. Kingsley."

"Dr. Kingsley? But he's an internist!"

"Dad said he was the most *worldly* person they knew and he'd have a good perspective on the matter."

"And you said?"

"I agreed. It seemed innocuous."

"What were Mother and Charley doing while Dad was talking?"

"Mom sat in her chair looking at her hands folded in her lap with that stern, worried look of hers. It was awful. I couldn't tell if she was going to cry or get up and hit me. But she looked up finally and said that they loved me."

"And Charley?"

"He made me so mad. He said he didn't believe me. That it couldn't be true. Listen, I need you to come over here and play interference for me. They've got to hear somebody support me. *I* need to hear somebody support me. Can you come over right now?"

"I'll be there in ten minutes. In the meantime, remember you've done nothing wrong. You've just told the truth. Okay?"

"I'll try to remember that. I love you, Yarrott."

On the way from my apartment to the house on Tyne Boulevard, I sorted through the tactics I would use. First of all, I had to settle whether or not I would tell them about me, too. No. That would be too much for them to handle. I'd keep that out of it. As I drove up the driveway, with a dry mouth and cold hands, I was as nervous to walk inside as I had ever been in my life.

I encountered Charley in the front hall. I said, "Angela called and told me what happened. Where is she?"

"She got pissed with Dad about five minutes ago and stormed out. She's gone."

Uh-oh. I was alone with her mess. My God, I'd give anything to not be here. What should I say? What should I do? How should I not implicate myself?

Dad heard me come in and joined us in the living room, where we all took seats. "Did you hear what your sister told us, Yarrott?" Dad was clearly unhappy, but he sounded thoughtful, like a minister, not outraged or disgusted.

"Yes, Dad. She wanted me to come over to lend her support. It sounds like she might have sprung it on you too suddenly. Are you in shock?"

"I'm so disappointed right now I don't know what to say."

Charley made a fist and hit the arm of the sofa. "I'll tell you what it makes *me* feel. I'm disgusted. It makes me sick!"

"Oh, come on, Charley," I said. "It's not so bad. Jeez, these days being gay isn't such a bad thing. Remember, this is 1974, not 1954."

"I don't care how liberal you think you are, Yarrott. It's not right."

Dad added, "I have to agree with Charley. I don't think it's right either."

Mom was listening in the front hall and joined us. "I'm so hurt. I just want to know what I did wrong. What did I do? How did I fail so badly as a mother?"

"Mom, you had nothing to do with Angela's sexual orientation." I felt like I was getting in over my head, but I had to try at least to get them to reason. In the back of my mind, I felt like a defenseless man surrounded by angry dogs. *If I don't watch myself, I'll be torn apart by them.*

"How can you defend this, Yarrott?" Mother sounded hard and mean, like she'd just grown big canine teeth. The same tone of voice she'd use to humiliate me. She might as well have called me "little man." "I want to know *why* you defend this!"

Charley jumped into the attack. "Yeah, Yarrott. Tell us. I want to know. You queer, too?"

There. He had said it. He had addressed what had been bugging him for my entire twenty years of life. Inside my head,

I was terrified. I saw the three faces glaring at me and knew there was no possible way I could be honest with them. Not today, after Angela's announcement, and possibly not ever. I controlled my anger from spinning into vertigo and gripped both arms of the chair. I calculated how I would respond. I needed the best diversion from the topic inflaming them. "Charley, after all I have done for you, how can you say that to me? Remember, I have kept you alive now for almost five years. This is the thanks I get? Now, I'm the one who's disgusted." I stood up, righteously indignant, and stormed out the French doors to the terrace. I gulped a deep breath and calmed myself down. Charley followed me outside.

"Yarrott, I apologize. This is way too much to deal with today. I don't know what to think. The hardest part of Angela's saying she's gay is that it makes you doubt *yourself*."

I was suddenly mute. I did not want to be, but I was unable to speak. Did I just hear right? Did Charley just say he doubted himself? Did that mean his own sexuality? That was impossible. Maybe he meant it made him doubt his *thinking* toward sexuality. Maybe I had misunderstood him, or maybe he'd just said the most profoundly insightful and courageous thing in his life. But I was too freaked out, angry, and proud to turn around and respond to him. I kept my back to him.

When I could have walked through a door that Charley was only now willing to open, finally offering us a dialogue that could have brought us closer, I chose to defiantly strut away into the backyard. I did not understand my own behavior and obviously he did not understand his either. We both were angry because we didn't know what else to be—and totally unable to find our way to common ground.

Charley called after me, "Yarrott, wait!" I continued to walk away from him and Mother and Dad, got in my car, and sped back to my apartment, where I promptly did anything I could to divert my attention away from what had just happened. I called somebody, I don't remember whom, to see a movie or eat dinner out or just get drunk.

Angela stayed at her new girlfriend's house that night. It was Sunday night.

Tomorrow's Monday. Which means I have to be at the Red Cross at one for the platelet pheresis. Maybe we can get through the procedure early so I won't have to see Charley. Occasionally that happens. He'll arrive at the pheresis center to find his little bag of platelets waiting for him. Yes, I'll do that. I'll go to the Red Cross early because I don't know what to say to him.

FORTY-FOUR

Great Expectations

It was Lee Leffert who convinced my parents that I should be taken seriously as an artist. He was the bachelor brother of the Air Force general living next door on Tyne Boulevard. Tall, athletic, and erudite, Lee visited his family in Nashville once a year from the Midwest, where he was the headmaster of a private school.

Education, success, and wealth seemed to pour out of the house next door. The Lefferts were prominent people whose house and grounds were kept with the precision of a miniature White House. Even as a small child, I was mesmerized by them. I watched the Lefferts from our yard like a dope, my thumb in my mouth. Life on our side of the fence sure felt dreary.

Lee Leffert tossed me a rope to a more glamorous possibility.

Having founded the elite Anderson-Bromley School, Lee was, by any terms, successful, but he wielded little influence on his brother, the general. I rarely saw them together in the same room at the same time. They were as opposite as night and day.

Lee's influence on *me*, however, was more powerful. From a safe distance, it would look like a man throwing a rope to a boy barely treading water. From a distance, it would look that way. Until the boy speaks.

I first remember him when I was in high school. He showed interest in me when I was in middle school, and invited himself over to visit with my mother and me. He told her he was keeping an eye on me and at one point suggested that I might develop my talents better at his school. The idea of leaving home then scared me cold. Living with other teenagers, who I was sure were mean-spirited, spoiled, and intimidating, was positively abhorrent. Luckily, it was an idea that neither of my parents thought feasible, given the cost of room and board and the fact that they were already paying three other tuitions for my siblings. Nevertheless, Lee Leffert continued to watch my progress and insisted on our meeting once a year, during his visits next door.

My mother was not comfortable with him, complaining under her breath that she did not appreciate his familiarity with me, which she felt was unwarranted, not to mention uninvited. It was strange to her how he would sling a long leg over the arm of the wing chair in the living room, despite being dressed in a suit. He held court in our living room, asking me about myself and my progress while he beamed with interest. At the time, I was an emotional wreck at Montgomery Bell Academy and tried hard to conceal that I was a struggling, twitching mess, even lying to him about my grades. God knows I did not need *two* schools breathing down my neck. One was bad enough.

When I was college age, we began to meet alone. He announced to me privately that he was afraid my situation with Charley would ruin my chances of developing into the artist that I should be. He told me that I needed to make decisions that would benefit *me*. I had no idea what he meant. I was obedient to my dutiful blood donations, and in a fog. I was lucky just to make it through each week, straining under the weight of a dull academic load and my afternoons at the hospital. The notion of putting together a plan for my future felt pointless.

During my senior year in college, Lee wrote me with an offer to take me on a two-month trip to Europe that he was making in the following summer, 1976, with a handful of his students. The trip would consist of two weeks in London, a month in Italy, and finally two more weeks in Switzerland. In London, he was planning to see performances of opera, ballet, and theater every day. This would make a splendid first trip abroad, he said, and he was sure it would be beneficial to me.

He was so sure of its potential importance in my life, he said he would pay my way.

I saw stars. *Europe! Opera! A polished life!* How could I possibly say no?

At this point, I was living on my own in my own apartment, so my parents let me make my own decision. The big question, though, was what to do about Charley's platelets. The doctors at the Red Cross and at Vanderbilt felt that it was time to find anonymous platelet donors, in order to give me a break and to have available in case of an emergency. After all, what would happen to Charley if anything happened to Yarrott?

A call was sent out nationwide, through the Red Cross, for volunteers to be HLA-tested with Charley. Three people in different parts of the United States were found to be suitable matches. Charley looked me in the eyes and said, "I want you to go on this trip, Yarrott. It's been six years. You deserve it."

I was both excited about a temporary escape from donating blood and also reluctant. What would happen if Charley rejected all the new platelets? I would be half the world away, more than twenty-four hours of travel away. Could he bleed to death if the new donors did not work? Could my parents find me in time if they needed me? My mind raced with conflicting images of extraordinary new places and horrible new worries. The doctors at the Red Cross, my parents, and Charley all repeated that I needed to forget about my responsibilities in Nashville and *just go. Go!*

Oddly, the afternoon before I left on the trip, my father called me to his office. He was vague on the phone and said he needed to talk to me in person. When I got there he was tapping his fountain pen on a file folder, trying to put his words together. "There is something that doesn't feel right to me," he said. "Something about Lee. I don't quite understand why he has been so insistent on this trip for you. Don't get me wrong; you need a break from your life in Nashville. You need to go off and see the world. But why is it so vital that it has to be with *him*? You're a young guy; you look still a lot younger than your twenty-one years. Lee's a middle-aged bachelor. Do you see where I'm going with this?"

Man, Dad is so right about Lee. Why am I doing this?

"Come on, Dad. I don't think there's anything to be worried about. Even if Lee did try to pull something on me that was sexual in nature, I can handle it. Don't worry." *I swear if Lee pulls anything on me, I'll knee him in the crotch.*

"Well, I just needed to make sure your eyes are open. No offense, okay?"

"Oh, Dad, no offense taken. I really appreciate your concern." *My God, what if he's right? What if Lee is a lecherous wolf in Mr. Chips' clothing? What have I gotten myself into?*

On June 20, 1976, I flew to Chicago and met Lee and the others at the British Airways gate at O'Hare Airport. Unlike the sun-filled cabin of the flight to Seattle with my parents and Charley, this flight was at night and the cabin of the 747 was dim and elegant, as if lit by candlelight. I felt I was in swanky London the second I entered the plane. Lee and I had two seats together near the front. The students were enjoying their own private conversations in the back part of the plane. After takeoff, Lee replaced his shoes with his slippers, pulled down two red plaid blankets from the overhead bin, and nestled into his armrest, leaning in my direction. He had done this, crossed the Atlantic, a hundred times.

This is going to be fine. I should be ashamed of myself for having doubted him. I am so damn lucky to get this experience. Thank you, Lee. Thank you.

Just as soon as I had finished that sentence in my head, he began. "Let me talk to you about discipline, Yarrott." Lee pulled out three small leather-bound books from his valise on the floor. "I read fifteen minutes of each of these every day. Every day of my life. I've been doing it since I began studies at Cambridge in 1945. Here, look." Lee opened the three books—one in Latin, one in Ancient Greek, and one in Hebrew—and pointed to the stains, pencil marks, and creases from thirty years of daily usage.

I tightened my grip on my armrest. "You speak all three of those languages?"

"And two more, Italian and French."

"Gosh. Uh, what do you get out of reading ancient languages every day? What do they say to you?"

"You've never read *Plato*, Yarrott? You say your major is art history and yet you've never read Plato? What kind of education can you call that?"

"I guess a sorry one." Had we suddenly hit some turbulence? I was starting to feel defensive about Vanderbilt University, the place I normally hated.

"Well, it is never too late to start a good thing. Here, take a look at this." He pushed the dog-eared volume into my hand and instructed me to open it very carefully. Instead of leafing through it and being inspired, I felt like I was inspecting someone's yellow toenails. I held it for what I thought was enough time to be polite and handed it back.

"Impressive," I said perkily.

"I know it is. The knowledge can be yours, too, if you allow it in."

I had a sinking feeling that I had just made a big mistake by coming on the trip. Here was yet another moment in my education that made me feel stupid. And trapped. Stupid and trapped. Yet again.

The airplane landed in London the next morning during a foggy drizzle. The hotel on Leicester Square was World War II–era and threadbare. It was inexpensive but in a convenient location to the theaters. Lee and I had rooms on different floors. Agreeing to meet up for dinner in the afternoon, I went straight to my room and unpacked. The room was even uglier than the lobby, and very cold, but it had a private bathroom with a tub on a platform and a toilet tank suspended from the low ceiling. I had never before seen black and green linoleum squares cover the floor and then climb all the way up the walls to the ceiling. A modest light fixture hung freely over the medicine cabinet and I hit my head on it each time I stood before the mirror. I filled the tub with hot water and put a strange new coin into the slot on the wall-mounted radio. Mid-song, Melissa Manchester suddenly was belting out "Midnight Blue."

I can't believe this. I know this song. I slid into the hot water in my tub. I already feel less foreign. The first music I hear on the radio on my first trip outside of the U.S. and it's an American singer. I lay in the tub, washing the travel off me with a plain white bar of soap that I was sure must have smelled the same during the time of Dickens. I lay in the water looking at the room's sad, mismatched decor, and thought hard on the fact that I was now so far away from home, from Charley, from Mother and Dad. I began to feel guilty that I had flown so far away from them. Lying back in the water, I tried to relax and put into order all the pieces that got me there in that tub in that hotel room in London. This will be good. Look around. Smell, touch, taste, and listen. Learn. I dried myself off with the thin waffle of cotton and spread the towel out neatly on the rod so it would not mildew, like I did at home. I slipped into the soft bed and drifted off.

In the dark room, I woke up suddenly to someone pounding on my door. I could not remember where I was. My travel alarm glowing next to the bed said six o'clock. P.M. or A.M.? "Yarrott? Are you in there?" I recognized Lee Leffert's voice. *Oh, God, I was supposed to meet them for an early dinner at five-thirty.*

"Yes, Lee. I'm sorry. I fell asleep. Can you wait a second?"

"Well, I guess I don't have a choice, now do I?" He sounded exasperated.

Stumbling through the room, I put my clothes back on and opened the door while shoving my shirttail into my pants. "God, I'm sorry, Lee. I fell asleep."

"Well, I've told the students to wait in the lobby, so we need to hurry. You mustn't hold us up again."

Over the next two weeks in London, I was punctual without fail as we attended four operas, two symphonies, three ballets, and six theater productions. The daytimes were mine to spend as I liked, going to museums or walking through the neighborhoods. The drizzle rarely let up, but I learned to enjoy the interior life of London, stopping for cake and tea and occasionally striking up conversations with strangers. My time with Lee was kept to a minimum, as we met for dinner and performances. But he always seemed to be annoyed with me, despite the fact that I did not repeat my initial failure.

The day before we flew to Italy, he invited me to his room for chat. I dreaded the hour we were to meet. "Yarrott, I asked you here because I'm a little concerned about something."

"Gosh, Lee, I'm all ears."

"To get to the point, I've been watching you and I am concerned about you. I would like to ask you some questions. Will you allow me?"

"Of course, Lee. I'm sorry you've been concerned. What would you like to know?"

"Well, to be perfectly blunt, Yarrott, you seem, well, undersexed to me. You don't act like you've had much physical contact with other bodies. What is your experience so far?"

Why the hell is asking me that? I don't want to get that close to him. This makes me really uncomfortable. I shifted in the chair and thought about the best way to answer this. He doesn't know that I'm gay. I wonder what he feels about homosexuality. God, what if he's gay, too. Oh, God.

My mouth suddenly went dry. "I've had more sex than you think. I probably started later than most guys because I lived at home until two years ago."

"And exactly what is it that you have done with other people? You don't mind that I ask, do you?"

Jesus Christ. How is this any of his business? "No, I'm an adult. I can handle the questions. Well, I guess you might say everything. Oral. Genital. Everything. Some people I've liked, some I haven't. I'm not seeing anyone right now."

He pursed his lips to think and this was followed by a long moment of silence. "Well, I have to ask you: do you like young women more than you like young men?"

My heart started pounding so loudly I was afraid he could hear it across the room. I suddenly became very hot in my jacket and turned bright red. *I am proud about who I am, damn it. I will not lie. Too bad if he decides that his interest in my welfare has been a waste of time because I am gay. That is his goddamn problem.* "I like men, Lee. I like men better than women. I'm gay, Lee."

"Oh, I thought so."

"You did?"

"Of course. People with your interests in art and culture, people with your, uh, sensitivity to things usually are. It's no great thing." Picking up his books again, he said, "Here, look at Plato for example. He even *encourages* the sensual bonds between males."

"So you are...okay with it?"

He laughed, "Indeed. Let me tell you some of the other wise secrets that I know from studying the classics. It is proven that human beings are happier and live longer if they have body contact with other human beings on a regular basis. Body hugs are proven to be the best method."

"Body hugs?"

"Yes, let me show you. Stand here in front of me."

I immediately felt wary. Here I am in Lee Leffert's room, alone, and he wants me to give him a body hug, whatever that is. Good God, what have I gotten myself into? Obediently, I rose and stood next to him with my arms at my sides.

"Not like that, boy." He took my arms and pulled them around his back and then grabbed me so tightly that it was hard to breathe.

"Now rub my back up and down. Firmly and deeply. Down, that's right. Keep going down." I stopped when I felt his belt through his jacket. "What are you so afraid of, boy?" He pulled away and stared at my face with a look of great concern. "I say, why are you so...uptight? This is exactly what I thought was wrong with you. You are afraid of human contact."

"I really don't think I agree with you, Lee. I love hugging people."

"Not like *this*." He rubbed his cheeks on mine, pushing the side of his face up and down on mine, his whiskers scratching my skin. I pulled away but he grabbed my head and held it while he pressed away.

"The face is the most sensitive part of the body, even more than your cock. See how it unnerves you? Now, what would you do if I were to press against your cock, huh?"

"I'd feel really uncomfortable if you did that."

He pulled away and sat down in his chair. "As I thought, Yarrott. You are literally suffering from too little physical, bodily, sensual contact from other human beings. You chafe when you should be enjoying it, even getting an erection. That, in fact, would be most appropriate."

I sat down, so relieved that he had stopped that I became giddy. I did not want to insult him. After all, he had made this trip possible for me, and if there is anything I cannot stand it's an ingrate. "Thank you for showing me that. It gives me a lot to think about."

"Yes, think about that and consider reading the classics once a day. Furthermore, you could do with a little more exercising. Were you on a sports team of any kind?"

I nodded my head from side to side, embarrassed by my lack of physical, masculine enterprise.

"At the ballet tonight, our last night in England, I want you to closely examine the physique of the male dancers of the Royal Ballet. I want you to study their musculature, especially their buttocks and thighs. Then I want you to examine your own tonight in the mirror. I notice that your firmness needs to be improved."

He's right. Who would want to have sex with me? My ass should be harder. He's right. I'm a pathetic excuse for a man.

"All right, Yarrott. That should conclude our little talk. I would like you to become the best you can be, mentally and physically. For the rest of the trip, we will be sharing rooms together. I think you can use the guidance."

Uh-oh.

FORTY-FIVE

The Heart of Florence

Flying to Rome the next morning and taking the train to Florence thoroughly changed the world around me. I felt like we had switched the TV channel from ABC to PBS. I had never experienced life in a foreign language before and it was exhausting and overwhelming. I had to suddenly *think* more. I could not take anything for granted. I observed every action and heard every sound around me and struggled to remember the words and their meanings.

My brain found refuge in letting my eyes rest on the waiter at the pensione. The handsome Edoardo was an enigma, with one foot in the modern world and the other in a medieval feudal system. It was hard to tell what Edoardo actually felt about anything because his behavior toward the guests was old-world and deferential. The guests were always right and the servant's opinion was inconsequential. Since I spoke no Italian at the time, our conversations ended abruptly when we reached the end of his tiny list of English words. I learned *molto grazie* and used it much too often, usually in a nervous, obsequious gesture, as every conversation we had ended prematurely and awkwardly.

In his body and face, Edoardo was every bit a Florentine—and he was stunning. With a sharp blade of a nose, full red lips, and black hair that framed his face in waves, his likeness could be seen in frescoes all over Florence. I found him lurking in the background scene on a wall by Ghirlandaio. He peered out, amused, in the Uffizi, as a terracotta bust by Donatello. I even saw him in the face of Riccardo Muti, the dashing young director of the Florence Symphony. Edoardo's likenesses stood behind counters in shops selling fine leather goods, embroidered linens, and heavy mosaic tables. I saw them having after-dinner walks with male friends, arm in arm, sweaters thrown over their shoulders, slowly making their way through the crowd. Such dandies and so unafraid! Edoardo was everywhere.

I desperately wanted to talk to him about things other than historic churches and museums, but without a common tongue my desire was useless. I settled for eye contact as he maneuvered fried zucchini blossoms and lemons onto my dinner plate. The engaging expressions on his face were easily the most intriguing communication at mealtime. The teenagers in the group were hardly conversationalists. They had only college ahead and rebellion on their minds. That left Lee and me alone to glance awkwardly at each other across the table.

The Red Cross and Vanderbilt Hospital had assured me that if Charley did not do well they would call me back to Nashville. After three days of sharing a room with Lee and sitting across from him at dinner, I had begun to hope for a telegram.

Edoardo looked at me, and then carefully placed a flattened piece of brown breaded veal in the middle of my empty white plate. *I think he raised an eyebrow at me. Did he raise an eyebrow? He did, didn't he?* Suffering an absence of friendly contact and desperate for company, I began to confuse reality with wishful thinking. "Lei vuole un pezzo di limone, signore?" he politely asked. I looked into his face, smiled mischievously, and raised my own eyebrow. I tried to linger on the one syllable and carry it with meaning, "Siiii, Edoardo...per favore...one piece...and grazie mo-olto."

Later, in our room, Lee put down his Latin and looked at me with a knowing frown. "You're making a fool of yourself with the waiter. Keep it up and even the students will notice it."

"I don't know what you mean, Lee. I'm just being friendly."

"Don't be. Patrons do not behave like that. It looks foolish."

"I'm from a more democratic generation. He and I probably have more in common than you think."

"Don't be ridiculous, Yarrott. If indeed Edoardo is flirting with you, he's doing it purely out of a mercenary motive. He thinks you will give him a sizable tip when you leave. That's if he notices you at all."

"Lee, I really can't agree with you. But thanks for the advice." I rolled over on my bed and resumed reading my book *The Optimist's Daughter,* by Eudora Welty. I had started it on the plane. It reminded me of home.

The next day, my spirits improved when we visited the former villa of Bernard Berenson, the art historian. Villa I Tatti, as it is called, is situated on the outskirts of Florence, with terraced, manicured gardens. Breathing in the fresh air made everyone friendlier. The center of Florence had the grating energy of any large city. It was noisy, crowded, and anxiety-producing. Villa I Tatti felt a long way from that bustle—meditative, even. Lee had spent time in the rooms as an undergraduate at Harvard, after Berenson had made the house a center of study. As we walked through the first-floor rooms, he tossed off references to renowned art historians. Since I had just graduated with a degree in art history, I was acquainted with some of the names he quoted, such as Vasari, Sypher, Wittkower.

I spent time by myself, following tourists around the gardens of I Tatti and photographing them from behind. To me, the posture and clothing of the travelers was very telling. By what they wore and how they walked, people could seem world-weary or proud, satisfied or sad, confident or timid. I did not want to engage the people I photographed. I just wanted to look at them at a distance and preferably from behind.

We arrived back at Piazza della Republicca near the pensione in the late afternoon. A stagnant heat had settled on the city. Lee bought cans of Coca-Cola for everyone at a corner stand and we strolled slowly toward the pensione. He jabbed my side and pointed to the access alley running down the side of the building. A young man was helping a woman and a little girl into a small car. Picking up the child, he hugged her and kissed her, then handed her through the window to her mother in the car. It was Edoardo, and the woman appeared to be his wife, the child their daughter.

Under his breath, Lee said, "See? His family. Like I said. He only wants a larger tip from you, if he wants anything at all."

"Maybe you're right," I said.

It was the next morning that Lee suddenly performed his daily exercises in a jock strap and nothing else. Lying on the floor on his back, stretching his arms over his head, his long body took up the majority of the floor space. I stepped over him on my way to the bathroom and wondered why he suddenly had stopped wearing his gym shorts. He had the intensity of focus of a competitive diver about to bounce dramatically off the board, except that he was flat on the floor. With his knees locked and his feet pointed, he drew his legs up over his head and slowly continued his arc until his toes touched his fingers in the far distance. Given Lee's vast confidence, I could not take my eyes off his flabby, blushing ass hovering in the air over his otherwise bone-white body. I kept thinking that Plato did not quite have this in mind when he wrote about the glories of the male physique.

I acted as if nothing out of the ordinary had just happened and went about my business, folding maps and writing post-cards, except that I now sat at the desk, facing away from him.

At breakfast, I waited for Edoardo to bring us a plate of bread, butter, and preserves, but the signora brought it out instead. The waiter was nowhere to be seen.

"Buon giorno, miei amici! Spero una bella giornata. Have you fine things to do today?" She sang as she glided around the table, lowering in the center the ceramic pitchers of coffee and milk.

"Si, grazie," I said. "I would like to go to Santa Maria Novella today. I studied it in college."

"Oh, Signor Benz. That is a fine church. My parents were

married in one of the chapels. Look for the fresco of La Trinità by Masaccio. I was baptized beneath it. Tell me what you think of it tonight at dinner!" She moved to the other tables and continued her musical chatter with the teenagers.

"Wow, imagine that, Lee. I can't imagine that kind of family history."

Lee was not listening. After the signora was a safe distance away at another table, he whispered to me, "You may be wondering why I am no longer doing my exercises in my clothes."

I whispered back, "No, not at all. Do as you please." I was stunned that he'd opened the topic here, in the dining room, with others sitting at tables only a few feet away.

"I believe, and I am 100 percent certain of this, Yarrott, that you need proximity to a man's nakedness. I'm sure of it. You are so inhibited I find it appalling. You need to explore another man's flesh and I am the one to teach you."

I raised my voice and looked away from him. "You know, Lee, I have wanted to see Santa Maria Novella for the longest time, since I studied it four years ago."

"You are starving for physical touch. Aching for it. Look at you, so sadly rigid."

"Gosh, I can't believe that I'm actually going to see something of Alberti's today."

"Yarrott. Stop your nervous chatter and listen to me."

At that moment, something in me broke. Politeness, deference, passivity, whatever it was, it broke. "No, Lee," I shot back. "You have to listen to *me*." My mouth dried up and I stuttered, "Wha...what you do with your own body and your own nak...nakedness is your business, but do not involve me in it. I do not want to kn...know. You are the age of my fa...father. This is wrong. Ba...back off. Do you hear me?"

He paused for a long, terrifying moment. His normally white, remote face turned red and angry. "How dare you speak to me like that. Shall I remind you who is paying your way here?"

I was suddenly jealous of the teenagers at the other table, laughing with one another and oblivious to the machinations of a dirty old man. We had just finished our fourth week of the trip and had four more to go. I thought of all the people—besides Lee— who had worked hard to make the opportunity happen for me, like the doctors at Vanderbilt, the women at the Red Cross, but most especially Charley. He was risking his health, perhaps even his life, by taking the platelets of strangers from all over the United States. He was doing this to make sure that I got to see the world that this man was offering me.

The world with Lee Leffert had just become a place I had no interest in seeing.

FORTY-SIX

Closed Shutters

I remembered the conversation I had with Dad when he called me to his office. "Come on, Dad. I don't think there's anything to be worried about. Even if Lee did try to pull something on me that was sexual in nature, I can handle it. Don't you worry." I wished Dad were in Italy with me to stop this fiasco. I did not know what to do about Lee, his anger, and his mental manipulation. I did not know what to do about my expenses. I did not know how to change the plans that were already in motion. I felt scared, *very* scared.

Damn the smug man across the table from me. Damn the polished, arrogant man. Damn me for being so stupid. I should have known that this trip was too good to be true.

Heat rose off me in waves. I felt myself dripping with sweat under my shirt. I felt I was emotionally unhinged and about to use fists as my next ammunition. Lee's face was white again. His anger had subsided as mine had erupted. Carefully folding the linen napkin with my shaking hands, I dropped it on the table and stalked out of the dining room. I was sure, out of the corner of my eye, that the teenagers had seen me get upset. I passed the creeping glass elevator and hurried up the stone steps to our room to find my wallet and passport. The matching brocades of the bedspreads and drapery were no longer elegant, but conceited and authoritative. Down the corridor, the lingering scent of the potted gardenia had become funeral-sweet and sickening. I let the heavy glass door at the entrance slam behind me and angrily pushed through the crowded piazza, an ugly tangle of cameras, backpacks, and purses.

On a side street I had not used before I thought, *Good, let me get lost so I can finally be safe by myself.* Through residential neighborhoods I found my way to the wall around Florence, beyond which I could see hills in the distance and the white speck of Villa I Tatti.

Goddamn villa... Berenson, another ridiculous snob... Art history, a useless map for snot-nosed eggheads who want to humiliate me... I was definitely coming unhinged. Keep walking, Yarrott. Walk it off. Walk until you feel better, until you figure out what to do.

I calmed myself down by counting the doorways opening onto the narrow sidewalk. The noise of the ancient center was far behind me, but each time a scooter shot through the quiet street I jumped. Housewives by the dozens were leaving their apartments, swinging empty cloth sacks to shop at the big open market down the road. Passing the doorway of a corner store, I smelled the combination of fresh fruit and scented boxes of laundry detergent. It reminded me of home in Nashville, the security of my parents and the rational routines of each day when I lived with them. There *is* security found in the predictable. Dad left for the hospital at seven o'clock. Mother planned meals for the day. I headed off to class. I felt scattered now, at my wit's end with Lee on this trip. I was somersaulting in the air with no idea where I would land. *Keep your eye on the sidewalk, Yarrott. Walk, count, walk.* The streets were narrow and winding uphill. Laundry hung from the windows, big white sheets.

How would I cobble together the money for a room at another pensione? How would I buy a plane ticket to get home? How would I explain what had just happened? So many people were happy that I was finally getting a chance to leave Nashville, to not donate platelets for eight weeks, to see the world that I had studied in college. So many people sent me notes saying that this was my reward for being a dutiful son and brother. Walking, walking, it occurred to me that I had a duty to keep my mouth shut. If they knew what was going on here, they would be disgusted and horrified. My parents would see this as one more tremendous disappointment. One more problem that should have been something to celebrate. On a rustic hillside road with fields in front of houses and chickens in the fields, I could see Florence fanning out in the distance, a pale umber city under a blue sky. It stood static, quiet, and calm. It looked safe.

Maybe it wouldn't be so bad if I let Lee have his way. I can go home and not say anything about it to anyone. Who would know besides me? I wouldn't have to embarrass Mother and Dad or the Lefferts. No one would know. But how can I do those things with him? My God. He is a sixty-year-old man. But, technically, I am now an adult. Then why do I feel like I'm being molested? Aren't I too old to be psychologically damaged by the situation? I'll just have to take it in stride...like Jane Fonda in Klute. Remember? Jane reads her watch over the guy's back while she fakes an orgasm. That's it. That's how I'll do it.

At the moment Lee moved his hand across my leg, a screen unrolled across my eyes and Edoardo filled it completely. The hour spent that afternoon in the brocaded room with the shutters closed was spent with Edoardo on a beach along some coast of Italy. The shower I took afterward washed sand from my feet and salt from my hair.

That evening at eight o'clock promptly, I arrived in the dining room wearing my jacket and took my seat while Eduardo moved from table to table spooning out a delicate salmon risotto. When I caught his eye he smiled, as usual. I nodded and mouthed quietly, just to myself, "Grazie, Edoardo. Grazie, grazie molto."

FORTY-SEVEN

Remission

After four weeks of sharing hotel rooms with Lee, grimly lugging my baggage from England to Italy to Switzerland, the voyage was over and I returned home. The esteemed educator had finally quit the sexual chase with me once I capitulated that afternoon in Florence. From that point onward, his reaction was to seem innervated by the trip and uninspired by my company. I was relieved when I had completed the two months abroad without anyone else knowing about the true nature of the trip and its disastrous turn in Florence. Mother and Dad and Charley, the Lefferts, and all the people at the Red Cross could be happy for me that I had finally gotten my break from the platelet pheresis. Now I could forget about the damn trip and that damn Lee.

My introductory trip to Europe, with all of its psychological complexities and mixed feelings, brought with it an astonishing turn of events. Almost as soon as I returned in early August, Charley's blood counts, particularly his red cell and platelet counts, began to rise inexplicably. The doctors at first were stymied as to why, after so many years of zero production, his marrow would suddenly be stimulated to produce. After a few weeks, it became obvious that the exposure to one of the new platelet donors, one of the anonymous people who sent their blood while I was away in Europe, must have been the catalyst. What an extraordinary turn of events.

The rising of his counts continued gradually for three or four months, then leveled off at a subnormal but still safe level. During that period, I stopped giving platelets when it was obvious that Charley's counts were not dropping in the days after a donation. It was time for the doctors to draw some kind of a conclusion about what was happening. Charley and I held our breaths. Could this be the end to his disease?

Nobody before in medical history, certainly not with as profound a case of aplastic anemia as his, had lived anywhere close to the length of time Charley had, now going on seven years. There were no prior examples from which to gauge an outcome for him. Patients usually died within a matter of months, and if they were lucky enough to find a family donor with HLA compatibility, the donor usually turned bad after a few months because of the growth of antibodies by the recipient toward the donor. Charley and I were still the exception. A historic, completely unique exception.

Dr. David Jenkins, the medical director of the Nashville Red Cross, and Dr. Flexner, still the head of hematology at Vanderbilt, met with Charley and me in Dr. Jenkins's office and announced that they believed Charley was in a full-fledged remission, the permanence of which they could not estimate. Yes, it was a remission, a remarkable one, a seemingly miraculous remission, and it was not impossible that the remission might be permanent.

"We have already discussed this today with your father, who is, of course, thrilled. Charley, we believe you may have a long future ahead of you. Yarrott, we feel that you can make your own plans now." Doctors Jenkins and Flexner were red-faced and beaming, as if they were announcing in a news conference the successful splitting of conjoined twins—which, in a sense, they were.

Charley and I, not sure what to say to each other, drove back silently to Tyne Boulevard together to tell Mother the news. You would think that both of us would be screaming our brains out with hallelujahs. However, before that moment neither of us had allowed ourselves to think much about our future plans. We were unsure of our next steps. To be given orders now to make something of our lives left us speechless. I knew very broadly that I wanted to be an artist but I did not know in which media. My experience had ranged from poetry writing to filmmaking to sculpture, but I had studied nothing in depth. I had no clue how to approach a serious study of any of those fields. Charley was even more clueless than I.

"What are you thinking, brother?" I asked, reaching across the seat and tapping him on his shoulder. "Pretty cool, huh?"

"I dunno, Yarrott. I mean, what am I going to do for a living? I never finished my education. I don't even know what I'm interested in doing. To tell you the truth, this is making me feel pretty lame. Here I get my future back and I don't feel like celebrating. What kind of fucked-up shit is that?"

When we walked in the door, Mother already knew the doctors' conclusion. She immediately hugged Charley and held his face in her hands. A few moments later, she turned to me and started crying. "You've done so much for your brother. You're going to be rewarded in some way. Someday, someday."

A month later, Mother called me on the phone. "Can you talk to your brother, Yarrott? He's really angry and down. He wants to leave town, take off on his own, visit Mark and his other friends in Arizona, maybe live there, but Dr. Jenkins wants him to stay in town. The doctors really don't know what to expect in this remission and aren't sure if it's safe for him to move away on his own. Your father and I have talked to him but he sees us as law enforcers. We're just trying to do the best for him. Can you talk some sense into him?"

"I have no idea if I can, Mother, but I'll try." That morning, I called Charley at Joe's cabin, where he had been living for several weeks, since being given the news of his remission.

Joe answered the phone. "Hey, buddy, how you doing? Your brother? Man, he's been a beast lately. I don't get it. He's finally told he's well and then he hits the pits. Maybe it's all the dope he's been smoking. Maybe it's too strong for him and all this remission stuff is just too confusing."

"Can I talk to him?"

"Lemme see if he'll get up. Hold on."

In the background, I heard the Allman Brothers singing and a door creaking open. Joe had to coax Charley to the phone.

Groggy and annoyed, he put the receiver to his ear. "Yeah? Yarrott? What's up?"

"Hey. Mom wanted us to talk. Said you're feeling shitty. Something about Arizona and the doctors not letting you go out there. What a bummer. Want to get lunch today? Maybe see a movie?" I was genuinely concerned about him.

"Shit, Yarrott. Mom's right. I am really pissed. What do those guys expect of me, anyway? Fuck, if I can't live my life, what's the use of having it given back to me?"

Later, over lunch at a nearby coffee shop, Charley confessed, "Can you believe this? I'm finding now that I miss the people at the hospital. Our friends there. The staff. I miss them. I felt safe there. Now it feels like everybody's breathing down my back, waiting for me to make something of myself, grow into somebody."

"I know what you mean. I feel the same way," I replied.

"Hell. I never finished college and don't want to either. I really want to go out west to Arizona to see Mark. He's always writing that it's beautiful there, wide-open and clear. Sounds like a place where I could think and figure things out. But no, the doctors won't let me go. Fuck them."

"What do Mother and Dad say?"

"You know what they say. They agree with the doctors."

"What do you think you'll do?"

"Hell, I don't know. Part of me says if I don't take this chance, I might not get another one. But I don't want to be a fool, either, Yarrott. I guess I'll wait a while and see."

FORTY-EIGHT

Visual Merchandizing

Back at my own apartment later that day, I heard myself saying the same things as Charley. *I have to make some decisions. I have to act now. It's the middle of September and I still don't have a job. Since I got back from the trip, I've sat on my ass. I need to get a job. But doing what? What kind of job? Where? How?*

A friend had begun writing for the alumni office at Vanderbilt. She said they were still looking to fill two more positions. But she was an English major; she would know well how to write professionally. Did I, as an art history major? Was that even a relevant question? I applied for the job by writing a sample at home. As a test assignment, I was given a few pieces of background information on an alum and was then told to write a personalized letter to him requesting money to support a particular project. The letter I delivered to the alumni office the next day squarely failed the test. I was told it was terse, too direct, and it lacked charm of any kind. I would have alienated a potential donor.

Damn. Now what?

I had no idea how people my age operated once out of college. How do they get jobs? How do they know what they are capable of doing? How do they know what they want and aim toward a career?

Another one of life's blind spots fell right smack in my line of vision. Dad and Mother began to nag me about looking for work, but I didn't know where to begin. Should I go back to the restaurant and cook or wait on tables? Should I take care of people's yards? I had no other training. I had my menial experiences and then I had what I thought was damn good taste. What was *that* worth? How do you make *that* count?

The network news with Walter Cronkite complained nightly about the country's rising unemployment and something called a recession. Well, that was just great timing for all of us just coming out of college. Even if I *were* trained sufficiently in anything, the Ford administration declared that there would be no jobs for us anyway.

But I had to find a job and pay my own bills. Dad was standing over me tapping his feet, more impatient by the week.

Another childhood friend, Jeff, had recently started working at the biggest department store in the city, Cain-Sloane. There were several branches across town. Jeff said that the store gave entrance tests on the first Saturday of every month. *Maybe I could do something there. Maybe I could take the test and pass it and see where they could use me.*

I put on a suit and drove to the back entrance of Cain-Sloane in Green Hills, just two miles up the road from my apartment. It had been the store my family always did our Christmas shopping at. I always seemed to run into my parents' friends there and because of that could never buy anything secretly. What would it be like to work there and wait on my parents and their friends? I could not turn a corner in Nashville without running into an old family friend. I could not swear in public without someone hearing it and raising an eyebrow.

I found the classroom behind the employee cloakroom in the basement and took a seat at a Formica-topped desk, among twelve other individuals, some dressed up as if for church and some looking tattered, like they were straight out of prison. The starchly coiffed red-haired lady handing out the test saw my name and asked flatly and loudly, "Are you one of Dr. Benz's sons?"

"Yes, ma'am, I am."

Licking her thumb while passing out papers, the dour lady suddenly smiled. "Well, hon, you tell him hello from Nancy Gitts. He's been my doctor for thirty years."

No one looked at my test. I was hired on the spot and placed in the housewares department as a salesman, with a plastic tag that read *Mr. Benz—Housewares*. In the blink of a eye, I was giving people refunds on coffeemakers and hauling boxes of cookware to station wagons. I was polishing a pyramid of wine glasses every morning and counting the cash in the register at night. I was listening to housewives complain about their pressure cookers and inserting credit card numbers in machines for approval. And I totally rearranged all of the display tables. All the while I tried to avoid the glare of Miss Boxer, the sixty-year-old pantsuit presiding over Personnel. Also known by the employees as Boxhead, she was easily seen across the store, swaddled on top in a stiff cloud of lacquered hair. Whenever I saw her blonde coiffure touring the aisles out of the corner of my eye, I miscounted change, misdialed credit card numbers, froze up the register, and infuriated the customers with misinformation. Boxhead saw my mistakes and she was not one to suffer an employee's incompetence for long. She called me into her office.

"I see that you have some trouble with keeping your cool, Mr. Benz. We can't have that."

"Yes, ma'am. I do get easily flustered."

"Well, you have a choice here. I don't like you in Housewares. You stink as a salesman."

"Ma'am? Sorry, ma'am." My obsequious face turned red and I felt the heat rising from my shirt.

"But Housewares has never looked better, so I'm promoting you to Display, only it's now called Visual Merchandising. VM for short. Right? Go see Mr. Davis, who will be your director." She waved me out of her office, "Don't just stand there, go on over to Display."

I reported to a large studio at the end of the corridor, where the freight elevators were located. Crystal Gayle was crying out "Brown Eyes Blue" on a tape deck as I pushed through the double swinging doors looking for Mr. Davis.

"You sure you should be in here wearing your nice suit?" A solicitous voice came from a wooden rack suspended from the ceiling high over my head. The smell of spray paint, sawdust, and coffee gave the studio a chaotic air, like a backstage party. I heard the slapping of feet landing on the concrete and jerked around to meet Mr. Davis face to face. "You the guy from Housewares?" He looked me up and down, smiled, and held out his hand. "I'm Tim."

Mr. Davis was lean and handsome, a mustachioed guy seven or eight years older than me, in his late twenties. He wore snug blue jeans and a striped European shirt, tailored tightly up the back. His brown hair was carefully blown dry and swept over his ears like Julio Iglesias. He was friendly and he was bathed in Aramis.

"My, my, Old Boxhead sent over a real cutie. She said you had a real nice way with setting out merchandise. We can always use that around here. Your name is kind of strange. How do you pronounce it?"

"It's like carrot, but with a Y."

"Oooh. Sounds German. Kinda mean. I *love* it. Grrrrr..." He made an Eartha Kitt sound and pressed a shoulder into me.

I stepped back from him stiffly and laughed awkwardly at his joke.

"Listen, cutie," he said, suddenly dropping his grin, "let's get something understood, right from the get-go. I'm gay and don't mind showing it. Will you have a problem with that?"

"No. Uh, not at all. I'm actually gay, too."

"No, *really?*" He batted his eyes facetiously.

"I'm just not very out. That's all."

"Well, honey, I am and I'm proud of it." He picked a piece of sawdust off my shoulder.

"Gee, that's great. Really. It's just that my parents and their friends and their friends' friends come here to shop and I haven't told anybody about me. So, I'm quiet about it, okay?"

"Okay. Okay, I get it. Let's see what you can do with design."

For the next several months Tim Davis showed me how to use a band saw to cut out any shape and lay down layers of plastic and plywood and silver Mylar with a spray can of adhesive. We made signs and partitions and assembled sample tables and dressed mannequins. We climbed ladders at Christmas and covered the entire world in fake greenery and red lights. Every time I saw a friend of my parents' in the aisles, I darted out of sight and remained anonymous in my world of cheap decor.

To the Cain-Sloane store, Tim Davis was a miracle worker, a magician with glitter and paint. He could draw blood from a plastic arm. With mannequins he could assemble in ten minutes the finest dressed circle of women in Nashville. He was reptilian-quick with his hands, his eyes, and his wit. The man missed absolutely nothing, not the smallest detail, especially in the goings-on around the men's restroom on the fourth floor.

I had not known that men's rooms in department stores were understood the world over to be watering holes for thirsty cowboys, and that they inspired countless innuendos and euphemisms. When Tim Davis pointed it out, I could not believe what I saw. I saw ministers and school principals exchanging sleazy nods with all walks of life, all heading in the direction of the northwest corner of the fourth floor. Much of the time, Tim snorted with delight at his snippy deductions, but occasionally he would suddenly be overcome with a deadpan face and he, too, would disappear into that corner for a half hour. I would be left holding a detached arm and a cowl-neck sweater.

Several times I met Charley for lunch at the Captain D's across the parking lot. Once he asked me what the guy I worked with was like and I crunched the ice in my tea and wondered how I could answer. "He's ...I dunno, a little demanding, a little scattered, a little..."

"*Flighty?*" Charley added with a raised eyebrow and a sneer.

"You mean by that *queer?*" I asked.

"Well, you said it. I didn't."

"Would that matter, Charley?"

"Shit, yeah. You wanna work alongside some perverted asshole?"

"Is that what you call Angela?"

"Don't start on that one, Yarrott."

Our voices began to rise and we both stopped the conversation abruptly and focused on our fried fish sandwiches.

FORTY-NINE

Looking to the North

The days passed slowly at Cain-Sloane. I was much too self-conscious to be dressing mannequins. Often I had to change their clothes in front of passersby, my hand stuck up a lady's skirt in the sportswear department, and the shame of having played in my mother's clothes as a four-year-old still stung me. Being a college-educated, liberal minded, world-traveled sophisticate, I saw this display work as demeaning. Embarrassing and humiliating. Was I not better than this?

I decided that I needed to go to graduate school. I needed better stimulation and training. I believed that I had something, a talent or a way of seeing that was special, and it would never be developed while working in a department store. I figured the choice should be between filmmaking, creative writing, and sculpture, all three of which I had some experience with at Vanderbilt. I settled on sculpture. After quickly looking around for programs in fine arts, I chose three to which I would apply: Rhode Island School of Design, Columbia University, and University of Pennsylvania. My criteria were vague and irrational. I picked RISD because I had heard from Draper that it was simply the best art school in the country. I chose Columbia because it was in New York City and the program sounded abstract and intellectual and I wanted to think of myself in those terms. And finally, I applied to University of Pennsylvania for no other reason than Melissa Cannon, my favorite teacher out of my four years of college, did her doctorate in English there. I knew nothing of the graduate sculpture program. I foolishly believed that all of the graduate programs in an Ivy League school would be consistently competent. It was a risk and a dare—but graduate school was my ticket out of Nashville. It did not matter much to me if the program was solid or not. I convinced myself that I would make any experience worthwhile. I just needed to get out of the shadow of home and breathe.

Mother and Dad offered to contribute to my expenses for graduate school, as long as the program lasted just two years. Beyond that, "You're completely on your own." I figured I could cobble together student loans and maybe a scholarship to make ends meet. I did not care how I did it, as long as I did it.

Tim Davis began calling me The Professor once he learned that I planned to leave Cain- Sloane in the fall for graduate school. He began treating me with kid gloves, no longer as just any gay kid up for grabs. He said I was going to become something bigger, more polished and more important. He said my weird name would mean something one day. Each week he gave me bigger design assignments, and he took over all the mannequin-changing himself. He encouraged me to take some risks with the designs and see how far I could get before one of the store managers reined me in. Tim seemed to delight in knowing that one of us would not be tethered to the store much longer.

I made early March appointments for interviews with all three graduate schools and flew to New York to use Eddy's apartment as a base. Following his instructions, I nervously took a taxi from La Guardia airport to the Pan Am building and met Eddy and my violinist friend from high school, Connie, at the Copter Club on the top floor. The dazzling lights of Midtown shone up like stage lights in our faces and my heart raced with the possibilities that seemed to spread out in front of me.

Since taking the job at the Albert Einstein College of Medicine, Eddy had been renting an apartment in a new high-rise across the street from his lab. The building overlooked what was in 1977 one of the worst slums in the United States. In the sun's morning blaze from the thirty-fourth floor, the South Bronx lay scrambled at our feet, but from that height most of the ugliness was transformed into a fascinating gray and green quilt. From the apartment I took a subway to Grand Central, where I boarded Amtrak to Providence one day and Philadelphia the next. By the end of the week, I was beginning to adapt to mass transit on the East Coast and I could feel an outer shell beginning to harden around me as I navigated through the crowds of the graffiti-smothered cars. *I can do this. I can become as tough as anyone and as quick as anyone.*

When I returned after the three interviews in the Northeast, I felt a gathering of support and vicarious curiosity from many people at the store. Surprisingly, Miss Boxhead had become solicitous and almost wistful in her questioning. It was as if going to the North had been a goal or at least an abiding curiosity for most people there, but had always been thwarted. Graduate school no longer seemed a possibility but a certainty, despite the fact that I had not been accepted yet to any school. It was no longer *if* Yarrott were going, but *when.*

The first letter arrived and it was from Columbia, a simple half-page form letter politely stating my rejection. The next day, a second letter arrived, this one from RISD, again a rejection. By that time, I was certain that my studio portfolio from college, saddled with my uneven grades, had buried the chance of any school accepting me. I began to brace myself for a humiliating back-pedaling at the store. I had all but given my resignation, so confident I had been of moving away.

Finally, after several more days of waiting, a thick letter arrived from the University of Pennsylvania. I tore it open in the vestibule of my apartment building. Yes, I had been accepted; my escape to the East Coast was now a certainty. In the time it took to open an envelope, Nashville and home, Charley and his bone marrow, once as static as solid rock to me and as permanent, had instantly become ephemeral matter, provisional, to be carried away by time and wind. I had been living in the final days of my childhood and had not known it. Everything usual, accustomed, and familiar had just become my past life.

FIFTY

Iced Tea and Tears

The noon sun was bright and dry overhead. The day had given us a rare break from the humidity that normally hangs over Nashville in the summer. I pulled into the restaurant parking lot next to Charley's red truck. He was leaning against it with a smile, waiting. He gave me a big hug, squeezed my biceps, and stood back to see me in my loose khakis and white T. "You're looking damn good, little brother." He wore a denim work shirt, Levi's with a big silver buckle, and his handsome squared-off boots. Charley was fresh from his rented cabin on a farm outside Nashville in Williamson County. He looked relaxed. His usual gray pallor had been replaced by a dark tan. Geronimo was back.

"Hey, you too," I said. "Get a load of that buckle. Man, that is fine."

"Yeah, Joe gave it to me. I like the one he wears so he went out and bought me one, too. Groovy, huh? Listen, I'm really glad you could make lunch again today."

The restaurant was busy so we took a number and sat on the benches in the foyer. The lunch crowd in the Vanderbilt area was always swamping the local eateries on the weekdays. This place was noisy with high-strung students and gregarious businesspeople.

"Look at those fat suits over there," he said under his breath to me. "Damn, could they get any wider? That guy's tie is so tight he looks like he's just been hanged."

I laughed and turned around in the seat to face him, then asked, with a concerned look, "Is there anything special that prompted you to invite me to lunch?"

"Not really, little brother. I just realized I hadn't seen you in a while and you'll be leaving in a few months."

"Hey," I said, "that's great. I'm really glad you called."

The hostess came over and led us to our table. We both ordered iced tea and medium-rare steaks, with half heads of lettuce and blue cheese dressing. We ate the soft yellow dinner rolls while we waited for our meals.

"How's the job at the store? You ready to leave it?" he asked.

"And how. I know I've only been there nine months, but it feels like my graduation from Vanderbilt was five years ago. I keep telling myself that a degree ought to amount to something more meaningful than a job at Cain-Sloane. Can you imagine, me, Mr. Benz of Housewares? I can tell you all the colors and prices of Le Creuset cookware. Man, did I waste time this past year or what?"

He answered quickly, "No, you didn't. I'll agree that it's not the best place for you, but, hell, it's been a job. Now you've got a whole new chapter coming up. So don't whine about the past year. Besides, you might not have figured out grad school if you had found a job you really liked."

"Hey, when did you get to be so wise?"

"Come on. Seven years of aplastic anemia *ought* to give a person some wisdom."

"You think?"

"Shit, yeah. Sitting back and watching the world turn around you while you're stuck in one place—that kind of perspective has got to give a person some kind of wisdom, if the person doesn't kill himself first."

"Charley, I don't know how you did it. You've been through so much."

"*We've* been through so much, Yarrott."

"And Mother and Dad."

"Yeah, and Mother and Dad. I tell you, when I think about what they've been through with me, I get choked up."

"You? I thought you were hard as a tack. Never cried. You're all man."

222

"Whatever *that* means, Yarrott. A few days ago I drove over to see them. I wanted to tell them something flat-out in case I never had the opportunity again. Mom was there by herself. I took her for a drive around Radnor Lake and stopped the car at the overlook. I told her how much I loved her and how much I was grateful for them and I just broke down all over the place. It was actually kind of funny. She looked really uncomfortable and said 'Why, Charley, you don't have to tell me that.' I felt like an idiot, but I could tell it meant a lot to her. She reached over, grabbed my hand, and kissed it."

Our meals arrived and the waitress set the wood and metal steak platters in front of us. They were sizzling. She ladled out the dressing on our iceberg lettuce.

"Yarrott, one of the reasons I asked you to eat lunch with me was because I want to tell you something, too." He put down his knife and fork and took a gulp of tea. "I've not been very good about being up front with my feelings with you. I've been really hard on you. I've really been a selfish asshole. But you've got to know that I really, *really* appreciate you being there for me, at the hospital, at home, listening to me moan and complain. All these years. You've been great. I want you to know that I appreciate it from the bottom of my heart." His lip trembled and he took a deep breath.

I froze in mid-chew and stared at him. I thought of the time I had turned my back on him when Angela came out to them and he wanted to talk to me. I could not be that cold asshole now. I owed it to both of us to listen, to look at him in the eye, and to respond, no matter how uncomfortable I felt. I said, "Well, ol' bud. Thanks for telling me."

"I want what's best for you, Yarrott. You've been stuck here with me and you deserve to be off in the world making art and enjoying yourself. You have a lot to give and you can't do it here." He was letting a tear creep down his face in plain view.

Why couldn't I cry, too? This was the moment of closeness with Charley I had been wanting for years, but now that it was here I had an unemotional, detached feeling. I thought the

223

right response would have been to get weepy all over my steak and salad and to blurt out "It was nothing. I'd do it again for you." I owed it to him to cry back. All I could think was *Damn, I'm a lot more like Mother than I thought.* I held my iced tea glass in my hand and said, "Well, big brother, this means the world to me. Thank you." Then I took a long gulp of tea.

Over his piece of pecan pie, Charley cleared his throat again. "Is there anything at all I can do to help you with your move to Philadelphia? Money, packing, anything?"

"Really? Well, I don't know how I'm ever going to get my car up there if I rent a truck. I guess I'll leave it down here and drive it back when I come down for Christmas."

"You don't have to do that, Yarrott. Why don't you let me drive you in my truck? We can load up the back and hitch the car to it. It'll be a cinch."

"Charley, damn, that would be great! What a life-saver."

"It's the least I can do, little brother."

FIFTY-ONE

Images in the Mirror

He passed me the joint without taking his eyes off the road. The red pickup pulling my blue VW was just past Knoxville on I-40. He was singing "Ramblin' Man" along with the Allman Brothers tape in the cassette player, singing as loud as he could into the wind. I coughed on the smoke and joined him. This same song used to excite me, with its anxious guitar and high-pitched vocals. I always thought of Charley and Joe when I heard it. If ever there were two boys who were born to ramble, it was those two. Hearing it now, on my way to the Northeast Corridor, skipping out on Nashville, the Allman Brothers left me feeling really empty, bluer than blue, especially with the dope in my head. *I'm the ramblin' man now, finally leaving in the dust all the shit that trapped me: Old Boy Nashville, homophobia, illness, my whole family. So why am I so blue? Family. That's it. Family. This song is telling me that I am leaving my whole family behind. The first chord of it, the first line of "Ramblin' Man" whines like a turbine and blasts you like a hot gust of wind. Why do we have to be listening to The Allman Brothers now? They hurt like hell.*

I looked over at Charley. He was focused straight ahead, holding the wheel with just the wrist of his right hand, the way a lot of guys do it in Nashville. I never got the hang of it. I always needed to feel the security of at least one hand holding the wheel. *Okay, I'm a Nervous Nellie. God, Charley is so damn... competent. Driving this big load of furniture while pulling my car and without even one hand gripping the wheel. I am such a pussy.*

I looked at myself in the side mirror on the door of the truck. Even with my biceps pressed on the doorframe they don't come close to the size of Charley's. And he's been sick for seven years.

What I am going to do without him?

I looked at the similarities in our faces, the large lips and narrow jaws. Man, sometimes we really look like brothers. We've made such a big deal about being different, but look at the similarities. You can see them a mile away.

I'm going to miss him more than I realized. I didn't think he would matter to me one bit. I thought getting away from him was the best thing I could do for myself. I hadn't planned on missing him. Fuck...I hadn't planned on this.

I thought I hated him. All the times he beat on me, made me feel like a turd. I hated him. Or so I thought. What about all the platelets? Didn't that prove how much I cared? Hell, no! Giving him blood gave me an opportunity to look good. That was all. Or so I thought. What's this now? I'm realizing how much I care about him NOW?

A cold sweat settled on the back of my neck. From Tri-Cities, Tennessee, to Radford, Virginia, I could think only of what my life would be like without Charley in it. I felt my stomach stirring and gritted my teeth. I looked over at him, keeping time with the music by nodding his head. *He is completely unaware of what I'm thinking. Will he miss me, too?*

"Hey, big brother! Let me ask you a question."

"Sure. Fire away."

"Remember that time you beat me up after seeing *Bullitt?*"

"At Christmas, Hundred Oaks Mall? Yeah, what about it?"

"You sorry about it?"

After a moment pondering the question, Charley nodded his head slowly. "Yes and no. You were a little shit then, so you had it coming to you. So, no, I don't regret that. But the fact that that little shit became the person you are now bothers me. I mean, you turned out to be a really good guy. I regret it if you are still hurt by it. Are you? Still hurt by it?"

"What was so bad about that kid a long time ago? Was he really so bad?"

"That guy was a little shit, Yarrott. A little shit that fought with a nasty tongue."

"He wouldn't have been such a shit if he had felt he had anyone on his side. Hell, look what I had to go through! I was at Montgomery Bell and nothing looked good to me. You were a big bully from day one!"

A sudden anger intensified until we were on the verge of arguing and swerving off the road. Instead, we looked at each other and started laughing. "Guess some things we can't talk about, huh?" Charley said. He put his arm over the seat and squeezed my shoulder. "Let's put it away for good, okay?"

"Amen." I looked in the mirror again and watched, even sadder, as the two white lines on either side of the road converged in the distance behind us.

FIFTY-TWO

Stigmatas

I had asked Charley to drive me to Philadelphia three weeks before the semester began so I could acclimate to a new world. My first weeks there meant swimming upstream against some bewildering currents. I had to remember each day just why I had decided to move to Philadelphia in the first place. *Jesus, I'm on a satellite orbiting nowhere. I don't have any reason to be here.* I was not even sure what or where my purpose was anymore. Charley no longer needed me.

But Yarrott, you stupid fuck! You've fantasized about this moment a million times! I was lost. I stood paralyzed at the edge of a huge hole left by my missing family. The depth of the sadness shocked me. I thought of Draper just ninety miles away in New York. He would be making the rounds of bars and clubs and parties those same August nights. He would be laughing and dancing and fooling around. But me? I drank myself to sleep in my apartment every night. *What's wrong with me?* I was lost.

When the program at Penn finally began in September, I hungrily grabbed hold of the structure that it mandated. Outside of classes, students were expected to work in their own studios at school, from nine A.M. until five P.M. School gave me a full-time occupation and an instant community and I was relieved beyond words.

Since I was no longer donating platelets, I wanted the needle scars to disappear from my arms. When I looked down at them, I felt an automatic lump in my stomach, a sensation of being trapped, oppressed, and with an unidentifiable anger building up. I called them my stigmatas, where I was nailed to the cross. Occasionally someone would remark about them, and say I did not look like the usual junkie with my athletic build and rosy cheeks. Just explaining the scars brought back the lump in my stomach, so I would change the subject fast. When I traveled to Europe in the summer of 1976, I took a letter from the American Red Cross explaining the scars, in case I was ever stopped under suspicion of drug use. That never happened, and now I know that my scars looked nothing like a junkie's. The eight hundred raised dots in the skin were fairly orderly and piled on top of each other. On one arm they formed a Y shape about an inch and a half long, and on the other arm, an elongated I shape.

During my first Christmas back home from Philadelphia, I asked my father to surgically remove the scars. At first he refused, but after I persisted he obliged me one Sunday afternoon in his office, with my childhood friend Jeff keeping me company and watching the procedure. Under local anesthesia, Dad performed a plastic surgery procedure on each arm called a Z-plasty. First, he cut out the scarred tissue, exposing the veins. Next, he made a one-and-a-half-inch-long Z-shaped incision around the gaping hole and pulled the skin back together by slightly twisting and closing the Z. Ideally, this procedure removes a wide area of skin while leaving a fine hairline scar with no puckering. Jeff helped Dad hold the instruments and apply pressure where needed as long as he could, until he suddenly sat down, white-faced.

Keeping his cool, Dad said, "Put your head between your knees, Jeff. You'll feel better in a minute. I can handle the rest." Dad was now using both hands equally, reaching with his left for instruments over his right, which was pressing down on the wound.

Between his knees, Jeff moaned, "You sure, Dr. Benz? Sorry I wussed out."

"Don't worry about it. I've got it. Just take care of yourself, son."

Dad worked quickly, quietly, and efficiently. He softly explained each step and asked me if I wanted to watch, which

I declined. The whole thing was finished in thirty minutes, just as the anesthesia began wearing off, with one arm sewn back together with fifteen sutures and the other with twenty. The bandages wrapping around my arms made it impossible to bend them. "But, Dad, how will I travel back to school or smoke or write if I can't bend my arms?"

"Don't be silly. Tomorrow morning, I'll change the bandages and put on smaller ones. By the time you leave they will be glorified Band-Aids. And, good, I hope it does make it hard for you to smoke."

Back in Philadelphia the day after Dad removed the stitches, I found it increasingly difficult and painful to straighten out my arms in the mornings when I awoke. As it turns out, wounds in such elastic and bendable locations of the limbs are usually painful because of the healing occurring when the skin is at rest and the limb is folded. When the skin is stretched upon waking, the pain is excruciating. It was so every morning for months afterward. As it happens, I learned that my skin tends to keloid or overheal, leaving thick, ropey scars. Unfortunately, the intended hairline scars we aimed for ultimately became almost as wide as what was removed.

Right after I returned to Philadelphia from the Christmas break, I wandered into a meeting of a group called Gays at Penn one night on campus. With my heart pounding in my ears, I was introduced to a handsome and wild-haired anthropology graduate student from Temple University, named Mike. The romance became full-fledged later that month—on January 18, 1978, to be exact.

Center City was under three inches of snow, and another six were expected that night. Around the corner from Mike's apartment on Chestnut Street was a theater showing the first run of *Saturday Night Fever*. It was Saturday night. I was with not only a man with brains, but the best-looking one I had ever met in my life—a combination of Kris Kristofferson and Timothy Bottoms. I had the crush of my life on him, and from all indications he was interested in me, too. No arm incisions were going to keep me from wrapping them around this man—if he wanted me to.

I remember every minute in the theater as the snow fell outside. We brushed knees lightly and then brushed them harder. *Damn, that was no accident!* Then we brushed our hands together and let them stay. This did it. This one moment, this cue of mutual interest, was no accident either. Finally, Mike wrapped his warm fingers around my hand and we smiled at each other in the flickering light.

The next morning I woke up to a searing pain. Sometime during the night, my right arm had curled around Mike and was now stuck under the weight of his torso. I'd wanted us to wake up in a tranquil snowstorm, a romantic Sunday morning after our first night together. Instead, my arm was on fire under a man I hardly knew but wanted to impress. I rocked him back and forth slowly to pull my arm out, but woke him up. He moaned happily and rolled over to face me, putting additional weight on the arm. "Listen, Mike, can I ask you to sit up for a second? My arm's killing me. Please?"

I ran to the bathroom and pressed a cold washcloth on the incision, which was oozing blood from a scab. Counting all the cuss words I could think of in my head, I tapped my foot until the pain subsided. Mike stood in the doorway, puzzled and concerned.

"Hey, what's up with your arm, babe?"

He called me babe! My soul lit up, my heart skipped a beat, and my face turned red.

"I guess I should tell you about something that occurred in my past. No, no, not *that.* I'm not a drug addict!" I stood at Mike's bathroom sink and told him about the seven years with Charley in Nashville, keeping him alive with my platelets. He rested his hand on my shoulder as I recounted the years leading up to the remission and the recent surgery to remove the needle marks. When I finished, I looked at Mike's face; his lips were partly open and his eyes worried.

"Are you okay? I mean, after all those years, are you okay?"

"Strong as an ox. A very healthy ox."

Mike lifted my arm to his face and planted a kiss right on the incision. "Better now?

"You have no idea how much better."

FIFTY-THREE

A Serious Artist

For the next three years in graduate school, I was plugged into a system that had a defined goal, not to mention a beginning and an end. I could finally concentrate on being independent from Nashville and get on with my life.

While the focus of Penn's sculpture department was abstract formalism, in the 1950s vein of its department chair, Robert Engmann, we were still expected to continue studying figurative work on the side. I loved working with nude models. It made me feel that I was reeducating myself. Hanging out in a room with a nude person all day made me feel like I was catching up sexually with everybody else. I learned to talk to a naked man or woman and not turn red.

I believed I was a serious artist. With my mother's serious scowl, I would direct the model, "Please raise your arm for me. Thank you. Now, if you would, please twist and touch your shoulder. Yes, that's it. Thank you."

Purely formal work came easily to me. I was praised for it and felt proud of it. In the next two years, I departed into an increasingly minimalist visual language. At times, I would stand back and look at my accumulating work and wonder where its content was. My sculpture was beautiful and had a certain powerful dynamism to it, but it was obsessed with formal surface, and whether in stone, wood, clay, or plaster, carving the edges, contours, volumes, and textures satisfied me. There was nothing narrative in it. No stories. No conflicts. No life or death. No emotional tension.

On Sundays, Mike and I made pancakes and read *The New*

York Times. One day, I was feeling completely relaxed with him in our apartment and it felt a safe time for a confession. I put the paper down and explained that I had always struggled with nervous tics.

He looked up for a second and said, "Babe, what are you talking about? I've never noticed you twitching or anything." He continued his reading then looked up again. "Well, maybe occasionally. Just a little thing here and there. That's all."

Man, have I come a long way. I can even talk about it now without wanting to die. This is good. I'm hardly ticking at all.

FIFTY-FOUR

Sixteen Hours with Noguchi

"Why don't we invite Isamu Noguchi to speak?" I asked. "Are you nuts? He won't come *here*." My suggestion sounded ludicrous to Rick and he immediately dismissed it with a smirk. The other committee members of the lecture series chuckled. "You'd better come up with somebody more realistic, Yarrott."

"You architects are so easily cowed," I said, half joking. "I'm going to write him anyway. We've got nothing to lose, for Christ's sake."

"Okay, but have a backup speaker. You're going to need it."

There were four of us on the graduate school lecture series committee at the University of Pennsylvania—Rick, the committee chair, and the student representatives from the departments of architecture, urban planning, and fine arts. In my final year in the program, I volunteered as the fine art rep, thinking it might be a good way to spend time with students of the other disciplines. My colleagues in sculpture and painting were typically sequestered in their small studios all day, all year, while the architects and urban planners were out mixing in the world, getting internships and learning about their professions from practical points of views.

I had no clue what I was going to do after I graduated with a master's degree in sculpture in a few months. My friends studying architecture made me feel more hopeful about finding work and making sense of my education. The sculptors and painters seemed continually overwhelmed by the idea of making a living.

While a student at Penn, I spent a few hours each afternoon poring over big illustrated books on sculpture in the fine arts library. Unlike my dark, hidden oasis at Vanderbilt, the fine arts library at Penn was housed in a spectacular landmark building, had a world-class collection, and was usually full of students.

One of the most famous living artists in the world, Isamu Noguchi had just published an autobiography, A *Sculptor's World*, and a fellow graduate student, Jill, someone with whom I always had an easy rapport, came over to my table and dropped it in front of me.

"Here. I think you should read this. Something about your work reminds me of his."

It immediately gripped me. Elegantly simple, he described a difficult childhood, being torn between the cultures of Japan and the United States. I was inspired by his ingenuity and his hard-won self-confidence. Born in 1904, one year earlier than Lillian Hellman, he rose out of the same era as she, of world wars, immense social change, and artistic experimentation. Noguchi's childhood was at times Dickensian in its bleakness, as he was shuttled around the world, abandoned by his single American mother, and rejected by his Japanese father. Despite those abuses during key formative years, his creativity soared. I found in his story the proof that one can accomplish anything, given enough will. He was the archetypal survivor.

I composed a straightforward letter of invitation to Noguchi and sent it in January. After two weeks, I had not heard a reply, so I placed a call to his studio in New York.

After one ring, a velvet-smooth male voice answered, "Yes, hello."

"May I please speak to Mr. Noguchi?"

"Speaking."

I had expected to speak only with an assistant or, worse, be turned away completely. I was not expecting to actually talk with the famous man. My mouth immediately dried up. I hoped I would make some sense.

Politely, but coldly, Noguchi said, "I'm sorry, Mr. What-did-you-say-your-name-was? I don't remember receiving your letter. Even if I had received it, I am quite sure I could not possibly speak at your school. You see, I am busy with three upcoming exhibitions this spring. So sorry, but best of luck to you."

The conversation had ended as abruptly as it had begun. After putting down the receiver, I saw my hands shaking and I was suddenly freezing. I had spoken to the great Isamu Noguchi and lived to tell about it. As expected, he would not come to Penn.

I did not bother to tell the lecture committee that they were right. Instead, I went to the second artist on my list of speakers, Alex Katz, the New York figurative painter who had often appeared as a critic for the painting department. I was sure I would not be turned down and I was correct.

Two weeks before the date of Katz's lecture, the painter called me at school in the morning to report that he had injured his knee and that he was canceling all engagements for the next month. Katz was sorry, but would not be able to make it after all. I berated myself for getting involved with the lecture series. All the experience was giving me was heartburn. Later the same day, the secretary in the dean's office called to say a letter had come for me and I needed to come get it.

"Who's it from?"

"Let's see. On the back, believe it or not, it says Isamu Noguchi, 4882 Vernon Boulevard, Long Island City, New York. Do you know Noguchi?"

"Well, I spoke to him once when I invited him two months ago to speak. It's probably his formal response telling us no. I'll pick it up in the next day or so."

Two days later, the secretary called to remind me to pick it up. I ran across campus and found it on her desk. Walking back to my studio, I opened it, expecting the polite decline of our invitation. It read:

Dear Mr. Benz,

I am assured that I did not respond to your kind invitation, so I would like to accept. I am available to speak on May 1. Please advise.

Sincerely,

Isamu Noguchi

I ran immediately to the room in the architecture building where I could find my colleagues on the lecture committee and, after pausing to collect myself and slow down my breathing, I walked nonchalantly into their studio and placed the letter on the table. "See, guys. It never hurts to aim high."

I watched Rick's reaction as he read the letter and mouthed the words "Oh, my God."

On the morning of May 1, I drove my blue VW to 30th Street Station and found Isamu Noguchi standing on the curb with his girlfriend, a striking young brunette named Nizette, also a sculptor. Having seen his image countless times in the media, it was strange having the real thing riding around in my jumpy little car. He looked much younger than I was expecting a seventy-five-year-old man to look. He was small and lean, with smooth skin and a nearly bald buzz cut. He wore comfortable but expensive casual clothes, a tailored tan leather jacket, and tan leather lace-ups. He carried a sleek black valise holding his carousel of slides, which he laid on the back seat next to Nizette. He looked, at most, fifty years old; he had a quick spring in his step and a strong, steady voice. I thought of my father, seven years his junior, and how much older, frailer, and whiter my father seemed.

Noguchi showed interest in each student's work. He was neither patronizing nor dismissive. Rather, he spent a comfortable amount of time in each cell-like cubicle, listening and asking questions and occasionally offering suggestions. After five or six of these visits, my brain was tired, but he continued for fifteen critiques. In the meantime, I talked with Nizette and learned that she was a stone carver and had worked for a time in Pietra Santa on the western coast of Italy, where she and Noguchi had met. She had lived a life I wanted: traveling while doing her art, in a community of artists sharing their ideas. She reminded me of a young Georgia O'Keeffe with her fine-featured face and graceful, strong body.

After the last student, Noguchi turned to me and said, "Let's get that drink, shall we?" At the bar of La Terrace, across Walnut Street from the fine arts library, we only had a half hour to ourselves before word got around that he was there and a crowd gathered around us. He asked me about my background, about my parents' lives and how I got started in art. I told him about Charley and me, about our differences and the role of aplastic anemia in both of our lives. I described how I had felt like a racehorse kept too long in the starting gate. He was solemn while he listened and finally said, "Remember the positive part of your story, Yarrott. You see, frustration is a great motivator. It is one of the best motivators in the world. I know from my own experience."

The crowd became noisier and tighter. His pronunciation of my name played again and again in my head. Several people introduced themselves to him, and as the conversations grew bigger and louder, I lost myself in thought. *I've got to memorize what he just said. I can't really think about it right now. Didn't he say that frustration is one of the best motivators in the world? Just memorize it and think about it later.*

FIFTY-FIVE

New Countries

I finished the graduate program at Penn and was ready to step into another challenge. I felt like I had only taken one small baby step, to move from Nashville to Philadelphia. Life was just not all that different in the two cities, and I felt I had learned all there was to learn. I needed to keep moving. I was saving my money waiting on tables at a restaurant called Frog, surrounded by other artists trying to figure out their next steps.

Mike and I talked about seeing more of the world. He was at the point in his studies that he needed to decide upon a subject for his dissertation. It was time for him to choose a foreign culture to study in person. We spread open the *National Geographic* atlas on the dining table and lit up cigarettes.

"What about Kenya and Tanzania?" I asked. "I'd like to see the Serengeti Plain. I mean, imagine what the horizontal landscape would look like. Maybe it's like a humongous Noguchi sculpture. Raw and pure. I'd love to see what it would do to my thinking."

"Nah, sorry, babe. Every anthropologist does their field research in Africa. I want to do something different. Maybe in an Eastern Bloc country. Like Poland, maybe."

"Poland? Are you crazy? What the hell would *I* do in Poland? What's going on in the way of art there? For crying out loud, Mike."

"Well, you don't have to get freaked out about it. Let's find a place that can satisfy both of us." We wandered the Mediterranean with our fingertips, from North Africa to Spain to Italy to Yugoslavia to Greece to Turkey. Mike chewed on his thumb and turned to me, "You know, Italy has had a pretty fascinating change in economy since the end of the war. There hasn't been all that much written about it, either. How'd you like to work in Italy? Didn't you spend some time there a few years ago?"

I took a drag of my cigarette and ran my eyes up and down the length of Italy. I remembered the hellish two months I'd spent with Lee Leffert and cringed. But I also remembered the gorgeous weather every day, which buoyed my sinking spirits. And I remembered the rich and delicate food, which made me forget my entrapment. Finally, I remembered the Pantheon in Rome, and I heard myself saying aloud, "Two thousand years puts things into perspective, doesn't it? Yes. It would be wonderful for both of us. Let's give it a try."

In May, I returned to Nashville for my father's seventieth birthday and told my mother that my good friend Mike and I were going to live in Italy. She did not take me seriously and changed the subject. "But, wait, don't you believe me?" I said angrily. "We're first going to study the language in Perugia, then Mike is going to use his Fulbright grant to study a hill town and I am going to work for an American artist. We've saved our money. We've arranged everything. And we're leaving the U.S. in the middle of the summer."

"Of course, dear," my mother said as she finished wrapping my father's birthday present. "Of course you are."

Charley barbecued a chicken for me a few nights later, at his little house he shared with Joe in the country. His puppy Amos was chewing the tips of my flip-flops under the table. "Can you believe how Mother and Dad don't listen to us sometimes?" I complained.

"Yeah, I know, it's ridiculous. But don't let it bug you so much. Just enjoy your adventure. By the way, Mike seems like a good guy to have as a buddy. You two are lucky to be doing this together."

Maybe I should finally tell him the truth about Mike and me.

Is he ready to hear it yet? Come on. This is perfect timing.

Then the moment was suddenly lost. "Hey, I've got some news too, Yarrott." Charley's grin crossed his entire face. "Turns out I'm gonna head out west about the time you're heading to Italy. Mark has invited me to stay with him in Flagstaff. As long as I want. Finally, I'm going."

"Holy cow, that's wonderful, Charley! You've waited for three years now. Nobody's been as patient as you. You deserve a medal or something." I sat back in my chair and smiled at him.

Charley continued, "Yeah, and I've worked here long enough to get my electrician's license. Mark thinks I'll be able to get work pretty easily out there. Hell, imagine that. I bet people will think I'm Indian."

"What do the doctors say?" I asked.

"They're cool about it. I told them I'd keep in touch."

"I'd say this is perfect timing, Charley Boy. Really perfect timing."

FIFTY-SIX

At Home in the Wind

I stood in line with other students for ten minutes at the post office in Perugia. There were two pieces of mail for me, a letter from Mother in a thin airmail envelope and a postcard from Charley, which had on the front a silhouette of a saguaro cactus against a sunset. His tight and unruly handwriting was unmistakable. His message was partly smeared on the back because something had spilled on it.

Flagstaff, Arizona

August 3, 1981

Howdy, little brother. I hope you're well. I'm staying with Mark for a while. Things can get pretty wild (if you know what I mean). Seriously, I'm having a great time. I think I'll settle here for a while. I guess we're finally seeing the world, huh? Let me know how Italy's working out for you.

Love,

Charley

I read the card in the hot noon sun while sitting on the marble steps of the Università per Stranieri. The weird shapes of umbrella pines and Lombardi poplars marched along the Umbrian hillsides in the distance like Dr. Seuss characters. Charley and I had diverged radically from our lives in Nashville, and even the trees surrounding us proved that. I was relieved for both of us. Still, my reaction when I found the postcard waiting for me at the post office was a deep wallop of sadness and dread. *I hope he doesn't write me again. It makes me feel so mixed hearing from him. I don't know why, but it does.* But many more cards came. He wrote me diligently and I wrote back.

Flagstaff, Arizona   August 7, 1981

Dear Yarrott,

Thought you'd dig this postcard of the Grand Canyon. Incredible, huh? Mark and I just got back. Wow. That's all I can say. Wow. I've settled into his apartment just fine. There's four of us here now, so it's a little small but we can make it work for now. Just got a journeyman job as an electrician and the pay is fine. How's life in Italy? Are you working for the American sculptor yet? Say hi to Mike.

Love,

Charley

Perugia, Italy   August 24, 1981

Hey Charley!

Got the card from Flagstaff. Congratulations—you did it!! I guess we're both finally on the road now, huh? I'm glad you're out there. That's where you've always wanted to be. Mike and I are trying to learn our way around here in Perugia. We'll be finished with the language course in a few days. Six weeks all in Italian went by fast. We're sorry to say good-bye to all our international friends we've made. I'll be heading up to Todi to work with the artist Beverly Pepper for a while. Mike has an apartment waiting for him in Ancona on the east coast. It's about a four-hour train ride away. He'll do his field research in a hill town near there. Say hi to Mark and stay out of trouble.

Your brother,

White Cloud

Flagstaff, Arizona   September 20, 1981

Dear White Cloud,

Have you heard from Pocahontas lately? I understand she bought herself a Kelly-green Karmann-Ghia. I swear, our sister, she's out of her mind. News from Arizona: I love it here. Mark's been very generous to let me crash in his apt but I think I'll get my own place soon. Man, you wouldn't believe the views of the desert. I feel like I'm at home in the wind. Hey, what did I just say? Does that make sense? Hope you're running around speaking Italian now.

Hello to Mike.

Geronimo

Todi, Italy   November 1, 1981

Dear Charley,

I'm writing a real letter for a change. I've just spent the past month working for Ms. Pepper, doing odd jobs in her studio and making some architectural drawings of her sculptures. She's in the U.S. now with her husband, Bill, until December, and I'm housesitting for them. Mike came for a visit and stayed a week, but now he's gone back to Ancona. It's hard to watch him leave on the train.

I saw Anwar Sadat assassinated on Italian TV three weeks ago and couldn't believe it. It freaked me out. People are such animals. Being in this huge old villa by myself made me doubly freaked out. I've discovered I hate being out of touch. I think I'll be moving to Ancona sometime in the next couple of months. Todi is incredibly beautiful, and the Peppers have been great, but I want to spend time in Ancona. It will be nice to have Mike there, too.

Talked with Mother and Dad last week. Everything sounds good there, but without the Benz Twins, I'm sure Nashville is awfully quiet. Too quiet. Are you feeling okay? Say hello to Mark, Joe, and the big skies for me.

Love,

Yarrott

Flagstaff, Arizona   January 3, 1982

Yo, Yo Yarrott—

Happy New Year, Brother! Sorry to write only a card. I'm not much for correspondence. Your Christmas in Todi with Mike and the Peppers sounded fun. Not everybody gets to meet a Hollywood director. Guess I'll send this to you in Ancona. Glad you moved where there are more people. Good luck with making your own art and showing it around. A show in May sounds cool. I swear, you always know how to stay busy. Hi to Mike.

Love,

Chas.

Flagstaff, Arizona   March 11, 1982

Yarrott,

Thanks for the phone call on my birthday. How cool to talk to Italy from Arizona, huh? Now I'm 31 I can be baaad. Mother told me you've got a second exhibition lined up already? Wow man you work fast. I'm feeling okay, although I'm getting tired quicker for some reason. Maybe it's the altitude. Anyway, don't worry. I'm fine. You just take good care of yourself and enjoy your time there. Keep up the good work.

Love,

Your old, big brother

Ancona, Italy   July 1, 1982

Dear Charley,

Mother tells me you're feeling lousy these days. Sorry to hear that. Also sorry to hear you're not going back to Flagstaff. I know you loved it. Thank you, thank you for offering to pay my way to Eddy and Debby's wedding in Nashville. You'll never know how much I appreciate it. But I can't leave in the middle of this big installation project. In Italy, if you turn your back, the workers will disappear and you'll lose your opportunity. I'm sorry not to be at the wedding, but everyone knows I'll be there in spirit. I'll try to call the house right after the ceremony's over. Hey, I understand you've met somebody in Nashville, too. Vickie, right? Mother has told me a lot about her. She sounds wonderful.

Love,

Yarrott

Nashville   September 21, 1982

Dear Yarrott,

I'm spending a lot of time at Vickie's place these days. It's not Flagstaff, but it is pretty great. She's got a little house in the country outside Nashville with about ten acres and two dogs. Amos enjoys being over there a lot romping. I'll tell you, Vickie's my soul mate. I've never been happier with anybody in my life. I'm sorry I'm not feeling better physically, but I'm doing pretty damn well emotionally. Thanks to Vickie I'm not minding being gone from Flagstaff. The doctors have started me on some special treatments to reduce the iron build-up. Believe it or not, they are bleeding me a pint of blood once a month. Me! Bleeding me! Can you believe it?

Love,

Charley

FIFTY-SEVEN

Snap

In October, I called home from a phone booth off Piazza Cavour in Ancona and talked with Mother. She sounded tense. "Mother, what's wrong? I can hear something in your voice."

She paused for a moment, then continued. "Honey, it's your brother. It's Charley."

"What do you mean?" Her anxiety spread by electric wire ten thousand miles away.

"Oh, Yarrott, how I hate to tell you this, but his blood counts have been dropping. The doctors are now very concerned."

I was silent.

"Yarrott, did you hear me?"

"Yes, Mother." My heart was beating so fast and I felt hot in the little compartment. "What does this mean?"

"Well, you know what they're afraid of. That the aplastic anemia is returning. That he is relapsing."

❧

I found myself wandering in the medieval section of Ancona, where the streets are narrow and winding, where the passages are dark and ambiguous. I heard a cacophony of stray cats and pigeons and motor scooters. I smelled soot and piss and mildew. I followed the passages deeper into the darkness of the ancient heart of the city. I tried to get lost, but the city just was not big enough. I tried to get away from the news I had just heard but it just replayed in my head. *Don't make me listen to it. Don't make me keep it.*

FIFTY-EIGHT

Don't Borrow Trouble

Mike and I prepared ourselves to return to the United States and to resume living in Philadelphia. After my show of wall sculptures came down in Ancona on the first of December, we spent the next two weeks packing and saying good-bye over dinners with our friends. The beautiful blue skies of Italy gave way to a gray fog that lingered for the remainder of our time. In a dim, ambiguous winter light, there was a continual pulsing foghorn somewhere in the distance, out there in the Adriatic. The atmosphere of our last days in Ancona seemed dark, mournful, and heavy.

"I'm sorry all this is happening to you, too," I moaned into Mike's shoulder.

"No, don't think like that, babe." Mike rubbed my back. "It's a good time for us to go back to the States. With all my notes, I can write the book there just as easily as I can write it here."

Standing over an open trunk, I said, "God, I just wish we knew what to expect. I can't imagine how horrendous all this must be for Charley. He doesn't know what the hell's going on."

We picked up our mail and I found an airmail envelope waiting from Mother. Reading it on the walk back to the apartment, I turned to Mike and said, "Hell. She wants to invite Lee Leffert for dinner the day after we arrive."

"You mean the letch who took you to Europe? Why, for crying out loud?"

"Because everyone in Nashville thinks he's responsible for my living in Italy now. Everyone thinks he opened the door for me."

Mike stopped on the sidewalk. "But that's absurd!"

"I know. I know. But what else are they going to think? I never told anybody about what happened. They think Lee turned on the world's lights for me."

"Can you take it? An evening with him?" Mike asked.

"I guess I'll have to, won't I?"

We boarded an overnight train from Ancona to Brussels on December 15, 1982, and then flew from there to New York. We stayed overnight, then picked up my old VW bug that a friend was keeping and drove to Nashville. On December 19, when we finally walked through the front door on Tyne Boulevard, we had been traveling four days. Despite my stupor, home felt like a beautiful place with a heart and soul. Seeing Mother's radiant smile and tears in the corners of her eyes made me glad to be back. She even hugged Mike with a long, firm hold.

Leaning on her crutches in front of me, she beamed, "Look at you, honey! Say something in Italian for me. Say you're glad to be home!"

"Grazie per i nostri benvenuti, Mama," I said with the bravura of rolling r's.

"Will you just listen to that? That's just marvelous, honey. Say, Daddy will be delighted to know you've arrived. Let me call him at the office right now. He'll want to say hello."

In a short while Charley and Vickie drove up in his new blue truck. I had not seen him for a year and a half and he looked gaunt and gray. Standing in the doorway, he had a broad grin across his face. We hugged for a long time and I felt the warmth of his body folding around mine. He seemed truly gentler, relaxed, not on edge or defensive. He also seemed vulnerable, having lost weight and energy. Charley had softened. Despite his sick appearance, he remained taller and bigger than me. He pulled away and said, "Yarrott, Mike, I'd like to introduce someone very important to me. This is Vickie."

As I hugged her, she whispered in my ear, "Listen, I've got to tell you, your brother is so grateful to you for coming back. He just loves talking about you." I immediately liked her openness.

Charley and Vickie looked more like family than he and I ever did. With their long, straight dark brown hair parted down the middle and olive skin, both looked as if Indian blood could be in their background. Wearing loose wool sweaters, faded jeans, and leather boots, they were stylish and comfortable. *My God, they're perfect together. They seem like two gloves from the same pair.*

We made dinner together—Vickie, Charley, Mother, Dad, Mike, and I. It was easy and invigorating to talk while we made pasta and salad. Mike and I described our life together in Italy. I noticed Vickie looking at Mike and me and smiling. *I think she knows. Good. I like her.*

My mother put down the knife while she chopped and said, "Gosh, honey, I've just got so many questions."

Everyone asked about our life of the past year and a half, who our friends had been, where we shopped for food, what was the hardest part of living in another language.

I could see the big unasked question in my parents' eyes: How could two men be such close companions without wives? They marveled in our accomplishments abroad and recognized the support Mike and I gave each other, but it was obvious they didn't understand it. It helped that Mike's part of the adventure had been supported by a Fulbright grant. My parents were impressed with his academic credentials. In their eyes, academic prestige trumped everything, even sexually ambiguous relations.

I was tempted to open up and get things out in the open once and for all, but I stayed closed. *Not now. They've got enough on their plate now without having to deal with my sexuality. It's a bad place for me to have to be, but I don't think there's any other way. This is not the time.*

Vickie put her glass of wine down. "You guys ought to come out to our house to see the puppies. We've got two new Jack Russell terriers. We've named them Ruff and Reddy."

Charley added with a laugh, "They're little devils and get into everything. They scare Amos away."

I noticed how Charley had become relaxed and confident alongside Vickie. He seemed comfortable in his own skin. I was relieved and pleased that he had found such a satisfying relationship. On the other hand, the specter of his relapse hung over all our heads. Upstairs that night, in the guest room with twin beds, I climbed in the bed with Mike and wrapped my arms around him and whispered, "My God, what do you think will happen in the next year? To all of us?"

"Babe, don't borrow trouble. You can't change what will happen. Just be there for Charley as much as you can."

"Right," I said to myself in agreement. "Don't borrow trouble."

The next evening, Lee Leffert arrived with his brother and sister-in-law, my parents' next-door neighbors. He immediately grabbed my elbow in the front hall. "I'd like to talk with you in private, Yarrott. To catch up."

There was nothing I wanted to say or to hear. I smiled, but avoided being alone with him. During dinner, I noticed that none of the three Lefferts directed a single question to Mike. To them, he was invisible.

What is this? Do they think he's a Lenin or a Castro sympathizer because of his beard? I don't know why I'm sitting here quietly like this while Lee has a self-satisfied smirk on his face.

Lee addressed me from across the table. "Yarrott, aren't you pleased by what came from your first trip in Italy with me years ago? Did you ever think it would lead to living there?"

I smiled weakly, nodded, and continued to chew. What a bastard. It really is too much, allowing him to take any credit for our hard work in Italy. And cornering me the way he did in Italy years before was criminal. I just wish I had the guts to be honest. I wish I could just open up right here, right now, and tell everyone what he did.

Mother looked at me from her end of the table and nervously filled in the silence. "Oh, Lee, I don't know what we all would have done without your generosity. My goodness, isn't it something? Even Charley's remission came out of it!"

God, I can't take this. Mother, please don't go any further.

"You know," she started, "Yarrott would probably still be giving his platelets twice a week like he did for seven years if you hadn't taken him on that trip. And look now, six years later, he's gone to graduate school and lived in Italy! Isn't it something how things happen?"

FIFTY-NINE

Summer Storm

Six months later, in the summer of 1983, I was busy with my sculpture work in Philadelphia. I was receiving some serious attention and was starting to make some money. After winning two commissions that spring, I had an exhibition of my Italian wall sculptures planned for the autumn at an annex of the Philadelphia Museum.

Mike was making progress on his book in our apartment on South 22nd Street, but we argued about where we should live and how we should live. Our styles of living were becoming painfully incompatible. I wanted more space and in a better neighborhood and he insisted that where we lived, bordering a ghetto, worked just fine.

Hovering in the back of both of our minds was Charley's physical decline in Nashville. His red cell and platelet counts were dropping more each week and the doctors had no idea what was happening. My parents frequently expressed their concern about it on the phone but quickly followed up by saying they hoped I would not have to interrupt my career to give platelets again. Everyone, however, knew something bad was on the way.

My anxiety grew by the week, and I sought ways to relieve the tension. I took long drives along the Delaware River. I walked from one side of Center City to the other. I killed time by discovering new neighborhoods and new worlds. I found myself walking right into a piece of American history that I discovered on one of my drives.

Fort Mifflin is a star-shaped brick and stone fortress, a

forgotten yet vital player in the Revolutionary War. In a bizarre twist of fate and urban planning, it sits near the end of the longest runway at the international airport, overlooking the Delaware River and calling out to its ruined twin on the other side in New Jersey. I would often drive out to the airport and sit outside the shuttered-up fort, just feet from the end of the runway. Airplanes would take off and land right over my head. I could escape my present dilemma by watching planes escaping to far places. It was classic vicarious entertainment. The rear-mounted jets, like DC-10s, L1011 Tri-Stars, or Boeing 727s, coasted in low, not more than a hundred feet over my head. The largest planes would produce vortexes of wind whipping off their wings, like invisible tornadoes whispering angrily around me for a few seconds after the plane passed over. Watching from the ground was a thrill. It was a rush that bordered on the sexual. Looking up into the extended wing flaps and the open wheel wells reminded me of looking into private places of a lover's body, exposed and vulnerable.

Although Mike thought my fascination with airplanes was weird, he accompanied me a few times to Fort Mifflin. We could never find a way inside, but hiked around the dry moat surrounding it and discovered two in-ground magazines, brick-walled caverns dug out of the earth and used in the eighteenth century for storage ammunition. No other place in Philadelphia excited me the way the spectacular and forgotten fort did. No other place was authentic like Fort Mifflin. It was untouched. It was forgotten.

I tried to stay too busy to think about Charley. There was no safe way in my mind to consider the idea of revisiting platelet pheresis, so I refused to talk about the subject. The effect was emotional confusion. I cared about Charley, but I did not want to let his illness back into my life. I felt torn and conflicted and became brittle and explosive. Mike and I were quarrelling daily. I wanted to make real inroads with a career, make something of myself. I hated the provincialism of suburban Main Line Philadelphia. I hated the urban blight that haunted Center City,

Philadelphia. I knew that after I finished my projects there would be nothing left to do there but wait for Mike to finish his book. And Charley? I tried not to think about it. What would it mean to give him platelets again? If I found Philadelphia limiting as far as a career in art, what would Nashville be? I just refused to think about it.

The call came on August 3. It was Charley. "Hey, little brother, I've got a terrible request to ask."

I knew what he needed. "Platelets, Charley? Do you need them now?"

"How'd you know?"

"I guess I've been waiting for this call for some time. Listen, don't worry. I'll head over to the Red Cross here in Center City. I believe they'll fly them down to you by tonight. The important thing is to feel better. I'm okay with this. You hear?"

"God, Yarrott. I hated to ask you. Not again. Not after what you've already done."

"Charley, thanks. Just take care of yourself, okay?"

When I hung up the phone, I called down the hall to Mike, who was at his desk typing a paper. "Oh, shit. Mike! Come here. Damn. I need you. Shit. I need you!" He rushed into the room and put his arms around me. The day we'd dreaded had come.

At this time, I was completing my largest project, a temporary outdoor sculpture called *Ghost Armada*. It was conceived on a gargantuan scale, altogether three hundred feet long. It was comprised of about a dozen flat, geometric abstract shapes hanging from cables on the facade of a museum located along the Delaware River and seen from I-95. It was scheduled to be in place from the end of July until the middle of September. With many people involved in its construction, it required a major amount of organizing. The Friends of the Philadelphia Museum of Art helped raise money, in only six months, to cover the cost of fabrication. I look back on that time, astounded that *Ghost Armada* was ever built.

255

Charley wanted to come up and see the sculpture, despite his precarious health. By then, his doctors only told him bad news: they had warned him in July that his disease was becoming symptomatic of something worse than aplastic anemia. There still was no diagnosis, but they hoped to have conclusive test results shortly after his visit to see me.

Vickie drove Charley's truck most of the way from Nashville and they arrived at the apartment on a hot, humid afternoon just as a big storm was building, a nor'easter. In a strong wind, Charley jumped out of the truck and gave us a big grin. I saw the gap from a missing tooth near the front of his mouth. Two weeks before, he had suffered an abscess that was related to his deteriorating condition. He had a splitting headache and his nose was packed with a tampon, of all things. The poor guy was coming apart at the seams. Still, he insisted on going immediately to the site of the sculpture. Black clouds filled the sky with swirling patterns. Leaves on the trees turned their pale sides over in the updraft. A monster storm was on its way.

We made it to a site overlook just in time to see the sculpture before the downpour. In the two black-and-white photographs taken by Vickie, Charley and I are standing on the roof of a building in downtown Philadelphia overlooking the Delaware River. *Ghost Armada* makes an angular dance for three hundred feet across the facade of the building in the distance. I remember those minutes on the roof. There was a fine rain just beginning and I felt it on my face. Charley's windbreaker was red. His missing tooth gave him a pitiful grin. He was thin and tired. In the first picture, Charley and I have turned toward each other, both awkwardly recognizing this moment together and not knowing how to seize it. In the next, we have suddenly hugged each other with a fierce grip. It is an emotional embrace, eyes closed and solemn, and our appreciation for each other is clear. Vickie made sure to get that moment. She understood firsthand the importance of permanence of family and proof of family. She had already lost both of her parents in Minnesota and their deaths had thrown her siblings and her tumbling in the air as teenagers.

256

While Vickie's role in Charley's life could not have been more essential to his happiness, my mother initially treated her with suspicion rather than open-armed acceptance. Either Mother was particularly protective of Charley or she was jealous of Vickie, or maybe it was a combination of the two. To be in the room with the two women was painful, as each doubted what the other said, although they challenged each other with feigned politeness. When Charley moved into Vickie's little house in a rural area outside Nashville, my parents were accepting but not at all congratulatory. Now, the second time Charley had moved in with a girl, they realized they had no choice but to go along with it.

One of the common bonds between Vickie and Charley was chronic illness. Vickie's father carried the genes for polycystic kidney disease and he had succumbed to it at age forty-five, a few years before Vickie's mother died of a stroke at forty-three. Including Vickie, there were three children in the family, and all three developed polycystic kidney disease. When Charley met her, she was already on a transplant list and had started dialysis once a week. The two of them understood the common lingo of hospitalization, of needles and tubes, of heavy-duty medications, of having good and bad days, and of feeling apart from the normal, healthy world. Incredibly, both of them shared the same indomitable hunger for adventure, risking their health if not their lives for the views from treacherous places.

The winds turned into howling gusts as we ran to the car and rushed home. Just as we got into the apartment, a flash of lightning and thunder knocked the electricity out in the neighborhood. We sat out the storm with lit candles placed around the apartment. After dinner, Charley and Vicki went to bed early. They were worn out, Vickie from driving all day and Charley from bleeding all day.

I called Mother and Dad that night to let them know everyone had arrived safely. They both got on the line. Mom asked, "Was he okay after the drive? How do you think he looks, Yarrott?"

I found myself stumbling to answer. "He looks...he looks awful." Before I knew it I was sobbing into the phone. "He looks so damn vulnerable. I hate seeing this. I can't stand it. God, what can we do?"

Dad answered quietly, "I'm afraid there's not much we can do. I know it hurts to see him. I wish I could prevent this, Yarrott."

Mom ended the call, "Honey, you all try to have an important time together. Whatever you do, don't fight. Just enjoy each other, please?"

The next day, the four of us spent the morning at the Red Cross in Center City while I gave platelets to Charley. A few hours later, the sun came out strong and I drove all of us to Fort Mifflin. They wanted to see historical Philadelphia and, to me, the fort was the most authentic place I had seen my whole time in the city of historical places.

"Wow, this is incredible, Yarrott. How do we get in?" Charley grinned mischievously.

"I don't know. I've never found a way over the wall."

"Well, we gotta change that. Here, hold me up." Charley stepped into my locked hands and grabbed a row of bricks over his head. Mike and Vickie stood behind us, not sure of what we were doing.

"Hey, I've got a ledge here. I think I can do it!" Charley pulled himself to the top of the wall and sat down on the edge. "There's a whole courtyard inside here. And an old house. And what looks like a graveyard. C'mon up, you all. It's not that hard."

All the times I had been there before, I had never found a way inside the fort. I gave Vickie a hike up with my locked hands and Charley helped pull her up the rest of the way. *Where is his energy coming from? How does he do it?*

258

"You guys, it's really amazing," Vickie called down to us. "You gotta get up here. It's like staring at history right in the face!" Just then an Alitalia jumbo jet roared over our heads and a shadow passed over the fort. From their place on the wall, Charley and Vickie could see the plane's wings wobbling over the tarmac just before its tires touched down.

I heard from them the day after they returned to Nashville. Charley's voice was weak on the phone and Vickie was in the background. He was shaking. "Yarrott, we just talked to the doctors. Now we know what's wrong with me. It's leukemia. The aplastic anemia evolved into leukemia. It's bad. We've got to do something soon."

SIXTY

Chemo

On the morning of October 1, 1983, Charley dressed himself in his red cotton windbreaker, faded blue jeans, and old leather boots, and pulled around his waist the belt with the silver Indian buckle. With Vickie anxious in the next seat, he drove his blue Nissan pickup to the new Vanderbilt Hospital and parked. He signed forms in the admitting office and then the two of them found their way to the oncology unit on the eighth floor, to private room 8025. The tinted windows overlooking a rooftop courtyard blocked out every bit of noise from the outside.

That same morning, Mike and I carried my bags to the car and pulled away from our apartment. We were headed for the Schuylkill Expressway and the Philadelphia airport. "Where the hell are your siblings? That's what I'd like to know." Mike angrily turned off South 22nd Street onto Lombard Street. "That's the story of your life, isn't it? You do all the work. Get beat up. Give blood. Get beat up again. Give blood again. Now you're giving your whole career up, too."

"Stop it, Mike. I don't have a choice."

"You can ask them to help you."

"How? Eddy has his job in Los Angeles. How can he leave his lab and come to Nashville? And Angela? She's in graduate school, for Christ's sake. She can't fly up from Dallas every other day—she's got classes she has to make. She's becoming an occupational therapist. I've got the most flexible schedule. I can go."

"Babe, you've borne the brunt of Charley's illness from day one. It's so unfair it makes me crazy."

"Mike, I appreciate your feelings about this. I do. But I can't change anything. Come down with me if you'd like."

"No way I'm visiting there now. Not when your brother's so sick. No way."

We pulled up to the departures door and sat in the Beetle for the last few minutes. Opening the door felt like pushing a ton of steel. I did not want to get out. What lay ahead? "Mike, I love you. More than I can say. Be with me in this. I'm scared."

He reached around and pulled me to him. I could feel in his tense silence that he was on the verge of crying. He sniffed hard and held my head firmly with both hands. Looking me in the face, he said, "I'm sorry I lost it. Of course, I'm with you. Whatever happens, babe, remember I'm with you."

Dad picked me up at the Nashville airport a few hours later and drove directly to the hospital, where he left me at the lobby and then returned to his office and patients. I had not seen the lavish new hospital before. It had risen up like an octagonal brick eruption in the very same neighborhood as Spats, the restaurant where I worked with Terri ten years earlier. I could not believe the tidy circle made complete by coincidence, which life often makes in hometowns.

My first thought about the new hospital was about the brick floor I saw at my feet in the lobby. *Stylish, but its rough surface will make it difficult to roll a wheelchair. That's sure sacrificing function for form.* I was loyal to the old Vanderbilt, with its rabbit warren corridors leading up and down, cinderblock walls from the 1920s, heavy wood doors to patients' rooms, and the permeating smells of alcohol, soap, and clean linens. Times had changed. We were in the new, modern mode, which took its visual cues from middle-class luxuries like hotels and cruise ships. The Vanderbilt Hospital I grew up knowing was an Old World throwback, erudite, scientific, and clinical like a Thomas Eakins painting. The new place seemed frivolous by comparison. I found it hard to expect solid medical diagnoses and treatments in a facility that would have looked at home next to an airport or a ski slope.

I was distracted and ornery. Only a few hours before, Mike and I were arguing. It felt like we had been arguing for weeks about inane things. I was on edge, anxious about every angle of my life. While I had been receiving all sorts of opportunities for my sculpture, I was running out of money. Over the summer, I had begun waiting on tables for a catering company, to pay my bills. Financial insecurity made me irritable and impatient. The specter of Charley's relapse hung over us now with a gnawing uncertainty and a host of awful possibilities. Mike's work in anthropology at Temple University demanded his presence in Philadelphia. My work in sculpture demanded proximity to New York. Charley was doing everything possible to make sure a repeat of the seven-year trap of platelet pheresis would not happen. When the question of chemotherapy came up, he wanted to begin it immediately, with the kind of impatient resolve that makes doctors nervous.

Doctors McGee and Flexner were not so sure about what to do. Charley had so many complicating side effects from his long-term illness, they had trouble determining the best cocktail of drugs and the safest dosage for him. Because of hemochromatosis, iron build-up in his body due to his hundreds of red cell infusions, he also suffered from cardiomegaly, enlargement of the heart. Because chemotherapy is a dramatic assault on the body, it can easily kill an individual with a weakened heart. Selecting the right drugs, causing the least amount of damage on already compromised organs, is essential. Ultimately, the hematologists chose Daunorubicin, a chemotherapy often used in the treatment of acute myeloid leukemia and acute lymphocytic leukemia. The list of possible side effects was long and alarming: nausea, exhaustion, hair loss, lowered resistance to infections, bruising or bleeding, anemia, mouth sores, and sensitivity to the sun. The drug also can cause changes in the muscle of the heart, so must be used with extreme caution with someone with Charley's cardiac history.

Earlier in the week, he had called me in Philadelphia to report the doctors' conclusions and his voice was trembling. He said, "Yarrott, I have a strong feeling that I will live through it. I will survive this."

Chemotherapy would begin on the first of October.

There were no other options. A bone marrow transplant with me as the donor was not thinkable, according to the doctors, because Charley had most likely developed antibodies to me, which would sabotage the transplant. Also, because of his tremendous number of red and white cell infusions, he had been exposed to most red and white cell antigens, meaning that he would most probably develop host versus graft rejection or even graft versus host, no matter who the donor was. There were no other options.

The elevator at Vanderbilt opened on the eighth floor, oncology, and I followed the signs to room 8025. The corridor emptied onto a central core nurse's station, with patients' rooms sprouting from the core. Outside his room I heard Mother and Vickie talking, a quiet lilting within a warm, steady flow of tone. I paused outside, anxious, nervous, dreading the change in Charley. Mother saw me and broke into her gorgeous smile.

Clapping her hands, she sang out, "Why, look who's here! Was it a good flight, honey?" She hobbled over to me without her crutches and gave me a big hug. I caught Charley's eye and we smiled at each other.

"The artist is in from the cold!" he announced. "Man, you're looking good! Get a load of that hair! It's grown a lot just in a few weeks."

A lot of quiet movement surrounded him in the small room. Vickie was tying to the headboard a silver Mylar balloon that said *Get well soon, Charley—Love from the Clarkes.* Angela had come from Texas after all and was using the remote to raise the knees of the bed. They both stopped what they were doing and the three of us hugged together in a triad and giggled like three old chums at camp. Vickie whispered quickly in a tired voice, "I am *so* glad you are here now."

Charley leaned forward in the bed and opened his arms to me, tubes attached to needles on the backs of both hands. I held him for a long moment, stroking his bony back. "You doing okay, big man? Feeling sick yet?" I smelled iodine on him. His cheekbones were pronounced, his color gray, and the gap of his missing tooth stuck out like a sore thumb in his smile. The missing tooth bothered me the most. It made him look disheveled and pathetic and vulnerable, like the homeless people beginning to appear in Center City.

He scooted over and motioned for me to sit next to him on the bed. "No, I haven't felt anything yet. So far, so good. Maybe chemo's not as bad as everyone says it is."

"When did they start with it?"

"About three hours ago." He bit his bottom lip and made an exaggerated face of worry. "So any moment now I should start puking."

"Charley, your language!" Mother said.

"Well, let's get real here. They said this flight's gonna be real bumpy."

I changed the subject. "What do you think of the new hospital? You like it?"

"As if I could like *any* hospital. I guess it's okay. Smells like new carpet, though. It's been bothering me all morning. That could get old."

Mom jumped in proudly, "You know, this is just phase one. Vanderbilt is planning *three* more wings just like this one."

"Man," I said, "I've only been gone six years and I don't recognize my hometown anymore."

"Uh-oh." Charley looked up at me. "You need to get off the bed and hand me something fast, Yarrott. Here comes something. Hurry."

I shoved the brand-new trashcan under his face and watched as he coughed twice, gagged, and vomited into it. Mother wrung out a washcloth with cold water and wiped his forehead. "Damn. Sorry about that," he said. Well, I guess I'm just like everybody else with chemo."

He squirmed, settled himself, and then sat up straight. Pointing to the window, he said to me under his breath, "You think you could bring Amos over here sometime and let me see him from the window? They might let him into the courtyard downstairs."

264

"Sure. I'll get him in somehow. By the way, who's taking care of him?"

"Mom and Dad have him with the dachshunds. That's fine for now, but he won't get enough exercise for a young Lab. Can you walk him some, maybe throw the Frisbee?"

I thought of Charley and Amos and their close bond and wondered why dogs couldn't be kept with their masters as they suffer through chemo. It would be such fine moral support. The idea of Amos being kept from him at this moment of all moments felt sadistic and cruel. This room was fancier than prison, but a prison it surely was.

"Oh, damn, here it comes again. Lemme have the little vomit thing there. I should be using that instead." I stayed next to him on the bed as he coughed into the kidney-shaped plastic tray. "Okay, I'm fine now. Now where were we?"

SIXTY-ONE

He Knows

Over the course of the next four weeks, Mother, Angela, Vickie, and I alternated our visits with Charley in the hospital. His nausea became a fact of life that he quickly accepted without complaint, as he did with the other changes, such as the red splotches in his skin, his loss of hair, his bloating, and the white sores in his mouth. He was never a particularly vain man, which was a good thing. Just on the surface alone, this experience was devastating.

Crossing paths daily in Charley's room, Vickie and I grew closer. Often we would drive to a fast food restaurant and eat dinner away from my parents and talk. She and Charley had only been together for a year and my parents were still taking their sweet time warming to her. Mother, much more than Dad, could be territorial about her sick son and Vickie did not hesitate to show her annoyance at that. After all, Charley was almost thirty-three years old, mature enough to establish his own allegiance to a wife or lover. This being the tense and critical period that it was, boundaries and territories were very confused. Some days that mattered a great deal, others not at all. When death is in the air, romantic love sometimes is forced to play second fiddle to more imperial parental love. There were no established rules of etiquette to turn to and Charley was too sick to intervene. I refused to take sides, so I just listened to both women and kept quiet about what or who I thought was right.

The problems between my mother and Vickie were not long-lasting. Usually, their difficulties with each other had to do with the role of protector. Who would stay with him at night if he needed it? Whom did the doctors address with information?

From Mother, I heard, "If she's going to insist on acting like his wife, couldn't she try to dress a little better? She'll almost as bad as Angela, for heaven's sake."

From Vickie, "Couldn't your mother try to lighten up with her criticism?"

During the first half of Charley's hospitalization, while his condition was stable and the therapy somewhat routine, Mother and Vickie rubbed against each other easily and I heard about it from both sides. Later, when it was obvious that Charley's situation had become grave, the two women surrendered to each other in mutual anxiety.

Alone at the Wendy's in the Green Hills shopping center, Vickie and I talked about our respective lives. Hers had been difficult since both of her parents died by the time she was seventeen. Wounded badly, Vickie left Minnesota soon afterward by herself to start a new life in the South. "Never in a million years did I imagine myself falling in love with a very sick man. But I did and that was that. No regrets," she said. "Once I commit myself to something I do not change my tune."

"Charley's incredibly lucky to have you in his life. After he's finished with chemo, what are you two going to do?"

She looked at me, surprised that I'd asked. "Why, Yarrott, we're getting married, of course. You know what? I can't wait."

She was so open to me, I was giddy with confidence, so I blurted out, "Well, you know you have one more brother-in-law than you think. There's Mike. You know, he and I are... together."

"Yeah, I know." She smiled warmly and continued eating.

"I figured that by now you knew," I said, relieved with her response.

"When we visited you in Philadelphia in September, Charley really enjoyed himself with you and Mike. Heck, I did, too."

I rested my hamburger in the air. "What did Charley say about us, Vickie?"

"You mean, did he recognize you being gay? Not in so many words. But what he *did* say was how much he liked you and Mike together. He was impressed with your life, what you are doing with it. Gosh, isn't that just as important?"

"I guess so. But I'd like to be sure that he knows. Just for clarity."

"Yarrott, believe me, he knows and he's okay with it."

I continued chewing my hamburger. "Vickie, do you think I ought to tell my parents?"

She looked surprised. "You don't think they know about you and Mike?"

"I don't think they will believe it until I tell them. If I've learned anything, it's that people usually will deny what's in front of them if they don't like the truth. With my sister a lesbian and the burden of Charley's illness, I've just never had the heart to tell them. Their plate is so full already."

She thought for a minute and said, "I guess I agree with you. But that sticks you with the burden of having to be dishonest with them, doesn't it?"

"Sure does. I feel like they're children and I have to lie to protect them. But what choice do I have?"

SIXTY-TWO

A Second Try

As anyone who has witnessed it knows, the effects of heavy chemo on the patient can be unbearable to watch. Charley's energy seemed to fall out with his hair and his enthusiasm drained alongside his nausea. Still, just as it had years earlier, his condition improved immediately whenever he received my platelets, which I was now giving every three days.

In the five years we had been together, Mike and I had not been apart for more than a week before I flew to Nashville on October 1. It was difficult to be satisfied with a nightly conversation when all of the daily routines we enjoyed with each other were put on hold.

Initially, I was concerned that being under the roof of my parents' house would mean everyone regressing in their behavior: my acting like an angry teenager and my parents acting like obstreperous bears. But the seriousness of our task at hand made that fear irrelevant. Surprisingly, my parents and I had enormous patience with each other, listened to each other's complaints, and consoled each other. To me, we felt like peers struggling through the same unknown territory. The day-in, day-out routine of spending time at the hospital felt like a job. There was a certain pride in doing it well. After four weeks, the first round of chemo was almost over. Charley looked and felt bad, but not beyond what we expected. I flew to Philadelphia on November 2 to spend time with Mike for two weeks, and left my parents, Angela, and Vickie to manage with Charley and await the results of the chemotherapy. He was scheduled for a bone marrow biopsy on November 10. From that, we would know if the leukemia was wiped out or not.

Every three days I returned to the Center City Red Cross to donate platelets, and they were flown to Nashville. By that time, I was fighting a constant headache. Revisiting platelet donations was making me irritable and angry at the world. I had become testy and impatient toward Mike, and we did everything we could think of to divert our attention from Nashville and to rekindle what we enjoyed doing together. We had frequent dinners with friends, went to the movies.

On November 11, Dad called, greeted Mike warmly on the phone, then when I got on the line said, "Hey there, Yarrott. We had a nice visit from Eddy. He had to fly back to Los Angeles this morning. He was such a big help. You getting some well-deserved time to yourself?"

"I'm doing fine here, Dad. What's the news with Charley's biopsy?"

"That's what I'm calling about. Here, I'm going to put Charley on so he can tell you himself."

I could hear the fumbling with the receiver and then Charley's voice, flat and tired, "Yo, bud. How's it up there?"

"The big question is how are *you*?" I was stiff with anticipation.

"Oh, well. Not so good. It didn't work." Charley sighed.

"Oh, Charley. I am so sorry. What did they say, Dr. McGee and Dr. Flexner?"

"They said, in these words, 'We're going to take another slug at it.'"

"God. You okay with that? I mean, the chemo is so damn nasty."

"Yarrott, I don't have any choice. It's do this or die." He paused, then said, "Of course, it could also be do this *and* die."

It was night when I returned to Nashville four days later, on November 15. Angela was home from Dallas and picked me up at the airport and drove me directly to the hospital. I knew that Charley's response to the second round of chemotherapy had already been miserable, much worse that the first week of the first round. That was an understatement. Charley had become a different creature. His body was swollen with edema and he had lost the remains of his hair. Red splotches covered his face. The whites of his eyes had hemorrhaged solid red from capillaries broken during his vomiting. His speech was slow and slurred. I took one look at him and felt my knees start to tremble.

Mother and Dad sat quietly in the easy chairs under the window. They, too, were different people. They looked exhausted. Mother lifted her hand to me and smiled weakly, relieved that I was back with them. Both of them looked twenty years older. I wanted to cry. Seeing my family so worn out made me afraid for them and for myself.

The treatment was devastating what was left of Charley. Day after day, as his body broke down further he drifted farther away in a fog and seemed to be lost in his thoughts.

Two weeks later, on December 1, I returned to Philadelphia for five days to install my wall sculptures in a three-person show at an annex of The Philadelphia Museum of Art. This should have been a time to celebrate. The show was part of the Challenge Exhibitions, a series dedicated to emerging artists and considered a nice feather in one's cap and a great way to get some serious attention. Coming as it did in the middle of Charley's chemotherapy, I had no choice but to quickly assemble the work on the walls and do little else. I did not even give the museum a list of addresses for mailing out invitations. I was in no mood to celebrate. The museum said they understood my predicament and said that the other two artists in the show could use my gallery as overflow space for their crowds. I did not care. It seemed to me that self-promotion at this time, while my brother barely hung on to life, was unseemly.

Christmas was already in the air and a light snow was falling. Mike had to plan his own holiday by himself since I was committed to returning to Nashville in two days. We celebrated quietly with dinner at our favorite Italian hole-in-the-wall in South Philly. That was fine with me, as I had little room left in my head for pleasant food or gatherings of people. I was focused on Charley and my sad, withering parents, who desperately needed me in Nashville. Mike was gentle with me and

271

very attentive to my sadness. I did not tell him in words that I was afraid Charley would not survive, but he certainly understood it.

In a phone conversation with a friend, I described what Charley looked like now and the friend, in an effort to help me face what was coming, blurted out, "Charley is dying, Yarrott. He is going to die."

Angrily, I snapped at him for being pessimistic. "How can you say that? Goddamn you!"

On December 4, my three-person exhibition at Fleisher Art Memorial opened at six P.M. and the other two galleries quickly filled up. I had not sent out a single invitation. The gallery housing my sculptures stood empty while glasses clinked and people laughed in the next rooms. Mike and I made a quick appearance and sat for a few minutes among my wall sculptures, serene geometric forms floating like altars on white walls, the room empty as a chapel. I regretted that I had let illness impact what should have been a night of great satisfaction.

The next morning, as I packed for the flight back to Nashville, I realized our apartment in Philadelphia needed vacuuming. Cat hair had invaded everything. The kitchen smelled sour, like old milk had been dumped down the drain. The cat box was full. I was angry to see our apartment like this. I wanted to escape the gnawing, endless responsibilities of life. What I had been contending with in Nashville was more than I wanted to handle. I needed a break from thinking about making solutions. But Mike had his hands full, too, with the writing of his dissertation, teaching at Temple, and dealing with the holidays by himself. I had already missed him sorely as I sat in the hospital with Charley. I had needed someone there to remind me of living, of soaring in one's life and work, of having fun, of making love, and of laughing. My thoughts returned to Charley. For him, what was there? Vickie had certainly tried to divert his attention. She had often brought in flowers for him, pictures of Amos, feathers and rocks from their house, but these things had drawn little excitement from him.

Mike ran up the stairs to the apartment, the morning's paper open in his hands, yelling for me. "Babe! The show is reviewed in today's *Inquirer!* It's really good about your work and they gave *you* the picture!"

He was right. The comments by the critic were precise and full of praise for the sculptures. *Static but never dull, Benz's work treads a delicate balance between empty and full. Like a young Frank Stella...* In the center of the page floated my sculpture *Black Ravenna.*

"Okay, that's wonderful." I could not feel the satisfaction. "Damn it, Mike. The flight's in one hour. We have got to go." I shoved the review in an opening in the suitcase and zippered it shut.

SIXTY-THREE

The Dam Breaks

Charley stared at the television now, blinking quietly and ticking off the miserable minutes. The upbeat theme music of *Entertainment Tonight* goaded him at dinnertime, as if jeering at a lame loser. The irrelevant hype about handsome Mel Gibson and *The Year of Living Dangerously* underscored how Charley now resided on a distant planet. Late at night, David Letterman's new hip sarcasm was fun for earthlings, but for Charley, trapped in that bed on a faraway planet, it was indecipherable nonsense.

Cal Kingsley, a highly esteemed colleague of Dad's, an internist, and a longtime friend of our parents, stopped by Charley's room. He frowned and shook his head upon seeing such catastrophic changes. In the hallway, he congratulated me on the show in Philadelphia. My father had told him about it, apparently very proud of me.

Dr. Kingsley said, "You know, Yarrott, you are your parents' star. Your success will help them through losing Charley. You can be comforted in that."

I was angered. He said "losing Charley," as if it were already a certainty. It was so disloyal. He was giving up hope way too soon. And what he said about me being the star disgusted me—like winning the lottery when everyone else is dirt-poor. I wanted to shake off his compliment before it stuck to my shirt.

I said, "I do hope Charley is not fully aware of what's going on right now. He'd be awfully upset by the way he looks."

Dr. Kingsley jingled the change in his pockets, sized me up

for a moment, and answered firmly, "Yarrott, Charley is already gone. His brain has undergone so many traumas with the bleeding and edema that the person you see is not the brother you knew. His capacity for thinking now is just about zero."

I immediately became protective and defensive, like a bully had just called Charley stupid. "Oh, I wouldn't be so sure. He can surprise you, Dr. Kingsley."

"Yarrott, you really must accept the fact that he's already gone."

I bit my tongue and affably shook his hand.

"Righteous bastard," I muttered to myself as the tall former Rhodes Scholar ambled toward the elevators.

On the afternoon of December 19, while I was hooked up to the machine at the Red Cross in Nashville, Dot and other nurses I had known years before gathered around me in the donor chair to inquire about Charley's progress. Time had changed all of us. Their many children had become young adults in the intervening years. I was no longer a student, but was now twenty-nine. Dot and I still joked with each other, but also talked more seriously. She had known Charley and me during the first phase of his illness, and then through the remission, and now in the relapse. The past six years had brought change and growth for everyone else, but it had only cruelly teased Charley with a taste of health. Being a mother of five children roughly our age, Dot was sensitive to the emotional roller coaster that we had endured. A devout Catholic, she was also attentive to the spiritual importance of what we were going through. She acknowledged Charley's proximity to death and his very slight chances for survival. It did not occur to me at the time that that afternoon could be my last platelet pheresis. After seven hundred searing jabs since I was sixteen, the fat needle in Dot's hand would be my last one.

At five P.M., while the evening sky through the windows turned ultramarine blue, I stood with Dad at Charley's bed while the nurse plugged the bag of my platelets from the afternoon's pheresis into the IV. It seemed just in time, too, because

275

Charley's gums had begun oozing badly in the early afternoon and his bleeding was worsening by the hour.

"Not to worry, big brother...*here* I come to save the *day!*" I said, doing Andy Kaufman doing Mighty Mouse.

Charley rolled his eyes and groaned with a tone that I thought said "In that case, we're in big trouble." I chuckled and patted his shoulder. He stared blankly ahead.

Dad and I had planned to run out to eat dinner when the bleeding stopped, but by nine o'clock the oozing had worsened, complicated by a bad nosebleed. Charley had not been helped by my platelets. This was a stunning, horrifying change. My blood had always turned a dire situation around, had always proven the doctors' pessimism wrong, had been the unwavering miracle that prevented Charley's plight from turning tragic. What was happening in front of us was unthinkable. The doctors and nurses were stymied about what to do. At this point, it felt like anything and everything was worth trying, but with a hospital floor full of desperately sick patients, the amount of attention needed to help Charley now was impossible. The Red Cross had been notified of the crisis and were feverishly cross-matching red cells and random platelets to give him as soon as they found them. He was losing blood faster than he was receiving it.

"We've got to stop his bleeding somehow, Yarrott. Here, help me." Dad gathered a stack of washcloths from the bathroom and ice from the bucket next to the bed. "Let's put it out like a fire in the old days. Assembly-line fashion. I'll pack his mouth and nose with the cold rags. You rinse them out in ice water and give them back to me. If we repeat it rapidly enough, we'll lower the temperature of the affected tissue and get this damn bleeding under control."

We rolled up our sleeves and got to work. Dad raised the head of the bed so Charley was almost sitting upright. "We need to take as much pressure off his head as possible. You okay with all this, son?" he asked Charley. "It's going to be really uncomfortable." Dad placed his hand softly on Charley's

276

shoulder, and he nodded in approval of what we were doing.

For the next three hours, in a dazed, robotic motion, Dad laid cold wet cloths across Charley's nose, mouth, and sinuses, and tightly rolled more iced cloth to pack deep inside of his nose and over the gums inside his mouth. He constantly replaced the cloths and I constantly rinsed and dipped them in ice, working so fast that the constant ice lowered his temperature. Charley indicated that his head hurt with the cold but was adamant for us to continue. The feeling that we were accomplishing something, the three of us together, gave me a rush of satisfaction. It was an orchestrated flow of cooperation, a focused dedication to one another that buoyed all three of us in an otherwise desperate moment. The bleeding finally stopped.

At midnight, Dad and I met with a young intern in the corridor. The attractive, dark-haired guy only a year or two older than I spoke softly with a deep Southern drawl. "Yarrott, your father wanted me to explain to you what has been going on with Charley since we started his second round of chemo. I wish I could say things look good, but they don't. His heart is just not strong enough to cope with the strain on his system that the chemo is causing. He's displaying signs of serious cardiac failure. Not to mention that your platelets are no longer working for him. Unfortunately, at this point, whether or not the chemo has wiped out the leukemic cells is not the issue. His whole body is spiraling downward and there doesn't seem to be anything we can do to stop it."

"You knew this already, Dad?"

Nodding, Dad watched my reaction. I played the intern's words through my head again and took a deep breath. "He's not going to make it?"

"It's not looking good." The intern waited patiently for my reaction. Dad wiped his eyes and looked at the floor.

"Does Vickie know?" I asked.

"Not yet," Dad said. "I'll talk to her when she gets here in the morning."

I felt oddly detached, mechanical. Maybe I was too tired to feel anything. Maybe I was is in denial. I could *think* about what was happening, but I could not *feel* it. I became analytical and wanted more details. "What will it be like for him, if he dies? How will it happen if he actually dies?"

The intern continued to stand there, staring me in the eyes. "It will be a fairly slow process. Essentially, his lungs will fill up with edema as his heart fails."

"That sounds like drowning."

"Well, that's certainly an accurate comparison. Wouldn't you say, Dr. Benz?" The intern tried to pull Dad back into the conversation.

"It is like that, yes," Dad reluctantly agreed.

I thought of the terror that must accompany drowning. I could not shake the fear, the panic, the absolute torture of struggling to breathe. "Isn't there anything we can do to make it easier for him, so he doesn't have to be afraid?"

Dad answered, "There is not much we can do except give him more morphine. And that is...well, complicated."

The intern added, "Yes, increasing morphine compromises one's respiratory system. In other words it would hasten his death. But it is true that it would make him more comfortable."

"Dad?"

"He's right, Yarrott."

"Is it wrong to quicken his death if it means he won't have to be as afraid?"

SIXTY-FOUR

The Bone Bridge

At two o'clock in the morning, I told Dad to go home and get some sleep. I was twenty-nine years old and hearty. Dad was seventy-two and he was looking frail. The past three months had devastated him physically.

During the course of the night, Charley slept and I sat up in the chair, nodding off occasionally. Other than the nurse periodically taking his temperature and blood pressure, we were left alone with the door closed, the light of the bathroom slanting across the carpeted floor. Despite its cheery, modern walls and carpet, the room had a feeling of being very old and enduring, a feeling of enclosed safety. I remembered the same feeling of security from my childhood book *Goodnight Moon*. There was just the rabbit in the bed, the old lady in the rocking chair, the ticking of the clock, and the moon outside. This hospital room felt like the most important room in the universe. And strangely, despite his terrible condition, I felt secure being in the room with Charley. He was the person with whom I had shared the most maddeningly complex paradox: our lives together had become as physically close as twins, yet we had been foes and opposites. But now, with him in the bed, or what was left of him, breathing slowly, quietly, eyes closed, couldn't I say now that we had finally developed a true regard for each other?

As he slept, his face and hands were twitching like a sleeping dog. *You go, Charley Dog, you chase those damn squirrels.* I wondered what he might be dreaming. That is, if he were able to dream anymore or to even think at all anymore. I could not tell.

The room was still. There were no noises from the corridor, like muffled TV or conversations. There were no doors opening and closing. No whining wheels rolling under chairs or beds. There were not even intercom announcements, no "Doctor Doe, Doctor John Doe." Dim, silent, and cut-off from the living, the room was like a grave, an early grave.

I remembered another time when I felt buried alongside him. It was also around Christmas. Aunts and uncles had come to Nashville, and to make space for them he slept in my room in the basement. That night he told me what it was like to face death. We were down in my old room with the painted rock walls. After I switched off the lights, we lay on the twin beds and he told me what it felt like to have no future. I reached out in the dark and touched the hard, cold surface of the rock wall only inches from my face. That night felt like Charley and I had settled down together in a grave.

He breathed slowly, across the room, and I scribbled on my drawing pad. First, a few simple vertical lines, tripods, then lines connecting them, like the wires on high utility poles. The drawing grew more distinct the more I layered the black lines. Finally I stopped. There stood two towers, crosshatched and skeletal, connected by the sweeping arc of suspension cables and a roadbed. A bridge.

And that's how we've lived, Charley. For thirteen years. Because of our bones, no less. Could the two sides have been any more different? On a cellular level, we are one and the same. But on a larger scale, if the camera pulls back and sees us big, we are as different as black and white. The opposite sides finally met, though, in the middle, didn't they? We still crossed over this bridge, didn't we? From me to you and you to me, we crossed back and forth over this bridge so many times we can't count them. Didn't we? We fought and screamed and hated each other, but we met in the middle, no matter what. Didn't we?

I began a second drawing of something new. A box became a house and then became a skyscraper. As I drew, I continued to think about the first drawing. *Yes, that's right. We met in the middle. Didn't we?*

SIXTY-FIVE

Life Insurance

An exhausted Vickie stayed with Charley while Mother and Dad drove home for dinner and joined me. Famished and impatient, I pulled out a box of spinach soufflé from the freezer and dropped it in the microwave with a hard clunk. I slammed the door shut and read the instructions. "Damn, even in the microwave this takes forever. Shit."

"Honey, I heard that. Watch your tongue," Mother said without looking up. She was preoccupied, leaning on one crutch and quietly arranging three plates and silverware around the breakfast table. She moved to the counter and slowly pulled apart a head of romaine, neatly stacking the leaves inside the plastic salad spinner. Finally, she said, "I, *we*, have something to talk to you about, Yarrott. I'm afraid it's going to upset you." She looked at Dad, then at me. She was clearly anxious and changed the subject on herself. "Ed, would you pull out the meatloaf the Clarkes brought over?"

Dad looked annoyed. "Of course. Now go on, Elizabeth."

"Well, we tried to talk reason with him, but he didn't budge."

"Mother, what on earth are you talking about? Just get it out."

"Well, honey, it's hard to talk about. It feels disloyal. We should be hoping for his survival. Not talking about *this*."

Dad took control of the conversation. "Yarrott, you know your life insurance? The policies I took out on each of you when you were children? Well, Charley has decided to leave the bulk of his to Vickie."

"And not to you, Yarrott," Mother added. She paused for my reaction, but I was slow to respond. I was exhausted. Even the idea of microwaving dinner seemed too great an effort.

She continued, "We believe he ought to leave the money to you. My Lord, with all you've done. And he's only known her for what...a year?"

Dad corrected her. "A year and a half."

"Well, it's not a very long time. Your father and I tried to talk sense into him a few weeks ago, before he went downhill so badly. Charley's a very stubborn guy, as you know."

Dad sounded more approving. "He's adamant about leaving something to Vickie. She lost everything when her parents died. She really needs it to get on with her life. She needs it to finish school. She'll need it when she goes in for a kidney transplant in a year or two. It's understandable. It's even commendable. Although...it doesn't seem fair to you."

"That's an understatement, Ed."

Dad ignored her and continued, "Yarrott, Charley said helping Vickie gives his death meaning. He needs that."

Mother hobbled over to me without her crutches and looked me in the face. "Well, say something. Are you hurt? Angry? What?"

I said, "I've got to think for a minute. Let me think." During the months of his hospitalization, I hadn't considered that Charley would have any money to leave behind. I had completely forgotten that we each had a sizable life insurance policy in our names. "Gosh, how much are you talking about?"

Dad answered, "Two hundred thousand."

I felt faint. Despite my exhaustion, my numbness, I knew this was a huge piece of information and full of meaning. I should be strongly reacting.

Mother quickly continued, "Personally, I think it's wrong, honey. You have put your life on hold for so long. For him."

"Is the whole two hundred thousand going to Vickie?"

"No. Half of it goes to her. A quarter goes to you and the rest is divided among Eddy, Angela, your mother, and me."

"Fifty thousand dollars is supposed to go to me?" This was more money than I was used to thinking about.

"Yes, that's right," Mother said with an apologetic tone. "It should be much, much more."

I heard myself assuring her, "But that's more money than I ever thought I'd have." Thinking of my life in Philadelphia, I immediately saw how fifty thousand dollars would bring relief to my constant financial insecurity. Besides, I did not want to feel betrayed. Not at this time. Betrayal by Charley, with his death imminent, was more than I could handle. It was easier to accept his decision, good or bad. Of course, give the greater amount to Vickie.

"But, that's not all, Yarrott," Dad continued with a solemn tone. "We've never talked about our resources and what Charley's illness all these years has done to them."

I was surprised. "I thought you always got professional courtesy or whatever it's called for doctors."

"Yes, that's right, but that's just for the doctors' fees. That doesn't cover hospital and laboratory bills. After we hit the ceiling of the insurance each year, I paid all of it."

Mother put down her drink and put her hand on my shoulder. I could feel her ice-cold fingertips through my turtleneck. "It has used up all of your father's retirement money."

"That's right. I have no retirement fund. And no savings. All the treatments at the hospital over the course of so many years...well, you can imagine."

Anger surged in me and my attitude finally flip-flopped. That ungrateful asshole. Not only did he bleed me dry, but he used up Dad's money, too. Then, to top it off, he leaves what money he has to his girlfriend! That's gratitude? That asshole.

Dad could see my face turning red. "But don't worry, Yarrott. I never intended to retire. Ever. There're all sorts of things an old surgeon can do. Like evaluating cases for the Social Security Administration. All sorts. But, whatever you do, don't hold it against Charley. He did what he truly believed was right. Try to believe that what he's doing will make sense one day. Perhaps he knows more than we do."

SIXTY-SIX

Bath

Tuesday, December 20 was dark and cold, and the large windows of Charley's room, tinted as they were, gave the impression of constant twilight. Snow was expected. On the bedside table, the ceramic Christmas tree was a sorry reflection of the holidays gearing up outside. The box of Snickers I kept in the dresser had just one last bar. I had compulsively eaten them over the past few days and my pants were now very tight on me. I looked in the stainless steel mirror of the hospital bathroom and saw a puffy oval face and a head in need of a haircut. I saw the reflection of Charley through the doorway behind me. His face was stuporous and vacant on the bed just a few feet from me. I looked at both of us in the same framed mirror and wondered how long, how long we would be in the same dimension together. The news of the insurance money and Dad's finances had lost its impact on me in the carpeted inner sanctum of death. *Is this really happening? Is he really slipping out of this life?* Charley was vulnerable now. An infant. Harmless. Defenseless. Meanwhile, a big truck was careening down the highway and Charley was lying right in the middle of the road. *Can't we stop it somehow?*

Weird, obsessive thoughts troubled me, like horseflies around my face. The fact that all this was occurring at Christmas felt like a sign of something. *Is he, are we, being punished? Was Mother right when we were kids, that we would be punished for being so mean to each other? Why am I the one with a pink, healthy body while Charley's is gray, swollen, and starting to rot?* I sat back in the chair, tried to calm down, and realized I was twitching my head.

For the second night in a row, I stayed overnight in the room, giving my parents and Vickie a longer, much-needed break. At midnight Charley's eyes were closed. I pulled out my drawing pad and continued with sketches for new wall pieces. Minimal, solid black forms seemed right to me for the way I was feeling, but everything I did looked too elegant, too smooth, too appealing. Something was making me disturbed and ashamed of my work, of its self-important shapes and meanings, its personal and esoteric language. What was I communicating that had any importance whatsoever in the human experience? Absolutely nothing. Yet I had been so proud of myself. Proud and self-centered and self-congratulatory. I whipped myself across the back with self-recrimination.

Charley motioned to me that he wanted help to the bathroom. Yet again. I mustered my energy. He had become pear-shaped and very heavy. I saw that his legs, too, were becoming engorged with edema and it hurt him to put weight on his round, soft feet. Pivoting him around and gently kicking his IV stand out of the way, I got my hand caught in the tube of the Hickman catheter jutting from his sternum. "Oh, shit. Did that hurt you, Charley?"

"Nuh. Dodn't." His mouth was dry and his lips cracked. I smeared some Chapstick on them.

In the bathroom, he looked like he'd forgotten why he was sitting on the toilet.

"Baf plea? Baf nah?" He looked up at me from the toilet with a crazy smile on his face. He wanted me to give him a bath.

First I had to wipe him. He was dry. He had had no movement. Again, his need to get to the toilet was a misfire. He either was confusing the sensations of his bodily functions or he was completely stopped up. Or perhaps both.

"Okay, Charley. I'll get Kathy the nurse and we'll take you to the hot tub. That'll feel good tonight, wouldn't it?" It was way past midnight, but in the purgatory of fluorescent light and stupor, it made as much sense as anything.

With his IV pole teetering alongside us, I pushed his wheelchair into the physical therapy room down the hall. In the middle of the floor sat a boxy contraption, a vertical bathtub the size of a washing machine, with a rubber-sealed door on the side. Kathy helped me pick Charley up and pivot him onto the seat of the tub. He felt as big as a bear, bulbous and hunched, with arms and legs too swollen for him to manage. We closed the door around him and sealed him in. He looked at me, annoyed, with a helpless, what-is-this-damn-thing-you've-put-me-in expression. The warm water gushed over his feet and began to fill the tub. His jaw fell open, he smiled, and then he mouthed to me, "Feels good. This feels good."

His inexpressive, dead-looking hands patted at his face, not sure what they were after. A tickle? A scratch? A pain? They waved aimlessly in the air. Were they knocking at flies? Clearing cobwebs? Gesturing to me to come close?

With a thin hospital washcloth, I pulled warm water across his back and under his arms and around the Hickman catheter disappearing into his chest. I soaped up the cloth and gently washed his face. He moaned, I think in the pleasure of the massaging of his skin. With a finger in the cloth, I cleaned his ears like they were small seashells, fragile, delicate, and curled. I rolled up my sleeves and dropped my hand into the water up to my bicep to wash the rest of him, dominated now by a gigantic, edema-filled scrotum, the size of a grapefruit. I carefully cleaned between his legs, as delicate in my mind as another seashell. He seemed to have no awareness of his nakedness, no shame and not a fragment of self-conscious pride.

The water drained out of the contraption and sucked loudly around his feet. He slumped forward and Kathy held him up as I quickly dried him off with lots of towels. I wrapped one around his head to cover his patchy scalp and pulled a soft terrycloth robe around his back. We lowered him into his wheelchair and I rolled him back to his room. By this time, he was beyond docile. He was technically conscious, but so relaxed from the warmth of the bath he seemed to be in a trance.

After an hour back in his bed, he became restless again, pulling at the sheets and patting at his face and scalp. He called for me repeatedly, believing that he needed to be taken to the bathroom. My back was sore from lifting him, so I suggested he use the plastic urinal. He was adamant about getting up. I took him to the bathroom, where he stood and strained out a few trickles of urine, then I brought him back to bed. A few minutes later, he had forgotten he had already gone to the bathroom and wanted me to take him again.

"Goddamn it, Charley, no. Not again. Not now. I just took you. Try to remember, damn it."

"Yarrott. Yarrott. Take me. I gotta go. C'mon, take me. Gotta go to bahroom."

"Damn it, NO." My anger slipped out at him.

"Damn ya, too." Charley turned his face to me, his eyes unfocused and floating about.

We were fighting, as usual. Despite everything. While there seemed to be a sacred intensity in the room, a solemn dimness, he was living life still. Our impatience with each other had been our manner and our pattern all of our lives and it was not about to change, no matter the circumstances.

"Can you believe how we argue, Charley? Still?" I pulled his hand down from his face and held it.

He looked straight ahead and was still for a moment. Then he blurted out clearly, "Yarrott, get some paper." I held my drawing pad in front of him and he tried to hold a pencil and write with it. His straining effort resulted in three scribbled, illegible jumbles of lines. He sighed and dropped his hand. "Here. This."

"What do you want to say, Charley? I can't read it."

His breathing sounded coarse, as if he were sucking his breath through a bag of sticks and rocks. He pawed the air gently, for me to come closer to him. I leaned over him and he whispered slowly, carefully in my ear, "I...love...you."

I was shocked and backed away from him. As with the times he'd approached me with surprising depths of honesty in the past, my reaction was to jump back, like I was getting too close to the fire. He looked at me through his fog and held a hand up. I took it and sat back down next to the bed. I leaned toward him and put my other arm around his head on the pillow. "Thank you, Charley. Thank you. Thank you. I hope you know that I love you, too. I love you, too."

His expression did not change. My eyes filled up and I continued, "I want you to hear something, Charley." I felt my bottom lip having a spasm. I fought to continue. "I want to be honest with you. This is what I want to say: I am going to miss you. So much I can't even describe." I rested my head on his shoulder, felt his warmth, and smelled his clean skin and the whiff of iodine from his Hickman catheter. After a long pause, so long that I thought that he had not heard me, he finally squirmed and reached up and rubbed his head.

He was quiet for some time, perhaps a few hours. My concept of time passing was upside-down. The rasping, rattling sound in his breathing became louder and the young intern stopping in took me into the hall. "The scratchy noise you are hearing in his breathing is gradual cardiac failure. His lungs are being compromised with the building up of fluids."

"Can you do anything to make it easier for him, more comfortable?"

"Just more morphine, but that will hasten his failure."

I heard myself repeating the words "No, we don't want that" and returned to Charley's beside. He looked at me and again motioned that he needed to be helped to the bathroom. This time, I felt honored to help him. I held him up, wobbling at the toilet, and aimed his penis over the water, but nothing came out. I hoped that flushing the toilet would give him some sense of satisfaction.

As I lowered him to the bed, Charley's scrotum, horribly swollen and translucent, was caught between his legs and he sat on it. He let out a mortifying howl and his eyes rolled back into his head. He collapsed in my arms, falling to the bed, and I fell on top of him. We were slipping to the floor and the IV pole was coming down on top of us. I screamed, "Help! Somebody help!"

Two nurses ran into the room and helped me pull him back up to the bed, and I realized he wasn't breathing. I panicked and screamed into his face, "Charley, come back. Come *to*. Charley!" The nurses stood by and offered no help. "Help

288

me," I pleaded. "Get the oxygen. Give me the mask. Turn the oxygen up high. Goddamn it, give the mask to me," I ordered. They obliged at this point and I wrapped the mask around his face. Then I remembered Charley had signed a no resuscitation form.

Suddenly, he coughed and wheezed through the rattling of his lungs. He opened his eyes.

"Charley, you almost left me! Damn you, crazy man." I wrapped my arm around his head and kissed his forehead. "Nurse," I said, "Can you please hand me the phone?" I called Mother and Dad at home and my father answered.

"Yes, Yarrott. Everything okay?" Dad sounded tired but calm.

"No, Dad. You and mother should come here. And call Angela and Vickie, too. All of you need to get here as soon as you can."

"Oh, no. Yes. We'll be right there. Hold on, son."

SIXTY-SEVEN

Winter Solstice

I lay alongside Charley on the bed, my arm around his head, calming him. He was anxious, struggling to breathe through his rattling lungs. His rasping breaths were becoming short and quick, like a small, nervous bird. Tapping one hand to the oxygen mask on his face, he waved the other at me, I thought to indicate that he needed to urinate. I held the urinal at his groin and rested his penis in it, but nothing happened. He jammed his head back into his pillow and moaned, then looked at me with angry eyes. He was miserably uncomfortable and restless. His lungs were filling like they were sponges. *How much does he understand? Does he know he's drowning?*

"Just try to relax, Charley. Try to relax," I repeated to him softly. He shakily moved his arm over to me and I took his hand in mine. I stroked his arm. "It's okay, big brother. Everybody's coming. They'll be here soon, Charley. Vickie, Mother, Dad, Angela. They'll be here soon."

The nurses quietly pulled the door closed and left Charley and me alone, his short, rasping breaths filling the room. Our time that morning was suspended, frozen. It is only after piecing together what happened that I say it was eight o'clock. I was aware neither of the time of day nor the passage of minutes. Outside the windows began a cold winter morning, December 21, the winter solstice. Inside the room it was as dim as twilight. The moment was suspended until I heard a commotion at the door as Angela rushed in, followed by Vickie. Farther away, I heard the metallic clicking of Mother's crutches frantically approaching down the corridor. She entered the room with Dad, grimly wiping their eyes as they gathered around the bed.

"Charley? You holding on there, son?" Dad asked, his voice breaking a little. He leaned over the bed and looked him closely in the eyes. Charley showed little recognition and instead seemed angry as he struggled to breathe. His chest heaved with each rasping inhalation. His head was pushed back on his pillow, mouth dropped open, chin raised.

I grabbed Dad's hand and pulled him gently toward the door. "Can we talk outside?"

I shut the door behind us in the corridor. "It's time, Dad. It's time to increase Charley's morphine. Look how he's struggling. Please, can we do it now?"

"I agree with you, son. What we're hearing in there is the death rattle. There is no reason to make him suffer more than he already has. Let me find somebody."

I leaned against the wall and took a deep breath as Dad talked with the intern in the nurse's station. *Do you feel how easy it is to breathe, Yarrott? Damn it. In...out. In...out. Smooth. Easy. Damn it. Charley's life has been one compromise after another, his health stolen, one piece of it after another. Now he's down to the last piece of it. Goddamn. It is unfair. It is cruel. If we can make it easier for him to die, we will do it.*

Back in the room, we slowly took our places around the bed. The intern injected the additional morphine into Charley's drip and then disappeared. Mother stood holding Charley's left hand and gripped his pulse with her right. Angela stood next to Mother at Charley's head and stroked his shoulder. Dad stood at the end of the bed and held both of Charley's feet. Vickie stood holding his right hand. I stood next to Vickie and held Charley's head in my left hand.

Charley looked at each of us with anger in his eyes as his struggle for breath deepened. He looked furious. Then all at once, his face began to relax. His breathing slowed and the fear and anger in his face seemed to disappear. He looked straight ahead and continued to draw determined breaths, even as the rattle in his chest intensified. His breaths grew longer and slower. In. Out. In. Out. In...

Each of us held part of him. We were utterly helpless as he fought. Angela leaned into his face and said calmly, "Charley, you can let go now. You don't have to fight anymore." He seemed to hear her. Deep, under his obscured vision, his tortured confusion, his panic, his anger, he *must* have heard her. Immediately, his struggling stopped and he exhaled slowly through what sounded like bubbles. I looked into his eyes and felt him drift away as if into a whirlpool. His chest heaved one last time and remained still. The expression in his face drained away, leaving his eyes glazed and empty above his open mouth.

After a long moment, Mother's tight voice interrupted our motionless silence. "His pulse has stopped. He's gone." A small, damp circle widened in Charley's lap. The awful grip of his body and all its pathologies had finally let him empty.

Angela reached across the bed to his face and with just the weight of her fingers, lowered his eyelids. I settled his head back on the pillow and cupped his jaw in my hand to close his mouth. Vickie gently placed his hand on his chest, holding onto his index finger for a long time before letting go. Dad continued to grip his feet at the end of the bed and quietly began sobbing to himself. Mother dropped down silently in the chair, stunned, still holding Charley's hand. Angela, Vickie, and I wandered outside the door and held one another, our triad, each of us trembling and unable to speak. In the bright light of the corridor, the sounds and movements of the hospital swept over us.

SIXTY-EIGHT

The Coldest Day

Voices were filling up the house downstairs and I had had no sleep for two nights. I lay on the twin bed in the guest room and stared at the ceiling. As I had just learned, life does not stop after one loses a brother or a son. There is no quiet moment of precious reflection. The world instead starts anxiously shrieking for decisions to be made. First in our face, an autopsy needed to be done. As perhaps the world's longest living patient with his critical form of aplastic anemia, the value to science of Charley's body was inestimable—as if his body had not been ruined enough. A moment after signing the autopsy form we left the hospital. Mother, Angela, and Vickie returned to the house with Charley's things. Dad and I drove through morning traffic across town to meet with a saleslady at the cemetery office, to select a coffin and make arrangements for Charley's burial.

"You know, of course, that we are well into the Christmas holiday schedule," she droned flatly into her event schedule. Scratching at her nose, she flipped the pages back and forth. "We'll have to get this done before Saturday the 24th. That's Christmas Eve. So, how about a burial on Friday midday? That'll give our workers time to complete the job and leave for the long Christmas weekend."

"Certainly," my father said, sounding agreeable but gritting his teeth. He was ever the diplomat, even now.

"Remember," he said, "my son did not want his coffin contained in a concrete vault. He wanted to be taken back to the earth, at least as much can be allowed."

"I hear you, Dr. Benz. I can't say I understand it, but I hear you and we shall honor the deceased's wishes. Let's take a look at the options for the deceased's plaque."

I spat, "His name is Charley. The deceased's name is Charley. Please address him as that, okay?"

"Yes, well, would *Charley* have liked this, for example?" She held out in front of us a laminated photograph of a bronze plaque decorated with a gathering of roses in each corner. Suitable for an old lady, maybe, but not my brother.

"Absolutely not." I sniffed. "Something absolutely plain, no flowers, no cursive, no italics, plain."

"*This*, then, is not too...austere?" She disapprovingly pulled out a sheet that was tucked in the very back of her sample book. It was a plain rectangular bronze plate with Roman capital lettering spelling out the name and dates, surrounded cleanly by a thin border.

"Perfect," I said.

~

I cannot imagine how the woman spent her work days, reciting her grotesque facts and figures, coercing people to buy more expensive coffins and plaques, feeding off these people who drive up in their cars right after the most earth-shattering event in their lives. Who *was* this awful woman, this saleslady of death, dressed in a black blouse with Saturn dangle earrings? On the way home, Dad and I scowled together at how weirdly she was dressed—in a word, celestial.

We earnestly tried to follow Charley's wishes, but still, we came up a little short. He had wanted the simplest of funerals, and to be laid in his jeans, flannel shirt, and boots, without being embalmed, in a plain wooden box buried directly in the dirt, no modern concrete shell to protect him, and buried under a tree. Dad and I got everything right except the plain box part. That was totally impossible. The only wood coffins available in the United States were heavily upholstered and fitted with bronze handles. Fortunately, there was already a big maple tree hanging over the Benz family plot. It was not the naturalist's burial on a country hillside that he had wanted, but it was close.

Mother, Dad, Vickie, Angela, and I decided that Charley's closed coffin would be brought home the next day for twenty-four hours. The visitation would begin on the evening of the 22nd and the funeral service would take place in the living room on the 23rd. While it sounded unorthodox and Victorian to do this in our house, it was the best way we could think of to honor his wish for utter simplicity. Charley's old friends Joe and Wilson, along with my friend Jeff, moved furniture downstairs to make room for what was ahead. They seemed surprised about the plans but were respectful nevertheless. Funerals in 1983 normally took place somewhere else. Anywhere but in your house.

I lay on the bed upstairs trying hard to turn off the voices and incessantly repeating images from the past forty-eight hours. I still felt responsible for Charley's welfare and comfort. I heard him calling me, needing to get out of bed. I saw the ceramic Christmas tree inside the dim of the room, smelled the odor of iodine, heard the rattling sound of his last breaths. Did I do well by him? Did I make sure he knew I loved him? Did I hurt him when I fell on him at the end? I was wired and my twitching was back with a vengeance. I desperately needed to shut myself off.

Dad came in to see how I was. "Able to get any sleep?"

"I don't think so, Dad."

"Here, take this. It'll help you." He had in his hands a blue tablet and a glass of water. Slugging down the pill, I saw how worn out Dad was. He was exhausted, but still maintained a dignified face.

"Will you stay with me until I go to sleep? I don't want to be alone." I felt safe with him, the way I sometimes had as a small child.

"Sure. I'm right here." Dad pulled up a chair next to the bed and I reached out with my hand. "I'm right here." He firmly gripped my hand until I stopped twitching and fell asleep a few minutes later.

Groggy from the long nap, I telephoned my high school friend Connie that afternoon to ask if she would be available to play the violin for the funeral in two days. She had played once before for Charley, the night before we flew to Seattle for the bone marrow transplant that never happened. This time, the voyage was definite.

"Oh, Yarrott. I'm so sorry. God, he fought for such a long time. Of course, I'd be honored to play. What would you like me to do?"

"It sounds kind of ludicrous, but he actually wrote down that he wanted Beethoven's Ninth to be played, the 'Ode to Joy.' Can you just play the line of melody?"

"Sure. That's not ludicrous, either. It's a celebration of life. I'll repeat the melody a few times and let it build a little. It'll be very appropriate for him. What about Barber's 'Adagio for Strings'? That'll be a good complement. I could play that as people gather in the church, then when you say, I could play the ode."

"One thing, though, Connie. We're having the funeral at home, in the living room. Casket and all."

"Really? Interesting. You know, that sounds just right to me. I'll be there early on the 23rd and you can get me set up."

That night, Dad turned down the thermostat to fifty degrees, in anticipation of housing a body not embalmed. In the morning, Eddy and his wife, Debby, arrived on the red eye from their new home in Los Angeles and pulled up to the house in a rented car just as we were sitting down for breakfast.

"My goodness, it's cold in here. Can't we please warm the place up?" Debby complained, hugging herself.

All of us turned around in unison and said, "No!"

The day ahead was full, writing an obituary and calling the newspapers to make sure it was printed. We also were expecting a visit from Dr. Strother, the minister from years ago at our family's church, McKendree Methodist. He was a gentle, sophisticated man—understated compared to the fire-and-brimstone preachers who were hired after him. We had always liked him as kids, had trusted him and had never heard him raise his voice in disapproval. Although he was in retirement on his farm, he agreed to officiate at the funeral since we were longtime friends. He arrived late, complaining of how slow he had to drive due to the ice on the roads. "The ground, my friends, is rock-hard."

Florist trucks pulled up to the house all morning. Mother called me to the front door. "Honey, this is from Draper to you. It's lovely." The white gladiolas stood out of the tall glass vase like an art nouveau statue.

The card said, "Know that I'm thinking of you. As always, Draper."

At ten A.M. a silver hearse drove up in the driveway and parked next to Dad's Oldsmobile. Inside was the hulking form of the coffin. The two mortuary personnel, Eddy, Dad, and I carried it up the stone steps to the porch and waited for Mother to open the front door. It was heavy like a couch, but easier to lift because of the handles on the sides. We squeezed through the doorway and waited in the front hall while the undertaker rolled out a folding stand on wheels and opened it up underneath the coffin. "Okay. You can let it down now," he instructed us. Then he wheeled it into the living room and parked it in front of the fireplace. He carefully laid a pall of white roses on the lid and turned to my mother. "Nice. Very nice. Would you like two stands of flowers on either side? Maybe big candlesticks, too?"

"No, thank you. The pall is fine, but otherwise we're leaving it spare. Just like my son wanted it," Mother said.

"Dr. Benz," I overheard the undertaker whisper to my father, "if you decide to view him, please understand that we thought it best to lay down inside the casket, under the body, a polyvinyl wrapping. Since he is not embalmed and wanted no cosmetic reconstruction, we could not guarantee that he would not...leak or spill some fluids. You understand, I'm sure."

After the furniture was arranged around the room's perimeter, our friends and the undertaker said good-bye. We were alone in our house with the lustrous pine coffin and Charley's body. The sickly sweet odor of roses wafted through the house. I could not help but remember the original purpose for scented flowers at funerals...before the days of embalming.

"I would like to see him," Dad said solemnly as Mother, Eddy, Angela, and I stood in the front hall, hesitant to enter the living room.

"Not me, Ed. I don't think I can see him," Mother stated flatly. "I'll come back after you all are done."

"Well, okay...if you think it would be the right thing to do," Angela replied to Dad.

I was caught numb and did not know if I wanted to see him or run out of the room. Before I could make up my mind, Eddy removed the pall of roses and laid it on the floor. Dad slid open the latches of the head end of the coffin and slowly lifted the lid. I saw first the plastic gathered loosely inside, then the plaid flannel shirt and blue jeans appeared out of the dark interior, then his hands, folded together across his chest. Finally, his face, his beautiful nose and prominent cheekbones, his deep eyes—closed as Angela had left them, his colorless lips relaxed, not frowning, not smiling. Then his black, thread-like hair, *No, that can't be hair, he had none left, what is that, stitches—oh, God,* I darted my eyes to focus on his hands, the long gray fingers lying on his chest. *Why is he so thin? No one could be so thin. His jeans are gathered under his belt like there is nothing inside him. He was not like this the morning he died. What has happened? Oh, God...the autopsy.*

Angela touched his hands and Dad stroked his face. I could not watch this. I moved behind them and buried my face in Angela's back.

"We'll have to keep this room very cold until tomorrow," Dad said slowly and evenly, as if in a trance. "Does everyone understand?"

Jeff and Wilson picked Mike up at the airport in the afternoon and drove him to the house. We had not seen each other since my opening weekend in Philadelphia two weeks earlier. To

Mother and Dad, Mike was still just my good friend and traveling companion. They welcomed his support of me but they did not know the full meaning of it. To find some privacy, we walked in the yard and talked. The ground was frozen and crunchy. I stuffed my hands in my jean pockets.

"You know, everyone in Philadelphia is asking for you and sends their love." He put his hand on my shoulder. "How are you holding up?"

"I don't really feel anything. The experience is so new and so big, I don't know how to think about it. There is a lot I just don't want to remember."

"Like what?"

"Like today we opened the coffin and looked at Charley. Everyone but my mother. I wish I hadn't seen him. Now I've got that picture in my head for the rest of my life. Damn it."

"Babe, why in God's name did you all do that?"

"Because my family's full of doctors. They're clinical. Nothing scares them."

"Excuse me for saying so, but their doing that is pretty fucked-up."

SIXTY-NINE

Colored Lights

The living room was full of people that evening, stopping by to pay their respects. It felt like Christmas afternoon, like a holiday open house, only this time a big pine coffin took up a large spot in front of the fireplace. The usual compliments were made to my parents, how they both looked so good—under the circumstances. They did not.

Mrs. Jeffries from three houses down rushed though the door and made a beeline to Mother in the wingchair. She had her red seasonal Bible under her mink coat. "Oh, isn't it glorious how Charley's gone to live with the Lord at Christmastime! My, it's awfully cold in here."

"So good to see you, Faye. Thanks for coming," Mother said cautiously. She quickly pulled at the elbow of the woman closest to her. "Marion, you know our neighbor Faye Jeffries, don't you? Won't you show her to the coffee?"

Everyone was particularly solicitous of Vickie, whom Mother and Dad introduced as Charley's fiancée. You could see the spasm of discomfort on people's faces. I watched everything from a strange, angry perch in my head. I could not stop my vicious thinking, like my facial tics but this time manifesting as thoughts in my head. *Bittersweet. So damn bittersweet. People must think this is the saddest damn house in the world.*

Someone called me to the kitchen. It was Claudia on the telephone in Florida. "Yarrott? Are you okay? I am so sorry about Charley."

I was relieved beyond words to hear her voice. She understood what Charley and I had been through more than anyone else. She saw it from the beginning, the very first platelet pheresis. She saw us in those early years. She was one who truly understood the depth and weight of our dilemma.

"Oh, honey, I'm there in spirit, believe me."

"I do, Claudia. I do." I hung up and wiped my eyes.

Charley had a huge number of friends in his life and they stayed with him through much of his thirteen-year illness. Members from his various sports teams in high school showed up and signed the visitors' book. I got a weird satisfaction from their shock as they came through the door and froze as they turned the corner into the living room and saw the coffin. *Yes, you feel this death tonight. You're alive and he's not. You be god-damned grateful.* I was angry at his friends the way he was often angry at them for having successful, healthy lives. I felt a warm, sadistic syrup in my throat.

I heard a quiet commotion at the door and saw a group of people stepping respectfully into the living room. *Now this touches me. My God, it's half the blood bank.* To see these wonderful people out of the context of the hospital was strange. I rushed up to Annelle and hugged her for a long time. She whispered, "God bless you, sugar." Then I moved to Ellen and Patricia and Bruce and Sandra and Georgia and Janet, each one just as solemn and warm. *It must be weird for them to see me without Charley. Well, there he is, folks, over there in front of the fireplace.*

Dr. Sergent, the young doctor who'd started the platelet pheresis with us thirteen years earlier, appeared in the kitchen with his wife, Carole. In the intervening years, he had returned to Vanderbilt from New York and had become a major figure at the hospital.

Grabbing my hand, Carole said, "Honey, how are you all holding up? My God, your family has been through so much."

"We're okay. A little tired. A little numb. But we're okay."

"Well, I've only been a bystander, but I've always loved your family. You, your brother, and your parents—all these years you have meant so much to us."

And Dr. Sergent to me. Remember those talks in the donor room with him? Remember him saying "I don't get what all the fuss is about gays"? Thank God I heard a good-looking, smart, straight man saying that when I was sixteen years old.

Dr. Sergent smiled at me and said, "We never imagined Charley's disease would turn into such an epic, did we, Yarrott?"

"Well, it's certainly been the defining story in our lives," I said, adding, "Yes, it sure was defining and...grueling." *What am I saying and why am I saying it to the Sergents? They're such sympathetic people. I guess I've got to be honest with somebody here. God, I wish somebody, just somebody would acknowledge the hell that Charley and I lived through together. What intense hell.*

૨૭

By nine o'clock, the visitation had ended and the house seemed much bigger. Mother told everyone in the family to make it to bed early for a busy day tomorrow.

"Anybody need ironing done?" she said, willing to help if needed.

My mother. Jesus. I can't believe it, she's thinking of ironing at a time like this. Her penchant for practicality just never stops. Dr. Sergent said something tonight—"Your mother is one of the most remarkable people I've ever met." I guess so. Look at her. Just look at her.

We had enough beds upstairs for everyone that night. Mike and I took the room with the twin beds, Eddy and Debby the old high bed, and Angela slept in Charley's room. It annoyed me that Mike and I had to sleep in separate beds to maintain the appearance of pals. I climbed into the narrow twin bed with him and wrapped my arms around him to feel his warmth. We lay there quietly with the bedside lamp on. The warmth of our two bodies said enough. After he opened a book to read, I crept back downstairs with a blanket around me to the living room. There I sat in the wing chair, with Charley across the room in his closed coffin. Quiet. No nurses. No medications to take. No need to go to the bathroom to be relieved. No relief needed. Just the ticking of the mantle clock.

I rubbed my hands together for warmth and felt the scar between my fingers that Charley's rage had once caused. One time among many. I saw the dark shape of the barn in the distance through the window. It had happened there, before his remission and while I was still giving him platelets. I had said something that triggered his fury and the next thing I saw was the tumbling glint of a plumber's wrench in the air, aiming like a weapon for my head. I threw up my hands to protect myself and the serrated jaw of the wrench struck flesh and bone with a thud.

"You could have killed me!" I heard myself blurt out in the stillness of the living room. "And of all people, why me?" I fought the urge to storm over to the coffin and throw back the lid and yell at him face to face. "You said I embarrassed you. God, you made me hate myself." The mantle clock ticked.

"You accepted me only when I played by your rules. So I walked differently. And I talked differently. You never looked at the ugliness in what you did." The floorboards groaned. I found myself on my feet, stepping closer to the coffin, angrier by the step. "Okay then. I'll apologize for you, asshole. I'll put words in your mouth. I'll say what I always wanted you to say."

In an approximation of Charley's voice, I said, "Yarrott," and startled myself by sounding exactly like him. In a half-whisper, I said, "Yarrott, Yarrott," as if he were just across the room, just in the other twin bed in my basement room from years ago. I could hear him with me. "Okay, Yarrott, you win. I apologize to you. You win."

I put my hand on the lid of the coffin. I saw the wrench come through the air at me, somersaulting and striking my hand. First came the deep, searing pain. Then the blood. Dad sutured the wound between the ring and little finger. Dad made Charley watch. Afterward Charley stormed off in his Jeep.

I shocked myself as I slammed my hand on the coffin lid. The roses shook. "Jesus Christ, why?" I felt the ache of bruises from the final pheresis inside the bend of my elbow. I felt the polished coolness of the lid. "Part of me is still in your veins. Hell, part of me will be buried tomorrow, too." The mantle clock struck eleven. The scent of roses lifted to my face.

I looked out the window at the strings of colored lights on the house across the street.

Sleet was clicking against the window and I gathered the blanket around me. Wind rustled through the trees and small branches tapped urgently against the house. Something vital sounded dammed-up, held back, choked outside somewhere.

"Yarrott..." Charley's whisper came from my mouth again. The likeness startled me again. The voice continued, "I love you." I straightened myself suddenly and backed away from the coffin.

"Yeah," I said. "I remember. I heard you. Two nights ago. Your last night alive." I rubbed my eyes and steadied myself against the wing chair. "You did. You said it. I heard you. Those were the very last words you spoke. Just three words. I...love...you."

"Yes. That's right." The calm voice agreed in the cold room. The clock on the mantle slowly ticked its wooden heartbeat. "And Yarrott...I spoke them *to you*."

I dropped into the wing chair and grabbed hold of the fabric on the arm, brocade that quickly took the warmth of my fingers. The words in my ears were echoing. *I love you. I love you. Who is speaking in this entangled world of ours, Charley? You or me?*

The weak glow of colored lights across the street traced the edges of the drapery in the room. Despite the sleet and snow, signs of life continued, a Christmas party winding down. Way across the road, I could hear the lilting voices of two women laughing and car doors shutting. An engine started, gunned twice, and the car pulled away on crunching ice. My ears followed these women as their car slowly continued down Tyne Boulevard. I imagined them rubbing circles on the windshield to clear their views and I wanted to be with them. I knew that warm air would soon be pouring from their dashboard heater. And I knew that in a little while they would be singing.

Epilogue

A few years after Charley's death, I drove down to Washington with a friend to see the newly built Vietnam Veterans Memorial. It had captured tremendous attention and stirred controversy with its stark, black-granite chevron digging into the earth like an enormous plow. Approaching the line of visitors, I noticed how an awed silence overcame people as they snaked down into the monument. There, in the middle of Washington, steps from the Mall, within smelling distance of hot dog stands and trinket venders, everyone in line suddenly became mute. We crept along the path and the walls of black granite grew deeper and higher until they engulfed us with the engraved names. Burly men stopped chewing their gum and blinked their eyes. Women pulled their small children close.

The crowd inched along slowly and respectfully. A man some distance in front of me leaned toward the wall and touched a name and then burst open like a dam, sobbing. We continued uncomfortably around him, leaving him alone on the path, separated from the reflective black surface by low stanchions and ropes. *When will this thing end? It's interminable. I don't want to see any more people break down. How embarrassing. For God's sake.* Then something caught my eye. A tiny piece of red yarn stuck to a name. I tried to imagine the circumstances driving someone to leave it. Was it a girlfriend? A mother? Then I remembered my own mother on Christmas Day a year after Charley's death. She'd had a few drinks that afternoon, driven to the cemetery by herself, and Scotch-taped a twig of mistletoe to Charley's plaque in the ground. I envisioned her hobbling across the frozen grass, struggling to bend down with her arms in the crutches, to leave a gesture at once so terribly nutty and unspeakably sad.

I looked left and right, up and down the black walls of granite littered with the left-behind toys, notes, snapshots, and flags. I thought of Mother and Charley and the inconsolable sadness of families multiplied by fifty-eight thousand and, suddenly, it was a convulsion from my own throat that was shocking me.

I was the last person I would have expected to cry at the names of soldiers, presumably straight, masculine American males, men who might easily have identified with Charley's hostile teenage behavior. But I now felt a mile-deep connection with these guys, many of whom were his contemporaries. These were not the hairy, wet, and naked heroes from the World War II volumes in my father's study. These were young men whose worlds gave way under them like rotten floors. I understood the unfairness of their short lives.

While my blood lengthened Charley's life by thirteen years, our imbroglio, our *fix* as Mother once called it, did more than that. It delivered to *both* of us an extraordinary connection with each other, despite our differences. Had he not become ill, we would never have had it.

∽

More than thirty years after his death, Charley's echo occasionally rumbles through my day. I stop and listen, sometimes saddened, sometimes inspired. I can easily recall the events that took place in our lives between 1970 and 1983. I remember the people, the state of medicine, and the state of mind. Then I shake myself back to the present and realize how much has changed since then.

Mike and I split up not long after Charley died. Exhausted by the emotional upheavals in our lives at that time and by the heavy professional expectations we had each placed on ourselves, we simply did not have the strength to be there for each other. Despite the tumult of that time, we are close friends decades later.

Vickie maintained ties to all of us in the family and became a second daughter to my parents after Charley died. She used the insurance money exactly the way he had hoped—to finish college, get a masters degree in social work, and pursue that profession. Five years after Charley's death, she had a successful kidney transplant and married a good man named Larry. Their life continues happily on a farm in central Pennsylvania.

In 1995, Dad died, just six weeks after discovering he had pancreatic cancer. He was eighty-three and worked until the end of his life, evaluating medical cases for a variety of institutions. At his funeral were many families who appreciated his generous attention as their surgeon during his forty-year career. While Dad and I were not close during the time of *The Bone Bridge,* we grew to know each other well following Charley's death. Traveling twice in Italy together, we found in each other some of the same cultural interests and fascinations about the world. Ironically, as Charley took after my mother in looks, I grew to finally resemble someone: my father.

Mother died after a stroke in 2002. Until then, her walking limitations had grown increasingly complicated, and she spent the last two decades of her life in a wheelchair. Her spirit was undaunted, however, and she managed her rebelliously independent life for seven years after Dad died. She never liked knowing that we worried about her. It was the same style in which Charley lived through his illness: self-determining, fierce, and proud. I could see how the car wreck she survived as a teenager cauterized her with a toughness she then gave to Charley and returned to for her own final years.

I finally came out to my parents a few years after Charley died. My father said, "I suspected all along that you were gay, but chose to think otherwise. I don't like the fact, Yarrott, but I'm glad you told me." That was pretty much his attitude until he died. Not terribly negative, but not terribly accepting either.

My mother was angry about it. "I just want to know why you didn't tell us earlier." In her emotionally detached anger, she never accepted my being gay. Neither of my parents ever admitted any gratitude for my protecting them from the truth. However well or poorly my parents responded to my being gay, the fact did not destroy them, did not end our relationships, and I was at long last free to be frank with them about my life.

My siblings and I talk about Charley and the impact his illness had on the entire family. Angela is now a regular random platelet donor at the Red Cross. She says she gives platelets to a stranger every six months because she never wants to forget what Charley and I went through. She lives on a farm near Lexington, Kentucky, with two hundred animals, and for more than twenty years she has been an occupational therapist. We continue to be confidants and friends, like we promised in my apartment that afternoon thirty years ago. Eddy and his wife, Debby, now live in New Mexico. Eddy remained in the biotech industry for thirty years in New York and California, first as a scientist, then later developing companies doing genetic research. As always, he keeps the rest of us informed on medical news. He has pointed out how the timing of Charley's illness occurred between two crucial scientific discoveries.

On one hand Charley was extremely lucky. Without the knowledge of matching the human leukocyte antigens, discovered shortly before he became ill, his life would have ended in 1970. But as the medical world learned not long afterward, the best way to cure him would have been a marrow transplant with a well-matched donor performed almost immediately, not routine platelet phereses. By the time he talked with the doctors at the Fred Hutchinson Medical Center in Seattle in 1973, Charley had already been receiving my platelets for two and a half years. He was too late for a transplant. Had he fallen ill not in 1970, but in 1973, he might possibly be alive today. Of course, looking back on it now, with his hundreds of red cell transfusions at a time when the HIV virus was stealing through the national blood supply, the odds are high that he was infected.

Medical knowledge in hematology has evolved considerably since the early 1980s. On the websites for aplastic anemia, one now reads that *twenty* donors are required to provide the platelets necessary to keep one individual alive for a year. Yet, for seven years, I alone provided the platelets for Charley, 104 times a year.

In the most rewarding, surprising detour in my adulthood, I found myself teaching high school in New York City at Friends Seminary for fifteen years, and then later in Los Angeles at Sierra Canyon School for six. It was a career I never planned, but am deeply grateful for having had. While teaching art history, architecture, sculpture, and photography, I saw what teenagers need during their tough years of adolescence.

When I think of a typical teenager, I see a balloon already tightly inflated. Add homosexuality to it and the balloon stretches further. Add keeping alive an antagonistic brother through frequent blood transfusions and you must wonder when the balloon will burst. By watching hundreds of teenagers dealing with their obstacles, I finally understood how very big my own obstacles had been and what it took for me to survive them.

One thing that sustained me during the years when my balloon seemed it would surely burst was the notion that Charley and I had an important purpose. Why else would two brothers, so opposite in every respect, have the blood of identical twins? I had fantasized then that our impossible conundrum, when finally over, would demonstrate something remarkable, perhaps even divine. I had also assumed that somewhere else in the world there would be other pairs of siblings trapped by the progress of medicine, as we were. To this day, however, I have heard of no others. Given the uniqueness of our situation and our radical physical and emotional differences, you have to wonder: Why *us*? Why Charley and Yarrott?

There is not a day that passes when I do not wonder.

PHOTOGRAPH BY VICKIE ERICKSON DASH, PHILADELPHIA—AUGUST 1983

About the Author

Artist, memoirist, and essayist Yarrott Benz has written about architecture's seminal role in art history and the psychology of visual trends. Having taught for many years in New York City and in Los Angeles, he now lives on a farm outside Lexington, Kentucky.

CPSIA information can be obtained
at www.ICGtesting.com
Printed in the USA
FSOW01n1050301115
14020FS